I0120911

Irish Unity:
Time to Prepare

BEN COLLINS

Luath Press Limited

EDINBURGH

www.luath.co.uk

First published 2022
Reprinted 2022

ISBN: 978-1-80425-061-7

The author's right to be identified as author of this book under
the Copyright, Designs and Patents Act 1988 has been asserted.

Typeset in 11 point Sabon by Lapiz

© Ben Collins 2022

For Dylan

Ní neart go cur le chéile.

There is no strength without unity.

Contents

Acknowledgements

I WOULD PARTICULARLY like to thank John Haden Tucker for his excellent advice and expertise, which has been invaluable for this book – one day we will write one together. Many people have been supportive throughout the process and they are listed below.

Firstly, I would like to thank those who fundamentally disagree with the central tenet of this book, but still took the time to read and provide advice.

Jude Perry is a good friend and someone who has an excellent understanding of politics across Ireland; my dear cousin Julie and political soulmate John Maguire have been hugely supportive over the long period I spent writing this book; Gabriel McCaffrey has been insightful on the process of reunification.

I am incredibly grateful to James Maloney MP, Chair of the Canada–Ireland Interparliamentary Group, for agreeing to write a foreword for this book and his colleague Jennifer Hartley for her help.

Dr Conor McGrath – a great lecturer and now a friend – provided useful feedback on an earlier draft, even though we take fundamentally different views on the merits of Brexit.

Dr David McCann took the time to read a complete draft and I look forward to thanking him over a pint at The Sunflower Bar; Professor Colin Harvey has, unfortunately, had to put up with lots of hassle simply for expressing his peaceful views on reunification. This is not right in any society, but he still maintains his passion and has been very generous with his time and advice.

The Think32 groups and Shared Ireland podcast have also been very encouraging; Gerry Carlile of Ireland's Future and Kevin Rooney of the Irish Border Poll website supported my decision to publish this book; Andy McGibbons welcomed me onto his podcast; John Manley, Political Editor of the *Irish News*, provided some early media coverage, for which I am grateful.

Lesley Riddoch was willing to read an early version of the book and put in a good word with the publisher when I contacted her out of the blue. Her generosity is the reason why this book was published rather than just rattling around in my head. Martina Devlin took the time to read a draft and give me some positive feedback as well, which was much appreciated at the time; Sam McBride and Jamie Bartlett also read some of the book in draft form, for which I am thankful; Will Dean is one of the best fiction writers out there and was always willing to share advice.

Conor Heaney agreed to review a draft and give me some detailed feedback; John Cushnahan has made a significant impact in both parts of Ireland during his lengthy political career – I am very appreciative that he has taken the time, on several occasions, to talk to me about his experiences and thoughts on the future.

I have been lucky to have spoken to people from across the political spectrum on the topic of Irish unity. I am grateful for the thoughts of those who, for various reasons, wish to remain anonymous. While you may not wish to be thanked publicly, I will thank you privately.

The Skool Dads were a real Godsend during the long days of lockdowns – thank you all.

My colleagues at Hume Brophy have not only been great to work alongside, but they have also been enthusiastic about the book; Robert Barnett took time out of his busy schedule to provide some advice; all the people who were willing to read review copies and provide endorsements have been very generous with their time. I will thank you each personally.

David and the entire team at the No Alibis bookstore in Belfast are brilliant people who share a deep passion for books. It is a real pleasure to spend time there, get their insights and buy their books. I recommend the place to everyone.

This book would not have happened without the faith that Gavin and the team at Luath Press have shown in me. Caitlin is an excellent editor and has limitless patience to endlessly improve my writing. Thomasin, Eilidh, Rachael, Kira, Scott and Alastair all helped to make this a smooth process. I am eternally grateful for that.

Lastly, I must thank my wonderful family who mean everything to me. My parents David and Rosemary and my brothers Jackson and Justin have always been supportive; my better half Alison and my girls Violet and Scarlett give me more joy than I ever thought possible.

Foreword

BEN COLLINS HAS written a timely book on the Irish unity debate. It is thought-provoking, borne out by his lived experience and enriches this important question.

There have been historic links between Canada and Ireland for hundreds of years and with 4.4 million present-day Canadians claiming Irish heritage, the Irish connection is an important one for Canada. As someone with deep, family connections to Ireland, I am a passionate advocate for strengthening those bonds. In fact, in 2021, the Canadian House of Commons adopted my motion to declare the month of March Irish Heritage Month in Canada, in recognition of the important contributions that Irish Canadians have made to building Canada and to Canadian society in general.

Canada played an important part in the Northern Ireland peace process and the signing of the Good Friday Agreement, which still provides a framework for the peaceful transition to Irish unity. Many Canadians played a part in the peace process, including Judge Peter Cory and General John de Chastelain. Canada considers Ireland to be a key partner within the European Union. We believe that the EU–Canada Comprehensive Economic and Trade Agreement offers a great opportunity for both of our countries to strengthen our already strong economic links. With Ireland, we enjoy strong commercial relations with two-way bilateral merchandise trade worth over $2.5 billion in 2020, making it Canada's tenth largest trading partner in the European Union.

Canadian parliamentarians are also committed to expanding the bonds between our two countries. Today, we face complex border issues and while there are challenges, a satisfactory resolution is possible. While it is for the people across the island of Ireland alone to decide their future, we stand ready to support any democratic process which leads to a peaceful way forward.

This book sets out how we must prepare now in advance of any referendum and should be welcomed by all as a constructive contribution to the debate on Irish unity.

James Maloney
Chair, Canada-Ireland Interparliamentary Group
Chair, Canada-United Kingdom Inter-Parliamentary Association

Glossary of Terms

Alliance: Liberal party in Northern Ireland; does not take a constitutional position.

Backstop: the arrangements that Theresa May as UK prime minister negotiated with the EU, to ensure that there would be no borders on the island of Ireland or between Northern Ireland and Britain after the UK had left the EU.

Conservatives: UK centre-right, pro-Brexit party. Also known as Tories.

Customs Union: the arrangement that allows for a group of states to charge the same import duties and provides for free trade within an agreed area.

DUP: Democratic Unionist Party for Northern Ireland; pro-British and socially conservative party, originally anti-Good Friday Agreement with historic links to the Ulster Resistance.

Fianna Fáil: Conservative, Christian, Democratic party in the Republic of Ireland.

Fine Gael: Liberal Conservative party in the Republic of Ireland.

Green: all-Ireland, pro-European party focused on environmental/climate issues.

Good Friday Agreement: peace agreement which facilitated the end of The Troubles in Northern Ireland following referendums in both parts in Ireland (sometimes referred to as the Belfast Agreement).

Hard Brexit: where the UK makes a significant departure from the EU in political and economic terms.

Irish Labour: centre-left party of the Republic of Ireland.

Nationalists/Republicans: elected or appointed representatives of a political party or group; favour Irish unity

nationalists/republicans: members of the nationalist/republican community; have pro-Irish leanings and/or background

No deal Brexit: where there is no agreement at all between the UK and the EU after the UK has left the EU.

Northern Ireland Protocol: the international treaty negotiated between the EU and UK to ensure there is no hard border on the island of Ireland; resulted in an Irish Sea Border between Northern Ireland and Britain.

Sinn Féin: all-Ireland party with historic links to the IRA.

SDLP: Social Democratic Labour Party; Northern Ireland pro-unity party; formerly had links with Fianna Fáil.

Single Market: a group of countries (in this context within Europe - the EU27, the three countries of the European Economic Area, namely Norway, Iceland and Liechtenstein, as well as Switzerland through a number of sectoral treaties) agreeing to trade without tariffs or restrictions among themselves.

Soft Brexit: where the UK makes a less substantial departure from the EU in political and economic terms.

UK **Labour:** UK centre-left party.

Unionist/Loyalist: elected representatives of a pro-union political party or group

Unionists and Loyalists: identify as British; favour being part of the UK.

unionist/loyalist: members of unionist/loyalist communities; pro-British/pro-union

UUP: Ulster Unionist Party; original party of government for first fifty years of Northern Ireland; originally pro-Good Friday Agreement.

Timeline of Key Events

OUTLINED BELOW ARE some of the key dates that provide context for this book. This is not intended to be an exhaustive list – that would be a book in itself.

1 January 1801: Act of Union between Britain and Ireland comes into effect; Parliament of Ireland merges with Parliament of Great Britain to create a new Parliament of the United Kingdom.

24–29 April 1916: the Easter Rising. An armed rebellion takes place in Ireland during Easter week. Launched by Irish Republicans who wanted to end British rule in Ireland and create an independent country. The British reaction to the Rising, whereby a number of its participants were shot by firing squad, contributed to a widespread change in public opinion against British rule.

14 December 1918: UK General Election (including Ireland). Ireland returns a majority of Sinn Féin MPs who refuse to take their seats in Westminster. Instead, they set up a new parliament in Dublin.

21 January 1919: first Dáil Éireann (which means 'Assembly of Ireland') meets in Dublin.

21 January 1919–11 July 1921: War of Independence. A guerrilla war fought between the Irish Republican Army and British forces. This included the Royal Irish Constabulary (RIC), Auxiliaries and former British soldiers recruited to help the RIC called 'Black and Tans' due to the colour of their uniforms.

3 May 1921: Partition of Ireland; creation of Northern Ireland by commencement of Government of Ireland Act 1920. It was originally envisaged that both states would stay part of the United Kingdom.

6 December 1921: Anglo-Irish Treaty signed in London by representatives of the British government, including the Prime Minister David Lloyd George and representatives of the Irish government, including Michael Collins. It provided for the establishment of the Irish Free State as a self-governing dominion within the British Empire.

28 June 1922–24 May 1923: Irish Civil War between pro-treaty and anti-treaty forces, who remained opposed to the partition of Ireland which was recognised by the treaty.

6 December 1922: Irish Free State of 26 counties officially established, ending the Irish War of Independence.

16 May 1926: Fianna Fáil party founded by Éamon de Valera and his supporters after they split from Sinn Féin, on the issue of abstention on taking the Oath of Allegiance to the British Monarchy. He advocated doing this so that he could keep his position as a Teachta Dála in the Irish Parliament.

8 September 1933: Fine Gael founded following the merger of Cumann na nGaedheal, the National Centre Party and the Army Comrades Association.

18 April 1949: Ireland formally leaves Commonwealth and becomes Republic of Ireland.

1964–72: Northern Ireland Civil Rights Campaign, challenging discrimination and inequality against Irish Catholics in Northern Ireland.

14 August 1969: British troops deployed to Northern Ireland, initially as a peacekeeping mission to restore order after RUC (Royal Ulster Constabulary) brutality in Catholic Derry/Londonderry Bogside. The army was gladly received by the Catholics/Nationalists there.

9 August 1971–December 1975: Operation Demetrius, aka internment. Just under 2,000 people were arrested and interned (imprisoned without trial). Of these more than 1,800 were nationalists who were accused of being part of the IRA. Only 100 were loyalists. The European Court on Human Rights found five of the interrogation methods used amounted to torture.

30 January 1972: Bloody Sunday massacre in Derry. British Army shot 26 and killed 14, all unarmed civilians during a protest march in the Bogside.

24 March 1972: Direct Rule introduced in Northern Ireland and Stormont Parliament collapses.

9 December 1973: the Sunningdale Agreement, which introduces power-sharing in Northern Ireland for the first time, is signed.

1 January 1974: Sunningdale power-sharing executive meets for the first time.

17 May 1974: Dublin and Monaghan bombs. UVF (Ulster Volunteer Force) planted three car bombs in Dublin and one in Monaghan which killed 33 civilians and injured 300.

28 May 1974: Sunningdale Agreement collapses after Ulster Workers' Council Strike.

1 May 1975: elections to Northern Ireland Constitutional Convention set up by UK government to deal with NI constitutional issues.

3–13 May 1977: United Unionist Action Council strike with aim of getting UK government to take tougher action against the IRA and return to a Unionist majority form of government in Northern Ireland.

1 March–3 October 1981: hunger strike protests by Irish Republican prisoners to demand reinstatement of political status.

20 October 1982: elections to a Northern Ireland Assembly take place but Nationalist parties boycott the assembly and so planned devolution never takes place.

15 November 1985: Anglo-Irish Agreement signed. Intention for the treaty to bring an end to The Troubles in Northern Ireland.

23 June 1986: Northern Ireland Assembly is abolished by the UK Secretary of State for Northern Ireland.

26 March 1991: Northern Ireland Secretary of State Peter Brooke informs House of Commons that 'a basis for political talks now exists'. Becomes Brooke/Mayhew Talks.

April 1991–10 November 1992: Brooke/Mayhew Talks.

15 December 1993: Downing Street Declaration, a joint declaration by Prime Minster of the UK John Major and the Taoiseach of Ireland, Albert Reynolds which affirmed the right to self-determination for the people of the island of Ireland.

29 January 1994: President Bill Clinton approves US visitor visa for President of Sinn Féin Gerry Adams.

31 August 1994: IRA ceasefire announced.

13 October 1994: Combined Loyalist Military Command announces ceasefire.

8 September 1995: David Trimble elected leader of Ulster Unionist Party.

30 November 1995: President Bill Clinton visited Northern Ireland.

30 May 1996: elections to Northern Ireland Forum.

10 June 1996: all-party negotiations begin in Belfast.

14 June 1996: Sinn Féin excluded from talks due to IRA remaining active.

1 May 1997: Labour landslide victory in UK election.

20 July 1997: IRA ceasefire renewed.

26 August 1997: Independent International Commission on Decommissioning (IICD) established to oversee decommissioning of paramilitary weapons.

10 April 1998: Good Friday Agreement signed.

22 May 1998: referendums in both parts of Ireland approve Good Friday Agreement.

25 June 1998: first elections to new Northern Ireland Assembly.

15 August 1998: Omagh bombing carried out by Real IRA, a Republican splinter group opposed to the IRA's ceasefire and the Good Friday Agreement. 29 people were killed; more than 200 injured.

11 February 2000: Northern Ireland Assembly and Northern Ireland Executive suspended.

30 May 2000: devolution restored to Northern Ireland Assembly and Northern Ireland Executive.

26 June 2000: IRA arms dump inspected.

1 July 2001: First Minister of Northern Ireland David Trimble resigns over lack of decommissioning.

10 August 2001: Northern Ireland Assembly suspended for 24 hours.

11 September 2001: terrorist attacks on New York and Washington DC.

21 September 2001: Northern Ireland Assembly suspended for 24 hours.

16 October 2001: Secretary of State for Northern Ireland announces that the RUC (Royal Ulster Constabulary) will be renamed the PSNI (Police Service of Northern Ireland) as part of Patten Report recommendations.

18 October 2001: Unionist Ministers resign from Northern Ireland Executive.

23 October 2001: IRA begins decommissioning its weapons.

25 October 2001: work begins on dismantling British Army observation towers in South Armagh.

2 November 2001: David Trimble fails to get sufficient Unionist support to be re-elected as First Minister.

4 November 2001: new Police Service of Northern Ireland comes into being.

6 November 2001: David Trimble secures sufficient support to be re-elected as First Minister and Mark Durkan is elected as Deputy First Minister.

14 October 2002–7 May 2007: Northern Ireland Assembly suspended.

7 October 2003: Cory Collusion Inquiry releases final reports.

26 November 2003: Northern Ireland Assembly elections. DUP and Sinn Féin become two largest parties for the first time.

28 July 2005: IRA announces end of its campaign and promises full decommissioning of all its weapons, to be witnessed by clergymen of Protestant and Catholic churches.

26 September 2005: IICD confirms that the IRA has fully decommissioned all its weapons.

13 October 2006: St Andrews Agreement which changed how First Minister is elected and set out new process for electing a Northern Ireland Executive minister with control over policing and justice.

28 January 2007: Sinn Féin special Ard Fheis approves a motion calling for devolution of policing and justice, support for the police services, PSNI and An Garda Síochána.

7 March 2007: Northern Ireland Assembly elections.

8 May 2007: Northern Ireland Assembly and Northern Ireland Executive restored with DUP and Sinn Féin as the two largest parties for the first time.

31 July 2007: British Army formally ends Operation Banner, its mission in Northern Ireland.

5 February 2010: Hillsborough Agreement allows Westminster to devolve policing and justice powers to the Northern Ireland Assembly.

12 April 2010: policing and justice powers transferred from Westminster to Northern Ireland Assembly.

18 September 2014: Scottish independence referendum held. Narrow 55–45 per cent vote in favour of remaining in the UK.

23 December 2014: Stormont House Agreement, which covered identity issues, fiscal policies and devolution reform.

17 November 2015: Fresh Start Agreement for full implementation of Stormont House Agreement, sets out how to address ongoing paramilitary activity.

23 June 2016: UK votes to Leave EU, Northern Ireland and Scotland vote to Remain.

November 2016: potential £500 million overrun for Renewable Heat Incentive scheme comes to light.

9 January 2017: Martin McGuinness resigns as deputy First Minister due to RHI (Renewable Heat Incentive) scandal and Arlene Foster's refusal to resign or step aside for duration of the inquiry.

16 Jan 2017: Northern Ireland Assembly suspended.

2 March 2017: Unionism loses its majority for the first time in an Assembly election.

23 May 2019: Unionism loses its majority of Northern Ireland seats in European Parliament election.

12 December 2019: Unionism loses its majority of Northern Ireland seats in UK Parliament election.

8 January 2020: Northern Ireland Assembly and Executive restored by New Decade New Approach agreement.

8 February 2020: Irish General Election takes place.

27 June 2020: Irish Coalition Government of Fianna Fáil, Fine Gael and Greens is formed.

30 December 2020: UK Government agrees to trade deal with EU which includes Northern Ireland Protocol.

2 July 2020: First Minister Arlene Foster calls for Deputy First Minister Michelle O'Neill to temporarily step down while an investigation is carried out over Bobby Storey funeral.

30 March 2021: Arlene Foster calls on PSNI Chief Constable Simon Byrne to resign over Bobby Storey funeral.

28 April 2021: Arlene Foster announces her intention to resign as leader of the DUP and as First Minister after her own party's MLAS turn against her.

3 May 2021: Centenary of partition of Ireland.

6 May 2021: Scotland Parliament elections return a majority of MSPs who are in favour of Scottish independence.

14 May 2021: Edwin Poots is elected leader of the DUP.

14 June 2021: Arlene Foster resigns as First Minister of Northern Ireland.

17 June 2021: Paul Givan is nominated as DUP First Minister and Michelle O'Neill is reappointed as Sinn Féin deputy first minister.

17 June 2021: Edwin Poots resigns as DUP Leader.

30 June 2021: Sir Jeffrey Donaldson becomes new leader of the DUP.

8 November 2021: PUP (Progressive Unionist Party) withdraws support for the Good Friday Agreement, claiming that consent principle is undermined because of Northern Ireland Protocol.

3 Feb 2022: Paul Givan resigns as DUP First Minister in protest of Northern Ireland Protocol.

5 May 2022: Northern Ireland Assembly elections; Sinn Féin becomes the largest party for the first time.

13 May 2022: Jeffrey Donaldson confirms that the DUP will not nominate an Assembly speaker which means the Northern Ireland Assembly cannot operate.

13 June 2022: Northern Ireland Protocol Bill which will unilaterally seek to disapply parts of an international treaty between the UK and EU is tabled in UK Parliament.

7 July 2022: Boris Johnson announces that he will stand down as UK Conservative party leader and prime minister.

5 Sep 2022: Liz Truss elected as new Conservative party leader and then appointed as UK prime minister on 6 Sep 2022 by HM Queen Elizabeth II.

8 September 2022: Queen Elizabeth II dies and King Charles III becomes the new Head of State for the UK.

20 Sep 2022: First phase of Northern Ireland Census 2021 released, covering passports held, ethnic group, national identity, language and religion.

4 May 2023: Local government elections in England and Northern Ireland.

19 October 2023: Intended date for next Scottish independence referendum, as previously announced by Nicola Sturgeon.

By end of 2024: Northern Ireland Assembly to vote on continued application of Articles 5-10 of Northern Ireland Protocol.

Preface

I SHOULD CONFESS right from the start that I was not born into a family that ever dreamed of Irish unity – far from it. I grew up and lived in East Belfast – a predominantly unionist part of the city – as the youngest of three brothers in a unionist household. Irish unity was only ever seen as something to oppose in our house, simply as we resented the idea of being forced into reunification by IRA violence. But despite all this, I always felt Irish – it was just something instinctive.

My father was the vet for Belfast Zoo and he also had a pig farm just outside Belfast which meant he could afford to send all three brothers to Campbell College, an all-boys public school in East Belfast. My first job, at the age of six, was mucking out pig pens on the family farm. This taught me two important lessons: one, you cannot get the smell of pig manure off your skin for a week, no matter how often you wash; two, I enjoyed working hard. I have always believed that every job since then has been downhill or easy.

Growing up during The Troubles, I vividly remember the daily violence and constant fear that there would be more carnage. When I left school, I moved to Scotland to study at the University of Dundee, in September 1994, just at the time of the first IRA ceasefire. When I came home from university for Christmas in December, I was struck by the sense of optimism and hope in Belfast city centre that I had not experienced before. In the best way possible, it did not feel like the city I once knew.

In Scotland, I was able to socialise and develop friendships with people from all across Ireland, in a way that had not been possible for me in Belfast. I realised that we had lots more in common across Ireland than I ever thought.

Despite the ceasefire in 1994, The Troubles lasted until the peace agreement of 1998; after three decades of war, the Good Friday Agreement was signed. I had followed the peace process for four years as an interested observer, rather than a participant – I did not get to vote in the Good Friday Agreement referendum as I was still a student in Scotland but, of course, I would have voted Yes if I had the option to do so.

The Good Friday Agreement was a historic compromise which was negotiated and voted for after much hard work by President Clinton's Administration, the UK and Irish governments and the support of the EU, as well as political representatives and ordinary citizens. Making right with your enemies can never be easy, but the agreement ushered in peace and a power-sharing government which, although not perfect, was a huge step forward for the people of Northern Ireland and indeed Ireland as a whole. It also helped to create better relationships between Ireland and Britain (the status of the UK and Ireland as neighbouring member states of the EU, often with common interests, helped to strengthen links too).

I did believe that in the run-up to the Good Friday Agreement, David Trimble was a lone visionary within Unionism, so as a master's student in political communications, I spent a couple of weeks doing work experience for the Ulster Unionist Party during the 2001 Westminster Election. While I was never a member of the UUP, I knew they needed to remain as the largest Unionist party, ahead of the DUP, so that the gains of the Good Friday Agreement could be maintained.

That same year, I joined the UK Conservative Party in Scotland and I felt comfortable with the Scottish Conservatives, who were more liberal and more pro-European than their English counterparts. I have always been a classical liberal in the sense that I believe in personal freedom, free trade and democracy which is as close to citizens as possible and I had joined this party in the hope and expectation that Ken Clarke, a pro-European and socially liberal MP, would become the leader. I was wrong.

In 2003, I left the Conservative Party. A new job with the General Medical Council (the UK regulator for doctors) meant that I was no longer able to be politically active, but I was glad to leave – I was becoming increasingly disillusioned with the party's growing Euro-scepticism. I was pleased by the formation of the Conservative–Lib Dem government coalition in 2010 but always felt that it was likely to be a one-term arrangement. It did not take long after the coalition ended for the extreme right-wing part of the Conservatives to flex their muscles. The party has marched, rather than drifted, towards being a right-wing, populist entity. While I still have friends within the party, I do not feel any connection with the Conservatives.

Back in Northern Ireland, I joined Alliance after being asked to do some leafleting for them in the run-up to the 2011 Assembly elections. I was briefly on their Executive Committee and also a member of the Liberal Democrats, as I knew they were a stabilising force in the coalition government, blocking the more extreme Conservative tendencies. But when I started a new job in 2017 as Chief Executive of NIFHA (Northern Ireland Federation of Housing Associations), I had to resign from both parties, to ensure that the organisation' maintained its status as being politically impartial.

I realised that I was in danger of becoming one of those people for whom I always had disdain – somebody who moved around multiple political parties. But in my defence, I did it for the right reasons. My views have been consistent – my belief in the Good Friday Agreement, socially liberal values and the benefits of being part of the European Union have always remained the same, so I have made judgments about which political parties are the best vehicle for me to pursue my beliefs. I am not willing to change my views just to stay within a political party.

At the time of the Good Friday Agreement, the British and Irish governments were joint custodians and, from a Northern Ireland perspective, this provided assurances for all parts of the community. However, the detrimental Brexit vote has fundamentally changed this. I had a long-term aspiration for Irish unity since the Good Friday Agreement, but it became an urgent necessity for me after the vote for Brexit. I recognise that some voted for Brexit who once believed – perhaps even still do – that the UK leaving the EU is a good thing. While I respect their opinions, I do not share that view.

The realities of Brexit are becoming clear and the increased friction in trade from Britain to Northern Ireland is causing problems – the loyalist violence that occurred at the time of the introduction of the Northern Ireland Protocol being just one example. The regional government in Northern Ireland has not fully operated since February 2022, as the DUP resigned the position of first minister in protest of the Protocol. As a result, only limited decisions can be made, the Northern Ireland Assembly is not functioning and there can be no Northern Ireland budget. The people of Northern Ireland are being used as a bargaining chip by the DUP during a cost-of-living crisis and when our health service needs urgent investment.

Looking at the island of Ireland through the prism of Brexit, living through a pandemic and the global reset and 'new normal' that has followed, those of us on the island, especially in Northern Ireland, will look at our current political structures and contemplate whether they are fit for purpose. I believe that a growing majority, from all backgrounds, will decide that they are not and that Irish unity is the solution to this problem.

So, this book is about building momentum for Irish unity. I do not claim to have all the answers, nor do I think that I alone have a monopoly on what is best for the island of Ireland. I aim to put forward my thoughts on why we need to prepare and plan now, to avoid the chaos of Brexit. Hopefully I can add to this important debate about our future prosperity in a positive way. Ideas on their own can be powerful, careful planning and implementation provide the best chance of successfully making change. I am an idealist, but a pragmatist in how I get there. The inspiration for this project was to encourage others to develop their thinking. It is not seeking to set out a prescriptive template for how we secure reunification. That is a process which will be developed by many people, as we plan and prepare in advance of a border poll.

I recognise that there are people who take a fundamentally different view from my desire for Irish unity – they instead want Northern Ireland to remain part of the United Kingdom. There is a range of opinions on the matter within even my own family and group of friends, so I appreciate that many readers may strongly disagree with the proposition that I am putting forward. However, I wish for people of all political viewpoints to feel able to read this book and engage with my suggestions, just as I want to hear the positive vision for remaining part of the UK. We do not have anything to fear by debating the issues respectfully and peacefully.

There may be those who say that I am a Lundy,[1] that others like me who come from unionist backgrounds but favour Irish unity are betraying Nothern Ireland. But despite my unionist background, I always believed that I was Irish as well as British. Whereas my sense of Irishness grew as I spent more time outside of Northern Ireland, my sense of Britishness gradually dissipated.

Despite my dual nationality, I often felt as though I was not 'British enough' for Britain – I experienced hostility in London for being Irish; I had security guards follow me around shops when I was a teenager on a school trip after they heard my accent. In business, some people talked to me in a patronising manner because I was from Belfast. Similarly, I have experienced discrimination because of my unionist background – I applied for a job with a public sector body in Scotland and felt confident I would get it until a senior manager in the second interview started asking me hostile questions about my work experience with the UUP. I was asked to explain how Orange Order marches could possibly be like Mardi Gras, as the person snorted with disdain. Needless to say, I did not get the job after that.

Whether they feel British, Irish, a combination of the two, or a different nationality altogether, I want the best for everyone across the island of Ireland. Many unionists will be opposed to unity, but I would urge them to consider, who are the people that have *actually* betrayed Northern Ireland? The answer is the British government and Boris Johnson, the former British Prime Minister, in particular. Amongst other failings, he led the government that put a border down the Irish Sea a year after coming to Belfast and saying no British prime minister would ever do that.

Irish unity is an idea whose time has come. We need to rebuild our economy for the post-COVID world, to address the climate crisis and deal with the consequences of a hard Brexit. The Good Friday Agreement allowed the people of Ireland to decide on their future for themselves; we are now a quarter of a century on from this groundbreaking peace accord, which was supposed to allow bothparts of the island to develop a peaceful and prosperous relationship, with the potential for Irish unity over time. But now, the United Kingdom's vote to leave the European Union, despite Northern Ireland and Scotland voting to remain, has brought the issue of uniting Ireland to the forefront. We need to talk about what Irish unity would look like, where all the people of this island can live together in peace, prosperity and harmony. The time to start planning is today so that we can avoid the chaos of Brexit. We need to prepare now or we will fail later.

There are many positives to reunification – economic, social and political. Over the course of this book, I will set out detailed, evidence-based arguments to prove why now is the time to prepare for unity. If there is to be Irish unity in the true sense of the phrase, a significant number of steps and fundamental changes will have to be undertaken. I aim to set a clear-headed analysis of what the issues are, with options to overcome them and the likely impact. While there will be references to the complex history of Ireland, the primary focus will be looking forward to the future, with specific and practical actions to move the two parts of the island of Ireland into one united country.

This book is a think piece based on my ideas as well as cold, hard facts and figures, intended to generate a discussion about how we can create Irish unity together. It sets out a passionate belief about why there should be Irish unity, how the campaign could be won and, crucially, how through careful planning and implementation we can make sure it is a success for all its people. Unionists and loyalists need to be part of this discussion. While we cannot force people to take part in the discussions, we must continue to provide assurances and demonstrate that there will be safeguards for all in a New Ireland.

Introduction

TO SAY THAT we are living through an age of disruption is an understatement – these are extraordinary times. The UK has decided to embark on a Brexit journey with no agreed destination; it is no longer a member of the European Union, but there is no consensus on what the future relationship should be. At the same time, we are dealing with the ongoing fallout from the COVID-19 pandemic. Throughout both of these major, catastrophic events, it has been clear that Northern Ireland is not a top priority for the UK government. As we only have a population of 1.9 million out of a UK population of around 67 million, we should not expect to be considered the most important priority; however, policy decisions on both crucial issues have been taken against the best interests of Northern Ireland.

The fact that everyone across Ireland must appreciate is that, although I do not believe there is any innate hostility to the region, the British government do not care about Northern Ireland or value its contribution to the UK. Brexiters were frustrated by the added complications that Northern Ireland caused for leaving the EU because Northern Ireland shares a land border with another EU country (Ireland), but they got the Brexit that they wanted by putting a border in the Irish Sea. Britain has more freedom in how it has left the EU and, in theory at least, greater flexibility to negotiate trade deals with the USA and others. Multiple opinion polls by Lord Ashcroft[2] and YouGov[3] show the extent of England's disinterest in Northern Ireland – Northern Ireland – Brexiters would rather see Brexit secured than keep either Scotland or Northern Ireland as part of the UK. Being separated by the Irish Sea, those in England perhaps do not feel that they have as much in common with Northern Ireland, as they do with Scotland and Wales. So, the future of the region is with the rest of the island.

The UK does not have a written constitution. However, the Irish Republic does and this incorporates the Good Friday Agreement which also covers Northern Ireland. It was our pathway out of violence, as a post-conflict society and it will be our route map towards becoming a settled society, where we can finally live in peace.

Our future, including any constitutional change under the Good Friday Agreement, was to be decided through solely democratic means, after decades of strife. Brexit has put all of this at risk – it has forced part of Ireland to leave the EU against its expressly given wishes, as Northern Ireland voted clearly to remain within the EU and the rest of Ireland did not have a vote.

To those who say the EU will collapse in the coming years, I would say look at how the EU27 maintained a remarkable sense of unity throughout the Brexit negotiations. Similarly, the EU stuck together during the COVID-19 pandemic and in response to the crisis in Ukraine. The EU is working collaboratively with its member states to address the cost of living crisis. For example, President von der Leyen brought forward plans to control the spiraling energy costs on a continent-wide basis, in her 2022 State of the Union address.[4] Yes, there are frictions and strains on the familial bonds; however, this is what happens in a family and ultimately the EU27 are committed to the EU - they realise its key role as the greatest peace project the world has ever seen. Of course, there is a challenge in ensuring that the ordinary citizen, who cares mostly about jobs, housing and healthcare, understands that the EU provides a crucial framework to deliver on these key areas.

In some ways, Irish unity is a localised question about uniting two divided parts of one small island, but it also has larger ramifications and a wider resonance. Just as the EU helped to facilitate German reunification, so can Europe do the same once more for Ireland. This can help to reinforce the benefits and importance of EU membership. This is a union that is not only the world's largest economic market but also a significant player in geopolitics, again as shown by the rapid response to the Russian invasion of Ukraine. There is a growing recognition of the benefits of EU membership – Ukraine, Moldova and Georgia all formally applied for membership in early 2022; Turkey renewed its call to be admitted as well.

To those who would say that talk of Irish unity is destabilising, I would say Brexit is the true cause of destabilisation – increased talk of Irish unity is just a logical conclusion of the instability caused by Brexit. The UK government has, on two occasions in late 2020 and again in early 2021, indicated its willingness to break international law through proposed clauses in its Internal Market Bill and then again by unilaterally extending grace periods under the Northern Ireland Protocol. This risked the EU deciding not to ratify the

EU–UK trade deal. These hostile actions by the UK government are destabilising the fragile peace in Northern Ireland and risk creating a hard border on the island of Ireland. If the UK government cannot be trusted with an international treaty, I do not see how we can trust them with anything else.

Brexiters do not like the Protocol for two reasons: firstly, it stops the pipe dream of a pure Brexit where every vestige of EU law or reference is removed from the UK; secondly, after initial adjustments, the Protocol is working well for the majority of Northern Ireland businesses.

Opinion polls have shown increasing support of the majority for the Northern Ireland Protocol.[5] People and businesses indeed believe that the operation of the Protocol can be improved, of course, but it is concerning that Shailesh Vara the Northern Ireland Secretary of State claimed in August 2022 that almost everyone he had spoken to said that 'the Protocol is not working'.[6] The Northern Ireland Business Brexit Working Group, which represents a wide range of business interests, has continued to emphasise that while they think adjustments can be made, they support the Protocol. They stated in a recent written submission to the UK Parliament:

> It should be remembered that the Protocol is success-fully delivering on one of its main objectives – the avoidance of a hard border on the island of Ireland – and this is bringing significant economic benefit to the NI economy. [7]

So, either the Secretary of State was badly informed or chose to say something that does not concur with reality.

Those who support Brexit do not want to see Northern Ireland doing well compared to the rest of the UK, which shows the continual and increasing damage that Brexit is causing.

The sad reality is that the Conservative Brexiters now exist as an anti-European cult where no variance from anti-EU vitriol is tolerated. Whether it is a weak prime minister or an ambitious cabinet minister, there is always an irresistible urge to burnish their Brexit credentials through hostility to the European project.

Brexit has opened Pandora's Box and so we must be prepared for rapid change. We live in an era of political volatility and while no one can predict with 100 per cent certainty what the future holds,

I believe that there will likely be Irish unity within the next ten years. Partition was the Brexit of its day – totally self-harming. Although there was never a referendum to seek the approval of people to divide the island, we will have one to secure its reunification.

The island of Ireland has been blighted by violence and threats of political violence since before partition – we need to leave such destructive behaviour behind as we build a new nation within Irish unity. There will be no peace or true prosperity until the malign influence of any violent political group is ended. Of course, people who were previously involved in such activity can have a future, if they renounce violence and focus on community building.

Building momentum

Several factors are gradually coalescing together to build momentum for reunification. The demographics are rapidly approaching a tipping point and this has been confirmed by the 2021 Northern Ireland census, which was published in late 2022. This means that for the first time in its history, Northern Ireland is no longer a state with a Protestant and unionist majority. While it is perhaps too simplistic to say that all Catholics want Irish unity and all Protestants want to stay part of the UK, there is a broad correlation. However, an equally significant implication is that a state that was carved out of the island of Ireland specifically to have both a permanent Protestant and unionist majority no longer has either. But, to truly be able to achieve Irish unity, we need to cherish our unionist and loyalist neighbours across Ireland.

Era of great change

We live in an era of great change, constant uncertainty and rapid technological advancement, yet society has suffered because we often choose to engage only with those who agree with us. If we want to deliver a New Ireland, we need to actively engage with people from across the entire political spectrum. Political Unionism may refuse to discuss the prospect of unity, but we know that civic unionism is already part of the conversation. We need to hold a constructive and respectful discussion about how we create this New Ireland – peacefully. Martin Luther King and Mahatma Gandhi showed that progressive change can happen by solely peaceful means.

These examples of peaceful leadership provide a template for us to follow in Ireland.

As we engage in such open discussion and develop upon the goals of this new, unified land, we must inoculate ourselves against the sort of rabid Nationalism that bled through England and led to the Brexit vote. We can take control of our destiny so that we never again need to experience such uncertainty or are forced into accepting a change in how we live our lives and interact with the rest of the world. It will take a generation to heal the Brexit divisions and I wholeheartedly believe that the only way out of this quagmire is through a unified Ireland, within the EU.

The DUP appeared to be in a strong position supporting a Tory minority UK government, during 2017–19, but they were not able to change a UK-wide approach. They sought to control the direction of travel for how Brexit would be implemented but failed to do so. Time and time again, the DUP have shown by their intransigence that they cannot be relied upon. They campaigned for Brexit and claimed that they were in favour of a trade deal with the EU; however, despite being in a confidence and supply agreement with the UK minority Conservative Government, they then voted against every option for a deal during that period.

The May 2022 Northern Ireland Assembly elections resulted in Sinn Féin, a party that wants Irish unity, becoming the party with the largest number of seats for the first time since Northern Ireland was created. This entitles them to nominate a first minister when a new Northern Ireland Executive (government) is formed. At the time of writing Unionists, particularly the DUP – who would be entitled to nominate a deputy first minister – are refusing to form a government. They claim that they will not do so until their concerns relating to the Northern Ireland Protocol have been resolved to their satisfaction.

The DUP were bitterly opposed to the Good Friday Agreement in the late '90s and they were strongly in favour of Brexit in 2016. It is, therefore, deeply ironic that they are now complaining that the Brexit that has been delivered, including the Protocol that they initially supported, now breaches the Good Friday Agreement. Sadly, they are trying to blame all those parties who campaigned for remaining in the EU for the damage of Brexit, especially when their reckless support of Brexit has truly caused damage to Northern Ireland. Through their actions in recent years, the DUP have helped to create the conditions where a pro-unification party are now the largest in Northern Ireland; they have fast-tracked the region on a path towards unity. They have even helped to create the conditions for Scottish independence and increased consideration of Welsh independence.

In the UK Parliament, Alliance and SDLP MPs voted against the Withdrawal Agreement; in the Northern Ireland Assembly Sinn Féin, SDLP and Alliance voted to withhold consent from the legislation that implemented the Northern Ireland Protocol, which created the Irish Sea border. While the DUP wanted Northern Ireland to be treated the same as the rest of the UK, the backstop negotiated by former Prime Minister Theresa May and voted down by DUP would have created less friction between Northern Ireland and Britain. The options have always been a border between the North and South of Ireland, a border between Northern Ireland and Britain, or the UK remaining within a customs union with the EU. The DUP opposed every possible version of Brexit while refusing to state what they wanted.

A clear majority of newly elected members of the Northern Ireland Assembly in the May 2022 election (53 out of 90) support the Northern Ireland Protocol; the EU has already supported the Irish government's view and the Biden–Harris Administration has unequivocally stated their support for the Good Friday Agreement and the Northern Ireland Protocol. Yet, the British government threatens to override the Northern Ireland Protocol via domestic legislation. While hugely destabilising for Northern Ireland in particular, this will prove to be the latest in a series of performative acts that have no lasting impact, other than further eroding the reputation of the UK as a serious country.

Impact of COVID-19

There is no doubt that the COVID-19 pandemic has significantly damaged and irrevocably changed our world. However, it has also fast-tracked progress in certain areas such as online shopping, remote working and the use of digital health; it has perhaps increased our awareness of the immediate danger posed by the climate crisis and its impact on humanity. For the island of Ireland, the pandemic also showed that public health issues need to be managed on an all-Ireland basis – viruses do not respect borders. The Irish Republic was quicker to move to a lockdown, whereas Northern Ireland alongside the rest of the UK remained open. As the two states on the island adopted, at times, contradictory positions, it meant that the benefits of these different approaches were undermined. A public health emergency, in this case, a global pandemic, shows in stark relief that a small island like Ireland should be united and have one health service, not be divided into two.

A UK Tory prime minister can either placate their right-wing base or the demands of Scotland, Wales and Northern Ireland for a softer Brexit – they cannot do both. Voluntarily walking away from the world's largest economic bloc and stopping the free flow of migration to and from that bloc, shows that Brexit is an illiberal project. It is not going global; it is being parochial.

Unionists are saying there will never be Irish unity; Nationalist politicians in the Dáil are saying we want unity but just not yet, or now is not the time. They are both wrong. We need to start preparing now because it is going to happen and it needs to be a success. This pandemic will end at some point, but the constitutional changes will be irreversible by then.

Unity within the EU

The EU may not be perfect, but it is a crucial framework for growing prosperity across Ireland. It truly is the most successful peace process in history, if we compare the continent of Europe before and after the founding of the European Union. As a complex framework of rules and regulations, the EU does need to constantly evolve – the only way to ensure this happens constructively is through membership, not by standing outside the tent and shouting.

The UK government passed the Nationality and Borders Act 2022.[8] As a result of new immigration rules, non-Irish EU citizens travelling from the Irish Republic into Northern Ireland will, from 2023, need to apply for prior travel authorisation.[9] This will be unworkable on the island of Ireland and risks damaging the all-Ireland economy – it puts extra bureaucracy on cross-border workers and may dissuade cross-border tourism. If the UK government were to follow through on its threats to effectively dismantle the Northern Ireland Protocol, it would not only restrict Northern Ireland's access to the EU market but also will make the Irish Republic semi-detached from the European Single Market too as extra checks may be required to ensure that inferior goods and products from Britain are not leaking into the Single Market via Northern Ireland and on to the Irish Republic.

Unity within the EU will protect the entire island from these negative repercussions being forced onto Ireland by the actions of a third country, ie the British government.

Northern Ireland, as part of the UK, would have to spend the next several decades adjusting to existence outside the EU, or arguing about whether to seek to re-join it. It makes far more sense to, instead, spend the next decades reuniting with the rest of Ireland as part of the EU. Prosperity for all of Ireland lies within the EU. This can be seen clearly if we compare economic statistics between Northern Ireland and the Irish Republic, in terms of overall growth and per capita.

National leaders across Europe – such as Emmanuel Macron, Olaf Scholz, Micheál Martin and Leo Varadkar – have come to the same conclusion, that their country's national interests are best served by playing a full part in the EU. William Hague, the former UK foreign secretary, said that the UK's membership in the EU helped to amplify its voice on international matters. We have already seen how the UK's status has shrunk on the world stage, such as its recent failure to have a judge on the International Court of Justice for the first time since its foundation in 1945. By comparison, Ireland successfully campaigned for a temporary seat on the UN Security Council for 2021–22. In a world that is ever more uncertain, these things matter.

Brexit and its potentially calamitous impact on Northern Ireland – indeed, Ireland as a whole – have necessitated that we speed up the process of self-determination. There has been increased discussion of Irish unity following the UK's 2016 vote to leave the EU, with increasing support being shown in a variety of opinion polls. Northern Ireland was pulled out of the European Union even though a majority of people in the region voted to remain part of the EU and the effects of being taken out are potentially catastrophic. Therefore, we should aim for NIREXIT from BREXIT – that is, a Northern Ireland exit from Brexit.

Politicians will follow the people

The Taoiseach Micheál Martin said, in August 2020, that Britain may get tired of Northern Ireland and that is why the Shared Island Unit, which he set up after forming a new government, is so important.[10] However, he said a border poll at this time would be too divisive. Disappointing, yes, but we need to use this time to prepare and set out a detailed plan for how unity will be successfully delivered.

Once politicians from across Ireland realise there is an appetite for unity, they will surely get on board to help build the campaign – we have seen this through the welcome proposals on Irish unity, recently launched by Jim O'Callaghan TD of Fianna Fáil and Neale Richmond TD of Fine Gael. One result of the peace process, from a Unionist perspective, was that it froze the discussion and agitation for Irish unity by Nationalist politicians across Ireland and in Irish America. The new circumstances caused by Brexit mean that these politicians are now beginning to engage, so now is the time to actively campaign for unity.

The post-Brexit era presents many challenges for the people of Ireland, as well as a once-in-a-generation opportunity. Many people across Ireland – from all political perspectives – have worked hard to make the peace process a success and secure the gains of the Good Friday Agreement. All of this is under threat due to the voters of England and Wales – people who have voted against their interests, for a variety of reasons, including concerns about immigration and an outdated sense of sovereignty.

Northern Ireland and the Irish Republic have been able to build a mutual understanding toward a growing all-Ireland economy over the last twenty years. Do we allow the vote of others to put this hard-won progress at risk and accept that Northern Ireland will not have the same benefits of EU membership as the rest of Ireland? Or do we commit to securing our future by planning and voting for Irish unity, to safeguard our European destiny?

Brexit is the death rattle of the British Empire

The vote for Brexit can be defined in psychology as an example of the Dunning-Kruger effect, where people of low ability (in this case the UK government) have illusions about their superiority over others and believe that their brainpower is greater than others. This is a result of the inability of such people to recognise their shortcomings. The theory is that as they lack self-awareness, they cannot objectively evaluate their actual level of competence or incompetence.

The UK has decided to stop immigration and aim for a smaller economy, less influence on the world stage and increasing isolation.

The UK post-Brexit is not seen as a major player, but as a country that has accelerated its own demise through an entirely avoidable process.

This vote to leave the EU is a flare-up of English Nationalism. It is the death rattle of the British Empire, a misguided view of English and Welsh people. English Nationalism has a narrow-minded view of the world which does not favour internationalism, other than to expect favourable trade deals because of England's supposed exceptionalism. This attitude is part of the Brexit delusion, that somehow political and economic gravity can be ignored, through sheer will-power. It is a scream of anguish from working-class people in the post-industrial wastelands across the UK who have not been able to tap into the benefits of globalisation. We need to break away from the dying British Empire and crumbling United Kingdom which is now coming under strain from all angles; we need to safeguard our future prosperity through Irish unity.

The capital should remain Dublin, but to ensure full integration, there are other changes I would suggest. Belfast should continue its economic integration with the rest of Ireland, to regain its rightful place as a business powerhouse for the island. As England damages its economy through Brexit, opportunities will emerge for the island of Ireland and with goodwill and a strategic approach, there will be benefits for all parts of the island. The country will be at its strongest when we can ensure economic growth across the North, South, East and West.

Being part of the UK is conditional for a lot of people in Northern Ireland, particularly nationalists and centrists or the non-aligned. Brexit shows that there cannot be true peace on the island of Ireland until British control has gone. At the time of the Good Friday Agreement negotiations, the Irish and British governments acted as joint stabilisers for the peace process in Northern Ireland. Now we have the UK government claiming that they are bringing forward legislation to protect the Good Friday Agreement when they do not have the support of the majority of Northern Ireland to do so.

In the most optimistic scenario, we can view Brexit as part of a transformation for the UK state. After some time, it will transform into a pro-European country when the full disaster of Brexit can no longer be ignored. But this is likely to be without Northern Ireland, Scotland and possibly even Wales.

Part of the reason that the Brexit debate has been so hideous, particularly since the vote, was due to the lack of planning and coherent vision beforehand – we need to have an agreed approach for Irish unity. The unity campaign needs to emphasise that people on the island of Ireland have more in common than not. We do not share commonalities with the 70-year-olds in Sunderland who voted Leave to finally defeat the Germans.

Part One: Setting the Scene

Preparing the Ground

Tús maith leath na hoibre
'A good start is half the work'

Irish proverb

FOR MORE THAN six years, Northern Ireland has been traumatised by the effects of being torn from the EU against the will of the majority. Its people are ready to reclaim their rightful position in Europe once more – recent opinion polls show that support for being part of the EU increased in Northern Ireland after the referendum. At the same time, support for Irish unity is at record levels.

The process of negotiating trade deals is complex and the UK government has chosen speed over quality on some of the initial trade deals they have negotiated. During this time, while seeking new trade deals to replace those which expired when EU membership ended, the UK will operate in a twilight zone – while London may be able to survive because of its historic role as a leading global centre of finance, a small peripheral region such as Northern Ireland will struggle, not least because 100 miles down the road there is Dublin, with its native English-speaking population, access to migrant workers and continued membership of the EU.

London has, until now, arguably been the financial capital of the world, predicated on several factors such as location, availability of native English-speaking workers, its status as a global, cosmopolitan city and – crucially – its membership within the European Union including the Single European Market (which the UK government helped to create). All of this was altered by the vote to leave the EU. While the UK government will seek to protect the position of London, there are many cities within the EU, such as Frankfurt, Paris, Amsterdam and Dublin, that have all stripped financial services away from the UK capital. This presents a huge opportunity for Dublin and the island through Irish unity: as a country in the Eurozone as well as the EU, with a low corporate tax rate and access to highly skilled workers, Ireland can offer certainty for inward investors.

Remote working became normalised during the initial lockdown and the time that has followed, presenting an opportunity for more balanced growth across Ireland. The Irish government formed in mid-2020 is committed to rolling out a national broadband strategy which will help to ensure we can take advantage of this new opportunity. Now, more than ever, people will be able to secure skilled jobs while savouring the beautiful scenery across the entirety of our island. Dublin was – before the COVID-19 pandemic – in danger of overheating, as it was at risk of running out of Grade A office space, housing and skilled workers. Remote working helped to alleviate these concerns, but reunification can help further. Northern Ireland can offer much-needed extra resources such as cheaper housing and access to a highly skilled talent pool. It will also be able to provide cheaper Grade A office space, should this market come back. Just as in the Irish Republic, we can reinvigorate our rural towns and villages, as well as our suburbs, across Northern Ireland.

Unity is now a credible option

Irish unity is now firmly in the centre of the Overton window, a concept whereby only certain things are acceptable for political discourse. Other political ideas such as the Irish Republic re-joining the UK or Ireland deciding to leave the EU, are simply too far outside the mainstream to be seriously considered. The crucial fact is that moderate unionists or 'post-unionists' are now giving serious contemplation to Irish unity, in part as a vehicle to regain full membership of the EU for the region. This is starting to happen through public debate – as we have seen in large set piece events such as those being held by Ireland's Future – which has an important role in providing a platform for discussion, engaging with interested parties and energising those in favour of a New Ireland. I know that at the same time, from my own experience, there are lots of private chats within groups of people from unionist backgrounds about being open to Irish unity. These quiet conversations are key to engaging with unionism.

Liberal unionists may have needed a nudge to consider the benefits of Irish unity. The vote to leave the EU based on the votes of England is a stark reminder that all of us across Ireland need to decide our future.

Northern Ireland will be uniquely squeezed by the UK's decision to leave the EU. Suddenly, Irish unity is the safe, secure option for a prosperous, stable and outward-looking future. It will also be one where the unionist community will have a real say in their own future as key players at a national level, with direct access through the Irish government to the EU, the UN and elsewhere on the world stage.

Now that the Brexit transition period has ended, we are beginning to see increased friction in trade between Britain and Northern Ireland. While we do not know, at the time of writing, the long-term impact of the post-Brexit trade arrangements between the EU and UK, it is clear that the relationships between Northern Ireland and Britain and between Northern Ireland and the Irish Republic will be changed utterly. The different arrangements for Northern Ireland such as the Northern Ireland Protocol will create momentum to move towards an ever-closer relationship with the Irish Republic. The all-Ireland economy is growing and Brexit will give it further impetus to deepen and strengthen economic activity across the island.

Unity is a credible option, not to create a fortress in Ireland but to build on Ireland's already open economy and soft power through its membership in the EU, to spread its culture and to seek new inward investment and opportunities for all the people on the island. By June 2018, 26 per cent of other EU nationals had left Northern Ireland following the decision on Brexit.[11] This is a terrible result of that negative vote. These are people who contributed to our society, who enriched our culture, working across a range of key sectors, including healthcare, the food industry and tourism. Ireland as an island is better because of the diversity of its people.

Unity is an automatic entry to the EU

The former UK Prime Minister Theresa May stated after the Brexit vote that there was an increased possibility of Irish unity in the context of Brexit. In a meeting with her Conservative MPs, Theresa May went further and said that a vote to remain part of the UK could not be taken for granted by the people of Northern Ireland.

The former Taoiseach Enda Kenny had it written into European Council text that Northern Ireland will automatically become part of the EU again in the event of Irish unity. In other words, there would be no accession process for the region. Rather, it would automatically become part of the EU again. This is an off-the-shelf solution that allows those who favour Irish unity to have a clear pathway forward. Both the EU and UK government have openly acknowledged that this right to become reunited within the EU is automatic.

The European Union after Brexit no longer feels obliged to be neutral on the question of whether Northern Ireland should stay part of the UK, or whether there should be Irish unity. In the past, because both the UK and Ireland were members of the European Union, the EU institutions did not want to take a position over a dispute between two member states. Now that Brexit has been delivered, that block to an expression of a European viewpoint has been removed. Imagine there continues to be a strong majority within Northern Ireland who wish to be part of the EU now that the UK has left the EU. If this is blocked by the UK, or if it simply proves too difficult to maintain the open border across Ireland, the sense of frustration could quickly escalate further towards majority support for Irish unity.

In these circumstances the EU, which has invested a significant amount of time, money and effort into the Irish peace process, will have no reason not to express an opinion when it relates to a dispute between a member state and a third country (which is what the UK has now become). Northern Ireland geographically, politically and economically is already semi-detached from Britain. A UK government, which has focused on delivering Brexit and fighting off the demands of the independence-supporting Scottish Government, is unlikely to have the resources or energy to resist Irish reunification. We have already seen senior UK Conservatives openly expressing their agnosticism about Scotland's continued membership of the UK. Therefore, why should we expect the UK government to put up a fight to keep Northern Ireland within the UK? In geopolitical terms, EU support for Irish unity could be a great way for the EU to show that it has got its mojo back after the shock of Brexit and the initially slow roll-out of vaccines during the COVID-19 pandemic.

EU support for Ireland

The EU quickly realised the potential impact of Brexit and acted to support the peace process in Northern Ireland. Michel Barnier, the chief Brexit negotiator for the EU, worked as a European commissioner on regional development nearly 20 years ago when the Good Friday Agreement was just bedding in. He understands the importance of the peace process. The EU made the border in Ireland (keeping it open) one of the three key issues which had to be addressed to their satisfaction before they would engage in future trade arrangements.

Throughout the negotiations, the EU has made clear that Ireland is the number one priority. Spain is not concerned about a reunited Ireland being part of the EU, as it believes the circumstances are different to the prospect of Catalonia, or the Basque Country, separating from Spain and seeking membership in the EU.

Ireland, as it stands, has formed strong, working relationships with other EU member states – France in particular. Ireland joined the Organisation Internationale de la Francophonie, one of 17 EU countries that are members or observers. This is another example of Ireland's focus on growing its influence through a variety of networks and leveraging its soft power. The French Ambassador to Ireland has stated that France is now the closest EU neighbour to Ireland post-Brexit. The two main pillars for the EU post-Brexit are France and Germany, so the Irish government has consciously focused on deepening links with France.

Ireland has carved out a role within the EU post-Brexit which is starting to take a formal shape via the Ireland-founded 'New Hanseatic League' which also includes Denmark, Finland, Sweden, the Baltic states and the Netherlands. This is focused on fiscally conservative countries working together on economic issues.

The EU would see the reunification of Ireland for exactly what it is – the welcome healing of a long divided and troubled isle. A vote for unity will be a vote for progressive politics and building a viable economic future.

Brexit hostility towards devolution

Brexit is innately hostile towards the legislatures of Scotland, Wales and Northern Ireland. The UK government has a Tory majority in Westminster because of Conservative MPs elected in England. They hold a minority of MPs elected in Scottish constituencies, a minority of MPs elected in Welsh constituencies and none in Northern Ireland; they hold a minority of MSPs in the Scottish Parliament, a minority of members of the Senedd in Wales and, again, none in the Northern Ireland Assembly. They have no elected representatives at any level in Northern Ireland. The Government that holds us all to account is not representative of us or our needs. This removal of powers from the devolved administrations goes against what was agreed in referendums in Scotland, Wales and Northern Ireland.

The UK 'Internal Market Bill', as originally tabled, was set to break international law due to its potential impact on the Withdrawal Agreement and the Northern Ireland Protocol. The Northern Ireland Secretary of State at the time indicated that the Internal Market Bill would break said law 'in a specific and limited way'.[12] The originally drafted Bill directly contravened an act passed into law by the UK government in the same parliamentary session and was against a clear manifesto commitment. Even though the offending clauses were removed, it is still deeply concerning that a UK government would behave in this way, in a blatant attempt to secure leverage in trade talks. In the run-up to and since the May 2022 Northern Ireland Assembly elections, the UK government repeatedly threatened to pass domestic legislation to override an international treaty which it signed. This is not helpful.

In June 2022 Liz Truss, then UK foreign secretary, tabled in Parliament the Northern Ireland Protocol Bill which, if passed, would enable the UK government to unilaterally override large aspects of the Northern Ireland Protocol. Both the EU and US administrations have warned the UK government not to follow through on this course of action.

This reckless approach creates uncertainty about whether the UK government can be a reliable trade partner. One of the key arguments for Brexit was the possibility of leaving the EU and its Single Market to secure better trade deals with other parts of the world. This has yet to be realised and now that the UK has admitted to an intention to break international law, it will become much harder to negotiate preferential trade deals. Just like buying a car or house, the riskier you are as a party to a commercial transaction, the higher rate of interest you are likely to be asked to pay.

In the years since Brexit, we have begun to see a political decoupling of Wales from England. Support for Welsh independence reached 39 per cent in 2021,[13] up from eight per cent just a few years ago. When Scotland announced that its independence referendum in would be held 2014, support at the start of the campaign for independence was only at 28–30 per cent. Over the course of the campaign, this grew until it reached 45 per cent on the day of the vote. Since then, of course, it has grown to as high as 58 per cent, which shows that momentum continues to build, despite the UK government's attempts to ignore the debate. I, with the majority of both Northern Ireland and Scotland, wanted the UK to stay together with the EU. If England wants to stay outside the orbit of the EU that is its choice, but this should not be forced on Scotland or any part of Ireland.

Shared Island Unit

The Shared Island Unit is a positive step towards building and strengthening how we deliver public services and grow the economy between North and South and between different parts of the community in the North. It will certainly help to prepare the way for Irish unity, but it will also be beneficial for all across the island of Ireland before unity happens. It will lead to more cooperation in how services are delivered in a coordinated way across the island; however, this does not mean it can be used as an excuse to stop discussions about unity. We must be allowed to have the democratic process develop naturally without impediment.

The fact the DUP warned against Dublin interference when the Irish government set up the Shared Island Unit and the UUP said they would not engage, are damning indictments of Unionism. Every time Unionist representatives refuse to engage with their neighbours on this island, they do themselves and the people they claim to represent a disservice. Let's have a proper, rational debate about what happens on the island of Ireland. Rather than being offended by any discussion about Irish unity, I want Unionists to attempt to convince me of the merits of Northern Ireland continuing as part of the UK.

Views on unification North and South

Northern Ireland's vote to remain part of the EU by a clear margin of its voters from across the political spectrum has not been respected by successive Conservative prime ministers. Northern Ireland's vote to Remain is the most progressive vote for the region since the Good Friday Agreement referendum and it deserves to be acknowledged as such.

The combination of leaving the EU and the creation of a hard border between Northern Ireland and Britain has created, and will continue to cause, a great deal of political and economic trauma for Northern Ireland. The fact that Northern Ireland has been given unique trading arrangements with the EU, where Scotland has not, will be a key driver for Scottish independence. This will, in turn, affect Northern Ireland further as Scotland is a significant cultural anchor for Northern Ireland unionists to stay in the UK. Many people may start to believe that Irish unity in these circumstances is the best way forward, myself included.

Under the terms of the EU–UK trade deal, the UK will now gradually diverge from EU regulations and law, whereas Northern Ireland will remain within the EU regulatory zone and EU law will continue to apply. While Ireland will remain part of the EU, the influence of UK law (as its court decisions were often used for precedence in Ireland) will gradually dissipate. UK cultural influence such as supporting sports teams like Manchester United, Liverpool and Everton will continue; people will still watch British TV and listen to British music, but economic and legal drivers will increasingly come from Brussels, Paris and Berlin, not London.

Concepts of Irishness

We are now more than fifty years on from the civil rights marches of the late 1960s, but we still do not have equality. The UK government attempted to unilaterally designate people born in Northern Ireland as British citizens, to allow them to stay in Northern Ireland without having to register, unlike other EU citizens. This contravened the Good Friday Agreement, which allows all people born in Northern Ireland to choose to be Irish, British or both. Concepts of Irishness – whether we are 'fully' Irish, or whether we also identify as British, in some way – must be respected by all: our MPs, the UK government and especially the people of the island of Ireland. The key point is that nobody should be forced to become one of these nationalities against their wishes. A court case brought by journalist, political commentator and campaigner Emma Da Souza in 2015 led to the UK government eventually confirming, in 2020, the rights of those in Northern Ireland to designate as Irish, British or both and not to have any nationality forced upon them. The UK government announced in May 2020 that all UK and Irish citizens born in Northern Ireland would be treated as EU citizens for immigration purposes. This was, however, only a temporary change until June 2021, the date the EU settlement scheme closed.[14]

Unionists are panicking about Brexit, in denial about the consequences of their own actions. Regarding Irish passports – which allow their holders smoother sailing through EU airport customs, for example – DUP MP Ian Paisley Junior said,, 'It's a European document with an Irish harp stuck on the front posing as a passport'.[15] This statement is not only factually incorrect but also shows a clear lack of respect.

Ireland, particularly Northern Ireland, is a fractious society. The political debate has been frozen in Northern Ireland for the quarter of a century since the passing of the Good Friday Agreement – at least until the Brexit vote. The campaign of violence by both loyalist and republican groups had exhausted any appetite for constitutional upheaval; politics in Northern Ireland just before the EU referendum had become inert, rather than stable. The lack of innovative thinking was disappointing, but it is understandable that people had become disengaged with politics and simply wanted to get on with dealing with bread-and-butter issues, living their daily lives. Brexit has woken people up from their torpor – the debate around Irish unity, long dormant except for a few diehards and gratuitous references by the main Nationalist parties at their conferences, is active once again.

Republicans had not fully engaged with the EU referendum in Northern Ireland – they were historically ambivalent about the EU and simply paid lip service to campaigning to remain in the EU. Voter numbers in republican strongholds were very low, but while in the referendum 56 per cent voted in favour of remaining within the EU, opinion polls since the referendum show up to 69 per cent in favour of doing so.[16] There is also a clear majority in favour of Northern Ireland securing a special status relating to the EU, which is not available to the rest of the UK. Despite the hugely promising economic opportunities this could provide for the region, the two main Unionist parties are implacably opposed to Northern Ireland being treated differently in any way from the rest of the UK. The irony is that, on social issues, Northern Ireland only has some of the same legal rights as Britain and Ireland because MPs at Westminster voted for them, despite objections from Unionist politicians.

The new Northern Irish

The fact that many of us have dual nationalities and therefore multiple identities is something rather unique to Northern Ireland and something that was facilitated and protected by the EU. Alongside Irish and British, the increasingly popular Northern Irish identity, which is an evolving one is not dependent on our relationship with or feelings towards the UK. Those who identify as such need not worry about giving up this identity post-unity – even after reunification, there can still be a sense of being from Northern Ireland. After all, people talk about being from Southern California and their state is not a divided one.

Currently, Northern Ireland is like the slightly embarrassing and truculent stepson who has been inherited after a divorce. Britain is the reluctant father that does not really want to be involved, but does not yet have a reason to walk away. Our region urgently needs economic, political and social reform but this will never happen for so long as it remains part of the UK. Northern Ireland is too dependent on money coming from Westminster and our politics is semi-detached from both British and Irish politics. The political debate needs to move beyond constitutional issues, to focus on how we deliver opportunities for all our citizens. This can only happen once the vote for unity has been secured. This island is too small to remain divided and the Irish are too great a people with too much potential to be fractured as a nation any longer. But our region is a contested space which encourages parties to fight for supremacy. We need to widen our engagement, as the Northern Ireland structure makes every election a sectarian headcount – we will never have true freedom across the island of Ireland until we are at peace with each other.

In light of the Boston College tapes court decision and the stated intention to prosecute British soldiers for Bloody Sunday, should there be a truth commission to deal with all of these issues? And what would the consequences be? While people will understandably still be haunted by the past, we must endeavour to not be trapped within it. Any reconciliation process runs the risk of opening old wounds that will need time to heal. Many dreadful things happened during The Troubles, but I believe that the best way we can honour the victims and those who died fighting to protect the peace, is to move forward. Remember those who were lost, but help our young people live for the future.

Challenge for Unionism

The DUP angered nationalists and centrists with the description of feeding a crocodile during the 2017 Northern Ireland Assembly campaign, when referring to acceding to demands for Irish language recognition. That was the first time Unionism in Northern Ireland secured less than 50 per cent of the vote – they only managed to get 40 assembly members out of a total of 90; Sinn Féin were only 1200 first preference votes behind the DUP and ended up one seat behind them. Since Sinn Féin emerged as the largest party in the May 2022 elections, some Unionists have said that they would refuse to serve as part of a Northern Ireland Executive under a Sinn Féin first minister. The roles of first and deputy first minister are co-equal; however, the symbolism of such a change would appear to be too much for the brittle confidence of political Unionism.

One of the problems with political Unionism is that compromise and pragmatism are seen as a defeat, but if the DUP walk away from the Northern Ireland Assembly, they will be left with no power base. They no longer hold the balance of power at Westminster. The UK government has already made its position clear by agreeing to an Irish Sea border through the Northern Ireland Protocol, as they want to be free to pursue trade deals with other countries while keeping their commitment to no hard border on the island of Ireland.

Cooperation or accommodation do not come easily to Unionism, which grieves for the loss of its majority. The DUP failed to do a deal to restore the Northern Ireland Assembly in February 2018; they were unable to bring their party membership with them. Unionists had a window of opportunity after the Good Friday Agreement was signed in 1998 to make Northern Ireland work for all. Instead, they fought amongst themselves and continued to show a begrudging reluctance to share power with Nationalists and the non-aligned. Ultimately, they agreed to go back into power in January 2020, but that was only after they lost their position of influence at Westminster. History will look back and wonder how they managed to throw away leverage with a minority Conservative UK government.

Political success is not secured by holding out for 100 per cent purity – it is achieved by knowing when to compromise, when to cash in your chips and claim victory. But Northern Ireland is a pressure cooker environment that encourages parties to seek victory over the other side, rather than work together from the outset.

There is a term for a situation in which the obligation to make a move in one's turn is a serious, often decisive, disadvantage – Zugzwang (taken from chess). This is what the DUP faced in agreeing to resurrect the Northern Ireland Assembly. Sinn Féin are on the rise across Ireland, not just in Northern Ireland – in the Republic's election of February 2020, they secured the largest number of first preference votes. The only reason why they did not finish as the largest party is because they did not run enough candidates. They will not make that mistake again.

The DUP, the largest Unionist party in Northern Ireland, has always struggled with the concept of sharing power and in many ways has been hostile to the equality agenda. They have used the Petition of Concern on several occasions to block proposals that otherwise would have passed such as abortion rights,[17] available elsewhere in the UK.

The challenge for Unionism – one which currently they appear unable to meet – is this: since the Good Friday Agreement, they must effectively share power with Nationalists to make the Northern Ireland Executive and Assembly work. If they are not willing to do that, then there can be no government. Essentially, Direct Rule is the UK government administration at arm's length and includes full consultation on all critical issues with the Irish government – in other words, joint authority by another name. Every time there is a new round of negotiations, Unionism comes back to the table with a weaker hand. Sinn Féin leads the official Opposition in the Republic; while the current Irish coalition government intends to serve a full term until 2025, we may not have to wait that long to see Sinn Féin in government on both sides of the border in Ireland.

If all Unionists had campaigned for remaining in the EU, it would be easier to sympathise with the situation they find themselves in. However, Brexit is a problem the DUP actively campaigned for and so they must live with the consequences. As the only major party in Northern Ireland that explicitly called for the UK to leave the EU, they own all of the downsides.

Even now, a quarter century after the Good Friday Agreement was signed, Unionism struggles to share power. While welcoming the concept of power-sharing, Nationalists have felt badly let down by the DUP in recent years. Moderate unionists and agnostics are not overly attached to Stormont – there have been too many scandals and it is too unstable a form of government. It has collapsed on multiple occasions, with lengthy periods of not operating. Businesses, in particular, want reliable politicians who are willing to take hard-headed, evidence-based decisions.

Due to the unique nature of the all-Ireland economy and the repercussions of the pandemic and in order to help ensure the best course through the Brexit process, the Northern Ireland Executive will be pushed towards ever more collaboration with the Irish government. The cross-border bodies and the North–South Ministerial Council will continue and will gradually increase collaboration on an all-Ireland basis.

The UK will continue to be preoccupied with Brexit, as the negotiations continue after the trade deal and likely breakaway of Scotland. In those circumstances, a border poll will merely confirm changes that have already happened. There will not be an alternative to cleave to the mother's bosom for Unionists as the Westminster parties will not want, or be able to afford, time to focus on them. Ultimately, the DUP are Ulster Nationalists and do not want full UK integration. Therefore, Irish unity will be the only realistic option on the table.

Unionism's shrinking voter base

In the 1960s and '70s the Mayor of Chicago, Richard J Daley, actively used the provision of public housing as a way to keep African American communities separate from his Irish and Italian white working-class groups in order to preserve his voter base. Over 50 years later, in Northern Ireland, keeping tribal voting blocs alive is still a key focus for the DUP, as their voter base is declining, while nationalist and non-aligned centrist (and pro-EU) voter bases continue to grow.

Northern Ireland has suffered because of its divided society since the partition era – it is stark how such segregation remains ingrained in the various institutions of the state. Sheffield Hallam University's research on welfare reform showed that Northern Ireland would be the UK region most adversely affected by the changes.[18]: housing is still 90 per cent single identity; education is still heavily segregated. Some unionists will be unfazed by this – some will even welcome this separation of people. However, there are soft unionists and post-unionists, as well as the moderate non-aligned centre who want to change this dynamic and encourage integration. For everyone across the island of Ireland to move forward, we need to be focused on inclusivity, not on what separates us.

Sinn Féin have been able to engage beyond their previous voting base by emphasising their support for progressive issues, such as a woman's right to choose and equal marriage. They have also been vocal about the need for Northern Ireland's vote to remain in the EU to be respected. It is ironic the DUP's support for a hard Brexit has helped to rehabilitate Sinn Féin for many moderate voters and turned them away from Unionism.

Unionism can no longer rely simply on a numerical advantage when it comes to policy issues in Northern Ireland and it should take this opportunity to negotiate the shape of Irish unity from a position of relative strength. There are too many representatives of political Unionism who are still irreconciled to the fact that they no longer represent the majority.

Change is happening and moderate middle-class unionists are changing their minds because of Brexit. UK government officials rarely state that they care passionately about keeping Northern Ireland in the UK. In 1989, Peter Brooke said the UK government had no selfish economic interest; David Cameron said that the UK did have a selfish interest in Northern Ireland. However, aside from an ill-fated link-up with the UUP in 2010, which returned no MPs, he took a hands-off approach to the region. Theresa May had talked about the 'precious union' while buying off the DUP votes. Yet, when it came down to it, she ignored the red lines of the DUP and agreed with the EU that Northern Ireland would be treated differently.

On the one hand, Unionists claim to want exactly the same Brexit deal as the rest of the UK. However, they were happy to have different social laws from the rest of the UK, as well as different tax laws for Air Passenger Duty, water tax and corporation tax. There was an unspoken hope amongst some within political Unionism, that if there was going to be a hard border it would not be between Northern Ireland and Britain. Invariably this would mean it is placed on the island of Ireland. They believed that the creation of a hard border and leaving the EU, along with the rest of the UK, would lock Northern Ireland into the UK for the long term, regardless of demographic change. However, in reality, they were sowing the seeds of their downfall.

Nationalism has embraced the need for Irish unity in the short term and many moderates previously equivocal on the future of Northern Ireland as well as soft unionists are now re-evaluating their views on what is best for the future of Northern Ireland. The demand for seamless passage across the island of Ireland is shared by the vast majority of its people, North and South.

Unionism's outdated views

The vitriol directed towards the DUP during their agreement with the minority Conservative government by a cross-section of mainstream UK politicians should be a stark warning for Unionism in Northern Ireland. When politicians, commentators and campaign groups became aware of the DUP's backwards views, there was a great deal of anger directed toward them. Such hostility shows that there is no groundswell of goodwill that they can tap into within mainstream British thinking. They do not support the LGBT+ community; they are against equal marriage and some of their members are in favour of creationism. Unionism, therefore, cannot be seen as liberal and progressive. The implicit and explicit message is that people want to see these rights for our citizens who are not welcomed by Unionism.

While a small number of Unionist representatives may claim to be socially liberal, this is not backed up by the actions of the main Unionist parties. When Arlene Foster took over as leader of the DUP and first minister of Northern Ireland, it was hoped that she would be a moderating influence who could lead Unionism on a modernising process.

But the DUP have shown time and time again that they are unwilling or unable to represent the views of the majority in the region. Their mindset is stuck in a warped, 19th-century view of the world.

Mainstream political thinking in the UK has been outspoken in criticising the reversal of the Roe v Wade case by the US Supreme Court in 2022. This severely reduced a woman's right to access safe and legal abortions and the decision was met with shock and anger across the world, including in Ireland, but Unionism in Northern Ireland has continually sought to stop women from having the same level of access to abortions as citizens in the rest of the UK. Northern Ireland was the only part of the UK that did not allow same-sex marriage or abortion until the UK Parliament legislated for these rights. The DUP opposed these liberalisations, whereas unionists in Scotland, by comparison, have been able to embrace progressive values whilst still advocating Britishness.

If Nationalism/Republicanism wished to create an ideal Unionist party from their perspective, it would be hard to envision something much different from the current DUP. The various platitudes about modernisation and reaching out to Catholics and non-unionists have been proven to be empty words with no deeper meaning.

There is nothing inherently wrong with believing in unionism - believing in the link between Northern Ireland and Britain. However, a part of unionism believes in supremacism over others because they have been brought up with ideas of British exceptionalism that they trace back to the Battle of the Boyne in 1690. Should Unionist parties seek only to represent these hard-line unionists, they will only alienate themselves further from the wider population of Northern Ireland.

If Unionism wants to grow its supporter base, it needs to compromise and reach out to non-unionists, instead of constantly retreating to its narrowing voter base. However, the siege mentality is alive and well within Unionism – circling the wagons may make unionists feel secure in the short term, but it is no way to live in the long term. When Unionists equate Unionism with being a Protestant, in cultural terms if not religious, this only undermines their ability to widen their voter base.

There is a historical context that helps to explain why Unionism finds itself in this predicament, voluntarily reducing its reach by appealing to one section of society by narrow religious affiliation. Eamon de Valera, leader of Fianna Fáil, stated in an election meeting in 1932 that Catholicism provided his guiding principles; James Craig, prime minister of Northern Ireland subsequently, in a debate in the Northern Ireland Parliament in 1934, stated that 'we are a Protestant Parliament and a Protestant State.'[19] Both of these approaches were wrong. Leader of the UUP David Trimble, after he became first minister of Northern Ireland in 1998, said: 'I believe we can provide a pluralist parliament for a pluralist people'.[20] The two previous quotes show one of the damaging aspects of partition leading to insular thinking and divisiveness; David Trimble's visionary thinking (along with the leadership shown by John Hume and others) led to the Good Friday Agreement, which in turn offered a pathway to prosperity and peace – unfortunately, this has not been fully realised more than two decades later.[21] While many people, including violent republicans and loyalists, can be blamed for this across the political spectrum, anti-agreement Unionists played a key wrecking role, as they had done at Sunningdale in 1974. This was an agreement between the UK and Irish governments to set up a power-sharing government in Northern Ireland. Unionists refused to accept the concept of power-sharing, criticised this as a form of defeat and encouraged unionist voters to believe that it would be possible to go back to Unionist-only rule.

The Unionist mantra now is that there will never be Irish unity – they have sought to discount the mere idea of unity without even a proper debate on its merits.

At one time, Unionists in Northern Ireland stated that they wanted to be fully integrated into the British political mainstream – there was even a campaign for equal citizenship in the 1980s to pursue this objective. Under DUP leadership, there is no longer a desire to fully integrate with the rest of the UK. I remember speaking with a DUP minister after the 2010 Westminster election and asking him why the DUP as a Unionist party did not join with the Conservatives to be part of a UK-wide party. His response was simple: 'they are different from us'.

Through my work, I attended the UUP conference where David Cameron spoke in late 2009 before the 2010 election that led to him becoming Prime Minister. He talked about the UCUNF (link-up between the Conservatives and UUP) and I remember thinking this was the last chance for Northern Ireland to become integrated fully into the UK politically and move beyond tribal politics into focusing on bread-and-butter issues. Instead, the UUP argued it was important that they kept their own autonomy. It could perhaps have made a difference to the UK union if one or two MPs had been elected on a joint ticket. However, not only Nationalists, but also other Unionists were opposed to this link-up being a success.

This sums up the dichotomy that continues to face Unionism and has been exacerbated by Brexit. What does it say about Unionist politicians who claim that they want to be part of the UK, but do not want to be involved with their politicians?

The June 2017 UK election result should have been an ideal opportunity for the DUP to move into the UK mainstream. Instead, they chose to stay on the sidelines and negotiate additional funding for Northern Ireland in return for supporting the minority government on certain key votes, creating concern across the political spectrum.

This confidence and supply agreement was out of the ordinary in many ways, but the most unusual aspect of the agreement was a mainland UK government relying on a Northern Ireland party to function. While there was a strong link between the Ulster Unionists and the Conservatives until the middle of the 1970s, there has not been a Northern Ireland MP who has served as a member of the UK

Cabinet for decades, since the end of the Second World War. The fact that MPs from Northern Ireland actively supporting the UK government was such an unusual occurrence says a lot about Northern Ireland's position within the UK.

Lack of representation for young unionists

Young people today are leading campaigns for equality; they are at the forefront of activism – take Greta Thunberg, the 19-year-old climate activist, or Amanda Gorman, the National Youth Poet Laureate and activist who was just 22 years old when she moved millions during her reading at President Biden's inauguration. Thousands of young people across the island of Ireland took part in climate protests and Black Lives Matter marches – young people around the world want to see positive change and they want to put their faith in progressive, forward-thinking politicians. But young unionists are not being represented by the DUP and their backwards, outdated views – even in 2022, former Northern Ireland Environment Minister and DUP MP Sammy Wilson is, bafflingly and ironically, a climate sceptic and continues to deny and belittle concerns over climate change,[22] the effects of which will be the most detrimental for young people and their future.

It will not be long until the lack of options and responsible leadership for young unionists pushes them towards unity for a progressive future. 82 per cent of people from this background are in favour of being part of the UK.[23] However, that means nearly 20 per cent are not in favour of remaining part of the UK – if these unionists move towards supporting Irish unity, especially as a means of securing a more socially liberal state, unity will happen.

Young unionists are just like every other young person in Northern Ireland, the Irish Republic, Britain and elsewhere. They have dreams and aspirations; they want to live happy, fulfilling lives. Unfortunately, within political Unionism, there is a focus on stopping change or even just refusing to act. The objections to GAA (Gaelic Athletic Association) sports teams using vacant sports pitches in East Belfast,[24] or stopping an Irish language pre-school being set up in East Belfast,[25] for example, do not help young people. Trying to prevent further integration and education will only harm their future. Political Unionism's focus on stopping change means blocking any progress at all costs. How on earth will this improve the lives of young people in the long term?

Sectoral groups

There are many well-researched reports already available on how to improve public services across Ireland such as the Bengoa Report on transforming healthcare in Northern Ireland,[26] or the Engineers Ireland report on digital infrastructure across Ireland.[27] We should also look at how healthcare is delivered in Canada, Australia and New Zealand. In Canada, there is increasing usage of digital health to ensure that healthcare provisions are brought to the patient. While Ireland is a smaller land mass than Canada, the principle of using technology to better serve citizens is the right approach. There are also more general publications on creating Irish unity such as reports by a Dáil and Seanad Committee on 'Uniting Ireland & its People in Peace & Prosperity',[28] or *United Nation: The Case for Integrating Ireland* written by the journalist Frank Connolly.[29] All of these can be used to feed into the work of the sectoral groups that should be set up to develop a range of options for unifying the island of Ireland.

Political Unionism is unlikely to participate in advance of a vote for Irish unity, but we are already seeing civic unionism engage in the discussion on unity. Unionists should be invited to help implement recommendations post-unity, but these recommendations should be as practical and depoliticised as possible. This will mean that although Unionist political representatives may refuse to contribute to this work in advance of a referendum, they will at least have been invited to do so.

Using the all-Ireland Brexit forum and sector group meetings as templates, the Irish government should set up a series of sector-working groups on how best to deliver Irish unity. This should be done before the poll is called. A Green Paper should also be published by the Irish government setting out the vision for a New Ireland.

These groups should be established for key sectors such as housing, health, education, infrastructure and the economy; they should have experts from private, public and voluntary sectors, perhaps from around the world. Each of the panels would be tasked with providing recommendations that drive efficiencies and integration should be cross-cutting in nature. Transparency is key and evidence sessions should take place in public unless there are specific commercial sensitivities.

The recommendations should be made in advance of the referendum, so voters know what they are voting for and the Irish government should have the authority to accept or adjust them – democratic accountability is key. If the Irish government chooses to adjust recommendations, they should explain publicly why they have done so. The final proposed structure of the New Ireland, after this extensive consultation with all parts of society, should be contained in a White Paper published by the Irish government. These proposals would then be implemented after successful referendums in both states on the island of Ireland for Irish unity.

This process will provide a transparent way of building momentum for unity and certainty on what it will mean. The resulting papers from each of the sectoral groups can be released during the unity campaign to focus the debate on practical steps and issues, rather than myths.

Template for unity

The joint campaigning by pro-Remain parties Sinn Féin, SDLP, Alliance and the Greens provide a template for the unity campaign. While all four of these parties may not decide to campaign for unity, there will be supporters from across the political spectrum advocating a vote for Irish unity.

While the Irish Republic continues to embrace a diverse, progressive and prosperous future, Northern Ireland is frozen in time. Too often communities in Northern Ireland are focused on the past, arguing over past conflicts, discrimination and other historic events. The COVID-19 pandemic must act as a wake-up call – we need to reorientate thinking so that society focuses on the pressing issues of the present, such as the climate crisis, housing, health and creating jobs which includes having a world-class education system for all our people.

The Northern Ireland Assembly was suspended for three years and was reanimated just before the COVID-19 pandemic hit the island. Unionism was unable, at the start of this health crisis, to agree to an all-Ireland approach, preferring instead to blindly follow the UK government's lead and their flawed approach of pursuing herd immunity without a vaccine being available.

We can no longer afford the duplication of services across the island or within Northern Ireland. Research conducted in 2007 identified that the duplication of services is costing Northern Ireland an additional £1.5 billion a year because of the segregated nature of society and delivery of public services.[30] It means our taxes are spent less efficiently on public services than they could be and there are barriers to trade across Ireland, where there should be none. We have to do more to give people opportunities to earn a living, too many people feel they have to leave the island of Ireland to progress their careers; too often we are afraid to challenge political parties for their lack of leadership. For Irish unity to work we need to move away from this clunky duplication of services and give people hope that they can fulfil their dreams by staying in Ireland. Of course, living in other countries will always hold an appeal and great personal learning can come from those experiences, but we do not want Ireland to be a place where the young, in particular, feel obliged to leave because of a lack of a rewarding future.

In the post-EU referendum world, Irish unity offers stability and continuity through continued membership of the EU. Membership provides economic opportunities and human rights safeguards that are just not available outside of the EU. The choice is between either remaining separated from the EU in a rump UK of 60 million people (as Scotland is sure to leave) or in the European Union with full, unfettered access to its Single Market of 450 million people.

The EU will be the framework to provide safeguards for Unionists after Irish unity has been secured. This will be an excellent opportunity for the EU to show the world – most importantly, Britain – that it still has a vital role to play.

Building blocks for unity

The difference in economic output between the two states on our island is stark – the Republic has been one of the fastest growing economies in the European Union, whereas Northern Ireland is one of the slowest growing regions and the UK has seen lower GDP growth than the major EU countries since 2015. Irish unity will provide much-needed additional capacity for the Irish economy, as Northern Ireland-based workers and housing become integrated fully into the Irish economy, giving a significant boost to both parts of the island. It is also the only permanent way to ensure that there is no hard border reintroduced on the island of Ireland.

It would be great to see more political parties contesting elections across the island of Ireland, such as Fine Gael, Fianna Fáil and Alliance. Sinn Féin does already, but they stand on a populist left-wing platform. Their growth potential is also restricted by their historic links with the Provisional IRA, although this is less relevant for the younger generation who have no memory of The Troubles. Democracy thrives when voters have a wide range of credible choices across the political spectrum.

The more steps Northern Ireland takes now to mitigate the impact of the Brexit vote, the better prepared it will be for Irish unity. The region's ability to take action is restricted by its lack of control over government policy. Instead, decisions are taken elsewhere. The more Northern Ireland falls in line with the UK's creep towards a hard Brexit, the more economic and social turmoil there is likely to be in the region. There is an emerging all-Ireland economy – that is an economic fact, not a political statement. The better the Northern Ireland economy performs, the more manageable Irish unity becomes.

The Economy

'Things take longer to happen than you think they will, but then they happen much faster than you thought they could.'[31]

Al Gore

THE ROAD TO Irish unity will be a long one, but in the interim, until reunification happens, we may see an increase in cross-border trade. The UK market is the second biggest for the Irish Republic after the USA and Irish firms are keen to ensure full access to this market post-Brexit. One of the best ways in which they can achieve this is by having a physical presence in the UK. Setting up an office in Northern Ireland, for example Belfast which is only 100 miles away from Dublin, logistically will be easier and cheaper than relocating to London. At the same time, we are already seeing examples of Northern Ireland-based manufacturing companies taking factory space just south of the border in Dundalk to enable their manufacturing to comply with EU requirements and ensure that the goods they make will meet the Single Market Rules of origin. These are two brief examples of how the two states on the island can begin to work together to minimise the negative impacts of Brexit.

Northern Ireland will not succeed by merely pointing their begging bowl in the direction of the South to Dublin rather than the East to London. Irish citizens do not want to be burdened with increased taxes to subside the North and its unwieldy public sector. However, the research paper 'Modelling Irish Unification' discusses the financial benefits of reunification, as the process of reuniting the economically poorer Northern Ireland with the more prosperous Irish Republic will generate economic growth across the island.[32] Furthermore, this research published in 2015 showed that a reunified Ireland would deliver an additional €35 billion over the first eight years and most of this would be within the area currently known as Northern Ireland.[33] With a New Ireland using the euro as part of the Eurozone, this initial injection of growth would help the North rapidly close the gap and catch up to the Irish Republic's levels of prosperity. There is a way that the island can work together to grow the all-island economy for the benefit of everyone.

Brexit, the COVID-19 pandemic, the cost-of-living crisis and the housing shortage all point to the need for an all-island approach on every issue that affects all citizens (of whatever country) who live across Ireland.

Rahm Emmanuel, former chief of staff to President Obama who went on to be mayor of Chicago, said:

> Never allow a good crisis [to] go to waste. It's an opportunity to do the things you once thought were impossible.[34]

Brexit is undoubtedly a crisis for all parts of Ireland, but it comes with huge opportunities for growth and positive change through reunification and the resulting benefits for the economy – if we play our cards right. Ireland has a good foundation of infrastructure, a highly skilled workforce, proximity to mainland Europe and easy access to the US and the rest of North America. Furthermore, as a small island, we do not pose a significant threat to the economies of larger countries. The Biden–Harris Administration has stated that a US–UK trade deal is not a priority, so it is likely that a US–EU trade deal will be negotiated first. Therefore, for all of Ireland, our future lies in working through the EU. These opportunities will not be wasted, but any plans for economic reunification need to be economically literate.

UK growth is trailing behind the rest of the G7 in terms of trade recovery after the pandemic. The OECD (Organisation for Economic Co-operation and Development) has forecast that out of all G20 countries only Russia, which is being sanctioned for its war on Ukraine, will have lower growth than the UK.[35] The Office for Budget Responsibility, which was set up by the British government to provide impartial forecasting, has said that the UK will have four per cent lower productivity than would have been the case if the country had remained within the EU.[36] While this full decline is yet to come, it will mean the UK losing approximately £100 billion in output when it is fully realised.

Thanks to the Northern Ireland Protocol, Northern Ireland is the only UK region other than London to have a higher level of income than it did pre-pandemic. If domestic legislation to override large parts of the Protocol is passed, Northern Ireland will lose its preferential access to the EU's Single Market for goods. Such an economically damaging move does not have the support of the business community in Northern Ireland, or of wider society or the majority of elected MLAs.

By January 2022, it was already apparent that the Northern Ireland Protocol was having a significant impact on trade across the UK and Ireland: imports from Britain into the Irish Republic were down 18 per cent on the previous year; imports from the Irish Republic into Britain increased by 20 per cent on the same period a year earlier; imports from Northern Ireland into the Irish Republic increased by 64 per cent to €3,679 million and imports from the Irish Republic into Northern Ireland were up by 48 per cent to €3,305 million compared to the same period in 2020.[37]

As the *Irish News* reported in July 2022:

> Cross-border trade has continued to soar in both directions after the Northern Ireland Protocol was introduced, new figures show.
>
> According to the Central Statistics Office (CSO), imports from Northern Ireland for January to May 2022 increased by 357 million euro to 1.9 billion euro when compared with the same time period of 2021.
>
> Meanwhile, exports to Northern Ireland from the Republic from January to May 2022 increased by 586 million euro to 1.974 billion euro when compared with the same time period in 2021.
>
> Imports from Britain increased by 831 million euro, to two billion euro compared with May 2021 – a rise of 71%.[38]

These changes in trade flows will help to prepare for Irish unity. The reunification of Ireland will be a process rather than a single event and the groundwork is already being laid now.

We can expect that there will ultimately be a deal between the UK government and the European Union, concerning the operation of the Northern Ireland Protocol despite tough words by various

British politicians and the tabling of legislation at Westminster. The UK simply cannot afford a trade war with its largest trading partner, especially as it faces rapidly rising inflation, low growth and a cost-of-living crisis for consumers. The Bank of England has forecast that the UK will enter a deep recession in the fourth quarter of 2022 which will last until the end of 2023.[39] The bank also predicts that UK inflation will reach 13 per cent during this time. Ireland's inflation is forecast to peak at 7.3 per cent in 2022 and then fall to 3.3 per cent in 2023 according to the European Commission's 2022 summer forecast.[40] Ireland's growth is forecast to be 5.3 per cent in 2022 and then four per cent in 2023. For the EU, the economy is forecast to grow by 2.7 per cent in 2022 and 1.5 per cent in 2023.[41] EU inflation is forecast to be 8.3 per cent in 2022 before dropping to 4.6 per cent in 2023. By every metric, the EU economy is larger and more robust than the UK one.

The UK financial services sector, which until now has been a significant contributor to the overall UK economy, will suffer post-Brexit – the 'passport' that EU institutions grant to banks enabling them to operate under UK financial regulations has been withdrawn now that the UK has left the Single Market. Some of the jobs which relied on this arrangement have begun to migrate to cities such as Paris, Frankfurt and Dublin.[42] Irish unity within the EU can take advantage of this.

We have to focus on this economic reality to help convince unionists that Irish unity is the answer. The UK and Ireland will have to rebuild their economies post-pandemic. The Northern Ireland economy is not able to function on its own, but it is clear that Ireland, as a member of the EU, will fare better than the UK. Irish unity will be able to open many doors which will remain closed to the UK.

Aside from these macroeconomic considerations, there are local changes that could be implemented to save the public purse in Northern Ireland through a joined-up approach: unity would abolish the duplication of services, such as separate community centres for different parts of the population or separate schools based on religion or background within Northern Ireland, which is effectively a segregation tax; Invest Northern Ireland and IDA Ireland compete for inward investment, but a New Ireland would not have this internal competition.

There are practical realities of the border in Ireland that would make a hard border impossible to monitor effectively. According to the House of Lords European Union Committee in 2016, the year of the Brexit referendum:

> It is estimated that there are up to 300 major and minor crossings along a 310 mile (499 kilometre) border, with 35,000 people crossing the border each day.[43]

In 2018 Ireland had the fastest growing economy of any country in the EU, at 4.5 per cent, while the UK had the lowest, at 1.3 per cent; the Northern Ireland figure was lower than the UK figure at 0.9 per cent growth.[44] While the cost of living in the Republic of Ireland is higher, there are more jobs and higher salaries than in the North – the average salary in the Irish Republic is €44,202[45] (around £38,000) whereas in Northern Ireland it is £29,000.[46] Through Irish unity, those in what is now Northern Ireland will have access to better paid jobs and therefore better pensions – in a research briefing for the UK Parliament, analysis showed that the Irish state pension is 16 per cent higher than that of the UK.[47]

Of course, some Unionists will point to the anaemic growth in Northern Ireland and claim that Ireland cannot afford to be united; they will say that Northern Ireland needs to rely on handouts from UK taxpayers if unity does not happen. But this does not exactly point to the success of the union for Northern Ireland – quite the opposite.

Northern Ireland will perform better outside the UK

The UK government's analysis has stated that the Northern Ireland economy – so long as it remains part of the UK – will be smaller post-Brexit, in every scenario, regardless of what type of Brexit is delivered.[48] Those in favour of Northern Ireland remaining part of the UK will point to the supposed importance of the UK Single Market; however, this economy benefited greatly from membership of the EU. As this has now been given up, being tied to the (now declining) UK economy does not hold the benefits it once did. No amount of trade deals will make up for the loss of unfettered access to the European Single Market. There will be increased friction in trade on financial services; the ability to visit, study, live and do business with EU countries will be more difficult.

Brexit was supposed to be about growing global trade, whereas the reality is that Brexit is, instead, leading to increased trade barriers within the UK between Britain and Northern Ireland. It is also increasing trade barriers between Britain and the EU. We were famously promised that Brexit would lead to more money for the NHS – the UK government has subsequently admitted that it will have to spend £1.5 billion a year for 50,000 new customs officers at ports of entry.[49] The challenge for the Brexiters is that the plan to build an entirely new trade policy around a trade deal with the USA has been undone by the defeat of Trump in the 2020 presidential election.

Unity will mean a reduction in public sector jobs as we will gradually, over time, remove the duplication of services. This will free up space and capacity for private sector growth. It is simply not sustainable nor desirable to keep a bloated public sector – high levels of public sector spending do not create riches; they cause dependency, as people will often choose the safe option in the civil service rather than get involved in private enterprise. People often have the choice of joining the public sector within Northern Ireland or going elsewhere to progress in their careers. We need to change this.

The economy across the island of Ireland has become increasingly integrated since the Good Friday Agreement was signed. Any change to that, or the installation of new barriers, will energise calls for Irish unity. Neither state on the island of Ireland wants to see disruption or damage to the Good Friday Agreement; there are a significant number of areas of cross-border trade covered in the Agreement.

All-Ireland infrastructure will bolster the economy

The ports across the island of Ireland are key to maintaining and increasing economic growth through trade and tourism. Further infrastructure investment will help strengthen economic and social links across the island of Ireland. There is a similar initiative taking place on the Korean Peninsula, where there is increased investment in rail infrastructure in order to strengthen transport links between North and South Korea.[50] As the economist David McWilliams has stated, we should focus on building all-island transport infrastructure.[51] It is a welcome development that the Irish government formed in June 2020 has committed to undertake viability research on a Belfast–Dublin–Cork high-speed rail link. If Ireland can secure investment in this rail infrastructure, the journey time from Belfast to Dublin could ultimately be reduced from over two hours to 30 minutes. An express service with free high-speed Wi-Fi would bring Ireland into line with world-leading train speeds and open a much larger work-force to Dublin. Belfast would benefit immediately as commuters could access high-end jobs in the national capital. It would also enable Belfast to further develop its role as a professional services hub. Eventually, high-speed train links could even be upgraded to other key cities like Derry and Galway – not all of this can happen at once, but it could be rolled out over a number of years.

The Belt and Road Initiative is a global investment strategy set up by the Chinese government which provides one possible funding opportunity; however, we would need to make sure that it represents good value in the long term and is politically acceptable, in light of increased tensions between China and the West. The EU may prefer to keep investment from within the EU for upgrading Ireland's infrastructure as part of the unity project. There is also the possibility of US or Canadian investment for a faster train link.

Particularly in a time of turbulence (during a pandemic, or the wider impacts of the war in Ukraine) infrastructure can be considered a safe investment and produce an economic multiplier effect. While we want to get to a journey time of 30 minutes between Belfast and Dublin ultimately, even if we can get to a one-hour journey time in the first instance, it will have a significant benefit for the island's economy.

Inward investment in infrastructure needs to be of sufficient size to appeal to foreign investors. Therefore, the Government should work with the public and private sectors to package these opportunities attractively. Using a 'Team Ireland' approach, offering investors the chance to help build Irish unity, will have a strong emotional resonance as well as stable, long-term economic returns.

To build the infrastructure and economy, we need to enable the island to function as one entity. After a successful vote for unity, there must be negotiations between the UK and Irish governments with the participation of the EU, during a transitional period. Irish unity would require a transitional structural fund which would provide the finances to build reunification, focused on further integrating the economy and public services across the island. Compared to the entire UK budget, any transitional fund is likely to represent a small portion. Ireland is a key trading partner for the UK (prior to Brexit it was a larger market for UK exports than Brazil, Russia, India and China combined). Therefore, the British government investing in Irish infrastructure after unity would provide a good return and could help the UK to regain some goodwill in the EU post-Brexit. In addition, the UK would be setting in place a process that, ultimately, would relieve it of the financial burden of Northern Ireland.

Housing is key

The quality of homes people live in has an impact on health, happiness and job prospects, therefore Irish unity needs to focus on housing – the housing association model that is used in Northern Ireland can play an important role. This allows charities, which operate as not-for-profit businesses, to get grant funding from the Government for newbuild social housing and match this with private finance. As a result, they can build twice as many homes as would otherwise be possible, using public money. They are also increasingly involved in providing other types of affordable, privately rented and owned homes. This mixed tenure approach is crucial to building sustainable communities.

The state regulator in the Irish Republic does not allow out-of-state control and therefore currently there is a divergence between housing bodies on both sides of the border in Ireland. We should be able to have fully integrated housing bodies which operate across the entire island. This would develop synergy across the island and effectively generate much-needed new homes, as these bodies would be able to leverage their assets from across Ireland to borrow private finance.

There is a significant economic multiplier effect through the construction of new homes for the wider construction industry and supply chain. It may be possible to negotiate a low-interest loan through the European Investment Bank for a national home-building programme. We need to build infrastructure for people to live in good-quality homes across the island of Ireland and there needs to be stronger regulation but less governmental control. The HELP USA initiative is targeted toward providing affordable housing and emergency shelters for low-income people and those who have experienced homelessness. It is funded through government support, from individuals, corporations and foundations. Low-income housing tax credits are also used, so it is a potential model to follow.

Housing needs to enable remote working. Due to the pandemic, more people than ever before are working remotely. It does not matter whether someone is working remotely in the suburbs of Belfast or Dublin, or indeed anywhere on the island of Ireland – this change is something that will embed a long-term cultural shift and should also help people based in Northern Ireland to tap into the Dublin job market, previously only accessible to those living within daily commuting zones of Dublin. Face-to-face networking will always have value, but post-pandemic remote working will likely continue for the foreseeable future.

This pandemic has allowed us to cut down on congestion, rejuvenate rural and semi-rural communities and help to address the climate emergency. Surplus public sector land should be used to build much-needed homes. As government departments are consolidated across the island, surplus land and buildings should be converted into housing, where possible. A national house building plan using modular construction should be implemented across Ireland. Housing is a key foundation stone for society and will help to ensure healthy and happy people.

Ireland as the EU gateway

The EU–USA Open Skies Agreement allows any EU airline and any US airline to travel between any part of the EU and the USA. This offers a huge opportunity for Dublin airport as it can be the gateway to Europe for US citizens in the longer term despite the short-term downturn caused by the COVID-19 pandemic. Already the fifth-largest airport in the UK and Ireland with a second runway now operational, Dublin Airport, in 2018, broke the 30 million passenger milestone for the first time (six per cent higher than in 2017).[52]

Tourism income is significantly higher in the South than in the North – reunification would increase tourism income in the North. There can surely be no better advertisement to attract tourists than to invite them to come and see a reunified and diverse country. The physical and mental barriers to travel from South to North and vice versa will lessen. The alternative under an Ireland that continues to be partitioned is that the diverging trend in tourism numbers will increase. For example, visitors from another EU country may decide to stay within the EU, rather than going through the hassle of border checks or getting the additional required visas to visit part of the UK.

The island of Ireland can benefit hugely by positioning itself as the English-speaking gateway to the EU for American and Asian companies. Through Irish unity, Northern Ireland will be able to tap into this huge potential without interference from the UK government, or questions over its location as a place for Foreign Direct Investment. While Malta is also an English-speaking EU country, due to its small size it cannot compete on the same scale as Ireland can.

The UK government will not walk away from its financial commitments to Northern Ireland overnight. Despite much huffing and puffing, the Government agreed to pay billions of pounds to the EU for ongoing commitments such as the British state pensions of citizens who live in the EU, as part of the withdrawal agreement. We can expect them to agree to funding similar commitments as part of a reunification process.[53] It is in their self-interest to do so. They would have a selfish economic interest in ensuring a stable transition to Irish unity including financial contributions.

The agri-food sector is part of an all-Ireland integrated market and benefits from the gateway status. Any hardening of the border will make this more expensive and less efficient, adversely affecting economic growth in this area, which has until now been a star performer for the economy. In a related area, farmers in Northern Ireland will see their access to CAP funding stopped.[54] It is highly unlikely that they will continue to receive the same high levels of funding from a UK government that will have more pressing needs for areas that will return MPs for the party of government.

Ireland has been named the fifth most open global economy in the world.[55] It rightly sees membership of the EU as the best way to protect itself against geopolitical shocks and a hard border on the island of Ireland would undermine this and slow growth. The only way to permanently remove this threat is through Irish unity.

There is no status quo option

Economic unification will be a reality before political unification. Britain will fundamentally change its trading relationships post-Brexit but for Northern Ireland, the reality is that we are embedded into an all-island economy. Ireland has an open society and open economy – the reunification of the island will help to maintain this. This is not a choice between Irish unity and the status quo – there is no status quo option. The pursuit of a hard Brexit by the UK government has ensured that there will be significant changes for the UK and Ireland. Whereas Brexit is about putting up trade and other barriers to the UK's closest neighbours, Irish unity is about safeguarding and deepening the integration of the economy, public services and infrastructure across the island of Ireland.

Various senior Conservatives have said that they want to repeal the ECHR (European Convention on Human Rights).[56] This would have profound implications for Northern Ireland, as the ECHR is explicitly written into the Good Friday Agreement. This provides human rights safeguards which are important now and will provide legal rights for unionists in a New Ireland. It is yet another example of how being part of the UK has adverse effects on the region. The Irish government, which is a co-guarantor of the Good Friday Agreement, will not appreciate this proposed move either.

Ireland wants to continue to grow trade with countries outside the EU, but this can only be done as part of the EU and the wider EEA (European Economic Area), which includes an additional three countries: Iceland, Liechtenstein and Norway. The reality is that Ireland will, in this time of increasing protectionism, be able to secure better deals as part of the European bloc than it would as a small island of 7 million people (post-reunification) on its own.

EU delivers free trade

Despite what some people say, the EU promotes free trade. Since the UK vote to leave in 2016, the EU has agreed on trade deals with multiple countries including Canada, Mexico, New Zealand and Singapore.[57] It is the world's largest economic bloc, enabling free trade between its 27 member states and the EEA countries, as well as Switzerland which is in the Single Market but not the EU or EEA. It is also focused on negotiating free trade deals with many countries around the world – the latest example of this is the investment partnership agreement with China. Senior Democrats in the US, including Senator Chris Murphy, have stated that the US should prioritise a trade deal with the EU over one with the UK. I would love to see unfettered free trade around the world but unfortunately, that is just not feasible.

Northern Ireland depends on trade with the EU more than the rest of the UK. The majority of this trade is, unsurprisingly, with the Irish Republic. Reunification would ensure that Northern Ireland could continue to have unfettered trade with the Irish Republic and the rest of the EU27.

The constant threat by the British government to trigger Article 16 or overwrite the Protocol unilaterally via domestic legislation has been incredibly destabilising. It puts inward investment in doubt and undermines Northern Ireland's potential to maximise the benefits of the Protocol. Irish unity is the only safe way to ensure that there is free trade across the island of Ireland permanently and with the European Single Market.

Any suggestion that Brexit will suddenly allow the UK to undertake unfettered trade worldwide, or with select countries, is patently absurd. As evidenced by the UK government's unsuccessful visit to India shortly after the EU referendum vote, wanting a country's money but not its people is not an effective strategy. So many nations, like the US during the Trump–Pence Administration, have become increasingly protectionist. As part of the EU, Ireland at least has the traction to make other countries and/or economic blocs take notice. Alone we will struggle to secure deals, although I am sure other countries like the US and China will be only too willing to asset strip the UK – given the UK government's desperation to secure trade deals quickly after Brexit, this may be the only option. We know that the UK's National Health Service would be at the top of any target list for a sell-off. The small number of trade deals that the UK has been able to secure are either rollover deals, so no better than terms agreed when part of the EU, or significantly worse. Examples of this are the trade deals the UK has agreed with both Australia and New Zealand by Liz Truss as foreign secretary. Both have adversely affected the British farming industry. Northern Ireland farming has some protections through the Northern Ireland Protocol.

A country such as the UK, which walks away from its largest trading partner and puts walls up to stop inward migration, must rely on the kindness of strangers and hope that it can unilaterally change the dominant and successful economic paradigm of the last 70 years. Personally, I think King Canute has a better chance of stopping the tide coming in while wearing his best finery. The impact of the COVID-19 pandemic only adds uncertainty in a time of extreme political and economic turbulence; it accentuates the folly of leaving the world's largest trading bloc.

Transformation of the Northern Ireland economy required

At the turn of the 20th century, before partition, Belfast was the larger and more significant economic powerhouse, compared to Dublin. There was a perception that Ireland could not survive without the economic might provided by Belfast. At one point, Belfast had the largest linen works, tobacco works, ropeworks and ship-building industry in the world.

Prior to partition, Belfast was a significant economic player in the world. Being part of a significant trading market – namely the British Empire – helped, as did having an island-wide structure. Partition divided the island of Ireland economically, culturally and socially. This was accentuated by The Troubles. The Irish Republican para-military groups targeted businesses in Northern Ireland because they wanted to ensure that Northern Ireland was not an economically viable place. This had a hugely negative effect on businesses, tourism and inward migration from elsewhere in the UK. No true Irish patriot can think that this economic ruination is a good thing. Similarly, those hard-line Unionists who favour a hard border between North and South, or any dilution in the seamless trade across Ireland, are not true patriots for the people they claim to represent. Ultimately, if we do not desire economic prosperity and strive to achieve that, we do not have the best interests of society at heart.

Currently, Belfast has a lower population than it did in the 1840s. I am one of the few people I know who left Northern Ireland to attend university and actually returned – most of my friends who left did not come back because of the limited opportunities and the sense that Northern Ireland was a regressive place. Thanks to comparative peace, it feels like Belfast may finally be on the cusp of significant growth, which has been hoped for for such a long time.

In recent years, Belfast has achieved some significant success in attracting investment as a professional services hub. Global law firms such as Baker & McKenzie, Allen & Overy, Herbert Smith Freehills and Citi have all set up legal services centres in Belfast; there have also been record levels of investment in FinTech and the city has become the top international location for US investment in cybersecurity.[58]

For too long, people across Northern Ireland have become reliant on the benefits system and to rectify this, we need to help them adjust to the globalised world. Northern Ireland is a post-conflict region and that has an impact that we need to address. We also need to help people get the skills to secure jobs in the highly developed knowledge economy. One northern economist likened this reliance on the public sector and its funds to the Stockholm Syndrome.[59] While that may be an emotive analogy, there is a real need give our people the skills they need to truly embrace the opportunities of the 21st century. If we have a more dynamic economy, we can invest more in public services and people will have more hope for the future and better lives in the present.

The current funding model for public services is unsustainable. Significant savings could be found through the full integration of all public services across the island of Ireland. While the Good Friday Agreement has helped to provide a framework for increasing cross-border cooperation, the reality is that under the current structures there will always be an incentive for and ability of Northern Unionists to block full integration. When Edwin Poots took over as a leader of the DUP in May 2021, he blocked the effective operation of the North–South Ministerial Council. This was done in response to Unionist concerns about the Northern Ireland Protocol. Then, at the start of 2022, the Unionist First Minister resigned which hampered the ability to make long-term decisions such as a multi-year budget. Since the May 2022 Assembly election, the DUP have refused to support the nomination of a speaker or a first and deputy first minister. As a result, hundreds of millions of pounds that could be invested by the Northern Ireland Executive into the struggling health service and to help with the cost-of-living crisis have remained unspent. This action has contributed to the destabilisation of the Northern Ireland Assembly.

Unionism is opposed to any form of economic border between Northern Ireland and Britain but it wants there to be a social policy border to stop citizens living in Northern Ireland from having the same access to abortion or indigenous language protection as those living in Britain. Their desire for Northern Ireland to remain a place apart is a strange manifestation of their Britishness.

New Zealand provides an example of what a reunited Ireland would look like as it is also a small, open, free-market economy. New Zealand got rid of farming subsidies and was a success, but this was a difficult and painful transition. As a country, we need to decide how best to ensure our ongoing ability to provide our own food supplies.

The Irish Sea border has, since the start of the new EU–UK trade deal, led to blockages in food supplies from Britain to Northern Ireland and caused supply chains to be reorientated from South to North on the island of Ireland. Food security is likely to be an increasing priority, especially in the context of the climate crisis.

Lower subvention figure

Unionism and others opposed to Irish unity will claim that the subvention figure – the regular payments the UK government makes to Northern Ireland – is an economic barrier to reunification. However, the figure of circa £10 billion a year includes a significant amount of non-identifiable expenditure. As set out in an article in the *Cambridge Journal of Economics*, these non-identifiable expenditures include Northern Ireland's contribution to the UK defence budget and the UK debt interest payments.[60] These total approximately 26 per cent of the overall subvention figure. It is reasonable to assume that Northern Ireland would not be liable for these costs after reunification. If we also add in pension liabilities, which would remain UK costs, it is possible to see the subvention being reduced by roughly 50 per cent.

While there may be a reduction in public sector jobs after unity, there will be a transitional period where Northern Ireland can focus on raising its educational attainment, attracting high-value Foreign Direct Investment and moving away from low-value jobs. Merely bringing Northern Ireland up to the same level as the rest of Ireland – by way of investment from the Irish government, the EU and potentially the US – in terms of educational attainment, foreign direct investment and productivity will create economic benefits for the entire island.

Eastern corridor

The eastern corridor from Belfast to Dublin will be the economic spine of the country and it provides a unique opportunity to grow a path of prosperity, which can then spread across the rest of the island. This was highlighted in the Project Ireland 2040 publication by the Irish government which set out the long-term vision for the island.[61] The link between Belfast and Dublin is crucial and should be the primary focus for seeking Foreign Direct Investment, as the majority of people on the island live in this area and it, therefore, contains most of the island's economic activity. This can be built upon by tapping into the Irish diaspora (those who live around the world and have Irish citizenship or ancestry, estimated at one hundred million people), and cultural tourism and by focusing on creating a shared future across the island.

Tapping into the Irish diaspora will be key to any success (the flow of trade between the Irish Republic and the USA is currently over two billion euro per week). One of the ways to achieve this could be reducing corporation tax on an all-island basis; in other words, bringing the rate in Northern Ireland, (19 per cent) down to the Irish Republic level (currently a headline rate of 12.5 per cent and an effective estimated rate of two to four per cent for multinationals due to 'profit shifting' rules). The reunited Ireland would have to be a small government, open and low tax economy to succeed. Northern Ireland has been stifled for decades by an overly large government and public sector, so this would be a positive step. The Biden–Harris Administration has proposed and secured a G7 agreement to increase corporate tax rates; Ireland may have to adjust its approach to securing foreign direct investment in light of this.

Culture as an economic driver

Music, literature and drama are vibrant across the island of Ireland – we are famous for these aspects of our culture. Tourists flock from around the world to visit the famous book of Kells, the James Joyce Centre and the Writers' Museum in Dublin; multiple tour operators offer excursions to 'Yeats Country' in Sligo. A report entitled 'The Contribution of the Drinks Industry to Tourism' by Dublin City University revealed that 83 per cent of tourists visiting Ireland named experiencing traditional Irish music as the 'number one activity' on their list.[62] Chairman of the Irish Tourism Industry Confederation Paul Carty (who is also the managing director of the Guinness Storehouse in Dublin) spoke of how Ireland must appreciate the draw of Irish culture for tourists:

> They want to come, and they want to experience what
> is uniquely Irish. We engage with people, we have this
> term called the 'craic'. And, it's around conversation,

fun, music and all of that. It's quite unique to Ireland, and something we should dial up and not play down.[63]

Belfast, as a culture hub, can also be a strong economic driver for the entire island. Irish unity can only be successful with economic prosperity and a vibrant Belfast – the Irish government knows that the southern part of the island will only achieve its full potential when Belfast is also a success. Belfast has achieved some significant success in attracting sports and other cultural events over the last few years. These have included the 2011 MTV Europe music awards, 2014 Giro d'Italia and the 2017 Women's Rugby World Cup.

In particular, there is a real opportunity to make Belfast the American sports hub in Ireland for sports such as basketball and ice hockey, building on the success of the Belfast Giants (the multi-time UK and Ireland league champions) and the Friendship Four college hockey tournament. Dublin has secured the Aer Lingus College Football Classic between Notre Dame and Navy; as Casement Park GAA ground gets redeveloped, Belfast will soon be able to offer a similar facility to host college football. There has also been talk of the NBA seeking to expand eastward – there is no reason why this could not happen in Belfast. NBA and NHL teams often attract circa 10,000 attendees at matches, which is certainly achievable in Belfast. The crucial aspect is the location, time zone and access to the European media market. Why not create the Belfast Titans basketball franchise?

US investment has been significant already and I believe that Irish unity would create the environment for more inward investment. Importantly, while Irish unity would be able to appeal to the heart, it would appeal to the head via sound financial decisions. The Irish, for hundreds of years, have emigrated to the United States and Canada. They helped to build America and contributed to creation of Confederation in Canada. Now we want Irish America and Irish Canada to help us build Irish unity. We are not looking for charity but for investment in our future, which will provide a significant financial return and a piece of history.

More than ever, Ireland will be able to play a key economic role as a link between the North American market and the EU. If, as seems likely, Scotland votes for independence within the EU, this would not adversely affect Ireland's ability to attract inward investment. There will be enough potential investment opportunities for both countries.

Unity will help to unlock the true economic potential of the entire island of Ireland.

Brexit is not taking back control

Brexit was supposedly all about taking back control of borders and limiting immigration. However, when the pandemic struck, the British government was incredibly slow at controlling the borders. They did not stop people from entering the country and did not even require them to provide negative COVID tests during the first months of the pandemic, unlike other countries. As a liberal, I am in favour of open borders, but ideology must not get in the way of public health requirements during a pandemic. The island of Ireland could have pursued an eradication policy by enforcing strict border policies from the start. I realise that would have a significant economic impact, but a healthy population can help build back a healthy economy quicker than one that has been decimated by the virus.

At a time when the UK government continues to turn its back on the globalised world and reduce immigration, there is a real opportunity for Ireland in continuing to do the opposite. Before the potato famine, the island of Ireland had a population of eight million. The Irish people have emigrated to other parts of the world throughout history and made their mark. We now have the opportunity to grow our economy by continuing to embrace the benefits of immigration, at a time when our nearest neighbour has decided to try and pull up its drawbridge. Immigration has been a key part of Irish culture for centuries and we can leverage this financially after Irish unity has been secured. This can be other Europeans, British people who want to live in Ireland or those from further afield. There is also the prospect of a unity dividend as Irish emigrants may wish to return home and be part of building the New Ireland.

Brexit means lower standards

A recent standout economic success for Northern Ireland has been the agri-food sector. This has been possible, in part, because of the generous Common Agricultural Policy payments to farmers in Northern Ireland, as part of the European Union, but there is simply no way that this level of funding will be available to farmers in Northern Ireland after Brexit. There can be separate debates about the merits of funding the food industry in this way, but nobody can argue against the importance of food security. As part of the EU, people in Northern Ireland were assured of the quality of food imported from the rest of the EU and indeed via trade deals the EU has secured with other countries. Post-Brexit, the UK is desperate to secure trade deals with other countries and there is a significant risk that one of the necessary compromises will be a lowering of acceptable standards for imported food, especially as the UK will want to have access to cheap goods.

It is becoming increasingly clear that what Brexiters refer to as 'taking back control' means deregulating and lowering standards wherever possible In mid-2020, the UK government voted against food safety minimum standards;[64] in August 2022, a cabinet minister proposed a change that would affect water safety in the UK. They tried to claim that getting rid of European regulations that govern private investment in UK water infrastructure may improve water quality, which is completely absurd. [65] The EU sets a threshold for the minimum standard required – removing this enables the Government and private companies to ignore the said requirement. Shockingly, the campaign group Surfers Against Sewage released a report in November 2021 that revealed sewage discharge into rivers had increased by 85 per cent over the previous year.[66] This already poses not only a significant health risk for UK citizens, but also endangers entire ecosystems within our rivers – I dread to think of the repercussions of any further lowering of water standards. Do we really want to cling to an establishment that cares so little for our welfare and our environment?

Unionist perspective

For many years, unionists who are opposed to Irish unity have argued that unity was not viable because the Irish Republic was too impoverished – they claimed Northern Ireland would suffer by being tied to a 'poorer' part of the island. Whether that argument ever had merit is now a moot point. Across a wide range of metrics, the Irish Republic is now performing consistently better than Northern Ireland. Economic output, the attraction of Foreign Direct Investment and salary levels have all increased in the Irish Republic and significantly so compared to Northern Ireland.

Now those opposed to unity state that Northern Ireland is itself too expensive for the rest of Ireland to support. They reference the – previously mentioned – large public sector in Northern Ireland, arguing that the Irish Republic would not be able to sustain this after reunification. It is important to state that such a large public sector is a direct result of the fact that Northern Ireland does not have a fully functioning standalone economy. The Troubles did not help the region grow its economy and successive UK governments tried to compensate for this by pumping in billions of pounds, which were redirected taxpayer receipts from Britain. The reality is that this largesse will not continue post-Brexit. They have promised to level up parts of England, where they can actually get votes and win seats to form a government. There is no political incentive for them to invest money in Northern Ireland when there are severely challenging economic circumstances for Britain.

If unionists continue to argue that the Irish Republic cannot afford Irish unity because of the region's large public sector, this should be challenged as admission and acceptance of failure. In the post-Brexit world, one of two things will happen to Northern Ireland. Either it will seek, alongside Britain, to chase after the mirage of 'Global Britain', or it will be part of a New Ireland, which is outward-looking and focused on the future as part of the European Union.

The unionist resistance to Irish unity is like the Maginot Line, put in place by the French before the Second World War. At first glance, it appears impregnable and the mantra is that their firm opinion against reunification will never be breached. However, a substantial minority of unionists are liberal, moderate and pragmatic. As the full catastrophe of Brexit becomes clear, a growing chink will appear and there will be greater acceptance of the benefits of Irish unity.

Special status could have saved the union

The DUP has argued that they want Northern Ireland to be treated the same as the rest of the UK post-Brexit. The difficulty with this approach is that it would only harm the economy within Northern Ireland, which is highly integrated with the rest of Ireland. In a futile attempt to prove their Britishness, the DUP and other Unionists argued that there should be no special status for Northern Ireland.

The refusal to contemplate a special status for Northern Ireland post-Brexit was damaging to the pro-UK case. Northern Ireland remaining in the EU while part of the UK, or at least fully in the Single Market and Customs Union, could have been a financial boon for the region, leading to rapidly increased financial growth. By ruling this out, the UK government and Northern Ireland Unionists have not only hardened Nationalist opinion against remaining part of the UK, but they have also caused many centrist voters, largely Alliance and Green, to openly contemplate the benefits of Irish unity.

The DUP supported Johnson's 2019 proposals, which were implemented in both the Withdrawal Agreement and the trade deal, for Northern Ireland to be part of an all-island regulatory zone. This led to the creation of the Irish Sea Border. So, when Unionists complain that this is the fault of Sinn Féin, the SDLP, Alliance or Greens, it is important to remember that this particular can of worms was opened with the DUP's support. Their denial, now that the real impacts of Brexit are being felt, does not change this fact.

There was always going to be a debate about Irish unity in the coming years. However, Unionism would be in a better position to argue against Irish unity if Northern Ireland's prosperity had been increased by a special status. The EU–UK trade deal has put up more barriers to trade between Britain and Northern Ireland than would have been possible under Theresa May's preferred arrangements. In a declining economy, tied to a declining state, next to the vibrant and growing economy of the Irish Republic, people are more likely to think constitutional change is desirable.

The Unionist desire for an identikit Brexit, where Northern Ireland gets exactly the same deal as the rest of the UK, is short-sighted and impractical. Northern Ireland is different to the rest of the UK for a number of reasons. It is the only part of the UK that shares a land border with the EU and more than 43 per cent, according to an opinion poll in July 2022, would vote for Irish unity tomorrow, while those who want to stay part of the UK are on less than 40 per cent with the rest being 'don't know'.[67] To pretend that Northern Ireland is as 'British as Finchley' when the Good Friday Agreement mandates a unique and qualified constitutional status, is wrong.

Unionism, if it wants Northern Ireland to remain part of the UK, must change to stay the same. The only way for Northern Ireland to mitigate the negative impact of Brexit while remaining part of the UK is to seek and secure a special status. It is a difficult choice for Unionism, but its followers must compromise now on their vision of sovereignty, or risk fast-tracking the momentum, economic and otherwise, towards Irish unity. Pragmatism has rarely been a strong suit of political Unionism but special status, where Northern Ireland is part of the UK and EU at the same time, could help to create a level of prosperity that further leads to citizens wishing to maintain the status quo. The early economic statistics from the first few months' operation of the Northern Ireland Protocol have shown increased trade for Northern Ireland.

Unionism's refusal to accept that Northern Ireland is different to Britain will not be forgiven by nationalists, centrists and some moderate unionists.

Symbolism and Cultural Identity

'It's not that the Irish are cynical. It's rather that they have a wonderful lack of respect for everything and everybody'.[68]

Brendan Beehan

WE NEED TO embrace the sense of irreverence which is intrinsic to Irishness; the dry humour which so many people across Ireland exhibit. Yes, there are differences, but we should not see these as a barrier to living together in peace and harmony across Ireland. When we talk about symbolism and identity, it is not just about how Irish unity should be represented. We also must acknowledge how we should accommodate existing traditions on the island and integrate the different strands of society, inclusively and respectfully, into a coherent whole. Let us not be defined by whom we oppose – we need to move beyond being set against one another. Instead, let's define ourselves as a diverse society on a small, beautiful island that is open, progressive and outward-looking. We need to celebrate our fellow citizens who have emigrated to all parts of the world to make it their own, as well as our friends and neighbours who have come from all over the world to live here across Ireland. Let us make strength through diversity.

If we look at political Unionism since the signing of the Good Friday Agreement, it has been dominated by negativity. There was either defensiveness about the need to sign it, or outright hostility. Never at any point did we see a wholehearted endorsement of it. There has also been a maudlin fascination with death and defeat. To celebrate the centenary of the founding of the Ulster Unionist Council in 1905, the then-leader of the Ulster Unionist Party laid wreaths at the gravestones of each of his predecessors. This form of commemoration does not point to a brighter future, but a trapped mindset focused on the past, with memories of loss. As James Baldwin said, 'People are trapped in history and history is trapped in them'.[69]

One of the key aspects of the unity campaign is that Irish unity must create a New Ireland – Northern Ireland cannot simply be bolted onto the Republic as it currently stands. In every possible way, Irish unity must be inclusive to succeed fully. While a straight vote could lead to unity, we must focus on how to integrate those from different traditions in such a way that everyone feels able to be part of one unified country. Many of the trappings of nationhood will be up for debate, including the flag, the anthem and the structure of government.

The flag

Unfortunately, for many people in the North, the Irish Tricolour – created by the idealism of Nationalism (green), Unionism (orange) and peace between (white) – has been sullied by its association with the Provisional IRA and other terrorist groups. However, this does not mean that the Irish tricolour must be removed – we want to build on the independent state created after the Easter Rising in 1916, not dismantle it. The flag and what it *truly* represents needs to be reintroduced to people in Northern Ireland – unionists need to see the flag of Ireland being reclaimed from violent republicanism. I believe that we can reclaim the Irish Tricolour and ensure that the flag represents its original meaning: recognition of different traditions on the island, connected by peace.

However, perhaps the people should be given the option of deciding if they want to keep this flag or to change it. As happened in New Zealand, a shortlist of options could be presented, but a change would only take place if there was sufficient demand, as evidenced by a certain threshold being met. In New Zealand, the public ultimately did not show sufficient support for a new flag and therefore they kept their existing one, yet it demonstrated that there could be a transparent mechanism for involving the public in such a process. Canada also went through a consultative process in the 1960s to develop a new flag. A parliamentary committee was set up to consider thousands of suggestions submitted by Canadians. After a shortlist of three was finalised, the flag committee recommended the Maple Leaf flag to both houses of the Canadian Parliament, who voted in favour of the design and it was adopted shortly thereafter.[70]

The public in Ireland could, similarly to Canada, be asked to come up with some suggestions, or these could be developed by the Irish government which could select a shortlist from which the public could vote to decide whether they wish to have a new flag – and anthem – or maintain the existing ones. There is also the example of the South African national flag, first flown in 1994, which is a potent symbol of multiculturalism. The key aspect in all of this is that we are building a New Ireland, which means using the foundations of the existing Irish State and expanding this in a way that helps to accommodate all the people who live across the island of Ireland. While we must make a New Ireland as accessible as possible, we do not want to go through a process of dismantling everything that has been built up over the last one hundred years.

I believe that there could be four new flag options.

Option one: green shamrock on a white background to symbolise peace across Ireland.

Option two: similar to option one, but with the Cross of St Patrick in the background, as recognition of unionist identity.

Option three: a green harp on a white background.

Option four: similar to option three, but with the Cross of St Patrick in the background.

The harp is currently used on the president of Ireland's flag and on coins and has also been used by the UDR and RUC previously, so would hopefully resonate with unionist identity.

There would have to be a failsafe mechanism where there would only be change if there was sufficient demand (over 50 per cent support for an alternative), otherwise, the current Tricolour would be kept. A nation's flag is an external representation of a country's brand; the flag is a key part of how a country promotes itself, so any new flag needs to be something that resonates as being readily identifiable as Irish. It also needs to have the support of its citizens.

Cultural tapestry

We need to find a way of accommodating the rich cultural diversity found across our island. There are those who are Irish, those who are British and a large number of immigrants from other countries.

Cultural expression should be an inclusive celebration, not triumphalism and not defined by supremacy over others. As people, we must move on from cultural warfare to cultural appreciation and celebration of the rich tapestry woven across Ireland. The Irish Republic has, through diversity and economic progress, moved beyond this friction to a large extent, but Northern Ireland remains stuck in this quagmire.

A unicultural approach to nationhood will not succeed – this has already been proven by the attempts of the two parts of Ireland to create unicultural states dominated by one religion and political ethos which have excluded, to a significant degree, the minorities within those states.

Cultural tourism offers real potential for Ireland – if we can show that we are a nation truly at peace with itself. There will be a series of cultural drivers, such as our men's rugby team which was ranked as number one in the world for the first time in 2022,[71] or television programmes such as Lisa McGee's *Derry Girls* on Channel 4 which is celebrated by people from all across Ireland. In this era of relative peace across the island, these will help to create a greater sense of inclusive Irishness.

Symbolism is important and it must be seen in this context as more than mere tokenism. It must be viewed as a clear statement and representation of the values of Irish unity. It must represent something that can bring all the people of the island together in an inclusive manner. Irish unity must not be merely about dismantling the structure of the partitioned Irish State; unity must be about building something better, something inclusive.

The dynamics across the islands of Britain and Ireland are changing. For example, Scottish flags and cultural closeness to Scotland were previously emphasised by unionist communities; Scottish flags have now been adopted by republicans since the first Scottish independence referendum in 2014.

As part of our nation's cultural tapestry, we must acknowledge that Irish is the indigenous language of Ireland. I do not personally speak it – I did not have the option to learn it at school, as this was restricted to Catholic schools in the 1980s and '90s. Those from a unionist background, until recently, had to pursue studies of the language on their own, or in what was perceived to be a nationalist setting, such as certain schools or language centres.

It is awful that the Irish language has been wrongly politicised both by some people who speak it and by some people who do not. Thankfully, Irish is now much more accessible. We are finally seeing the flourishing of the language through the likes of the Turas initiative (turas means journey in Irish). The Turas initiative is located in an area of inner East Belfast which is proudly unionist – it is an example of how a greater amount of people are now able to enjoy aspects of Irish culture. Furthermore, thousands of protestors attended a rally in Belfast City Centre in May 2022 to call for the passage of Irish language legislation which has long been promised and continually blocked by Unionism.

The Irish language should never have become a political weapon. The Ulster Unionist government, after partition in 1921, undercut support for the Irish language; at the same time, the Catholic Church opposed full integration of schooling for all children in Northern Ireland. There was wrong on both sides.

An Irish language act for Northern Ireland could deliver economic benefits and cultural enrichment. A court case in 2017 found that the Northern Ireland Executive was in breach of previous agreements by not legislating for an Irish language act.[72] Northern Ireland is the only part of the UK or Ireland that does not protect its indigenous language in legislation.

Culture can be used as a celebration of diversity rather than a cause for friction and war for supremacy. If we look at how the Māori language and culture have been mainstreamed into New Zealand, we can see the potential benefits of taking a similar approach in Northern Ireland.

Goodwill for Ireland

There is a massive amount of goodwill for the Irish – a reunited Ireland at peace with itself could capitalise on this, to grow inward investment and indigenous business.

Ireland already has a lot of caché and soft power in cultural terms and its successful campaign to secure a temporary seat on the UN Security Council, despite stiff competition from Canada, shows it is a country that can punch above its weight.

The Irish government have also launched their Global Ireland plan which sets out a series of objectives to double the international footprint of Ireland by 2025.[73] This is being done by opening new and expanding existing diplomatic missions around the world. Ireland spreads its influence through its soft power and this plan will focus on promoting Irish arts, heritage and culture.

The Taoiseach has a guaranteed meeting with the US President every year on St Patrick's Day; in both the United States and Canada, March has been designated as Irish heritage month. This is a unique opportunity each year to promote Ireland with important political and economic partners in North America.

Especially in the digital age, reunification would present Ireland with a golden opportunity to share its story of rebirth and growth. The brand of Ireland is strong, well-known and hugely positive and a New Ireland will be readily able to tap into this. There are lots of things we can improve to make Ireland better but there is no need to change everything. I am incredibly proud to be from Belfast, a city that has been through a lot and come through it with resilience, but like my late grandfather, Samuel Collins said, Dublin is the capital of Ireland. This must remain the case after reunification, but we also must tap into resources that exist outside the island of Ireland, such as the extensive network of people who are connected to Ireland but live elsewhere.

The Irish diaspora

The 100 million people across the globe who identify as Irish can and should support the quest for Irish unity. As Thomas Francis Meagher, an Irish and American patriot once said:

> It is not only our duty to America, but also to Ireland. We could not hope to succeed in our effort to make Ireland a Republic without the moral and material support of the liberty-loving citizens of these United States.[74]

The Friends of Ireland caucus in Congress plays a key support role for Ireland internationally, as they have supported the peace process since the group was created in 1981; the US government continue to show bi-partisan support for the Good Friday Agreement and the Northern Ireland Protocol. On a diplomatic visit to Ireland in May 2022, Senior US Democrat Richard Neal stated:

> The number one priority for the United States is to ensure the hard-won peace in Northern Ireland is preserved and reinforced. The Good Friday Agreement

worked because it had something in it for all sides...
America will continue to nudge and nurture this agreement. After all, the Good Friday Agreement is America's too.[75]

While President Trump viewed statecraft as transactional, like his
business activities, the Biden–Harris Administration is firmly on the
side of Ireland. Joe Biden is proud of his Irish roots and I believe
we can position unity as a natural progression for the Good Friday Agreement, especially as the UK government seeks to dismantle
human rights safeguards.

Presidential role

The president of Ireland has a key role as a lead ambassador for the
country, symbolising what the country is or aspires to be. As the role
was originally envisaged as president of the nation, for the entire
island rather than just the Irish Republic, the president should therefore be a persuader for unity. While the president must not interfere in
the day-to-day running of government, which is led by the Taoiseach,
there is an opportunity for the president to undertake longer-term
thinking. He or she is elected to seven-year terms, so has a unique
opportunity to use the Council of State and other advisory groups
to identify key issues and offer strategic long-term solutions. Their
role needs to be enlarged so that they can provide assurance that the
views and rights of Unionism will be respected and cherished when
Irish unity has been achieved.

A presidential candidate should campaign on all-Ireland basis
by seeking nominations from local councils in Northern Ireland as
well as the Irish Republic. Even though they do not, at this stage,
contribute to the official nomination process, it would send a strong
message and resonate with those who favour all-island politics

Historical Perspective

'Those who do not move do not notice their chains.'[76]

Rosa Luxembourg

THIS ISLAND HAS been weighed down by its history. We need to move on and look to the future. Yes, we should remember the past and learn from it, but we must not be held back by it. Sectarianism, discrimination and violence have blighted the island of Ireland for too long and we cannot allow ourselves to be stuck, restricted from progressing because of what has happened before.

2021 marked the centenary of the partition of Ireland. It is time to consider whether we want to continue with division or bring the people of this island together. It is pertinent to note that the 2021 commemoration of the creation of Northern Ireland did not have cross-community support as nationalists believe that partition was and remains to be a mistake and I wholeheartedly agree with them. The use of a Seamus Heaney portrait for the NI 100 celebration organised by the UK government is a form of cultural appropriation and another clear example of disregard for Northern Ireland – they did not bother to get their facts right. Heaney was clear that he was Irish, not British, in fact, he stated in his 1983 poem *An Open Letter* that he objected to being categorised as British: 'Be advised my passport's green. No glass of ours was ever raised to toast the Queen.'[77]

There are barriers in our way, some historic – terrorism from the past and unionist fear – and some new, such as making our way out of the morass of Brexit. Fear can be about the past, change happening now or what may take place in the future. But Irish unity is not breaking anything up, it is helping a fractured island to heal.

Growing up during The Troubles, as with the rest of the unionist community, I was determined that I was not going to be forced into Irish unity by terrorist violence or the threat of it. At the time, there was no space to think about a different future. But since then, we have had peace, however imperfect it may be, thanks to the Good Friday Agreement and we now have the opportunity to freely decide our fate.

Let's make peaceful, progressive change once more by preparing for a successful reunification process, together. We will only be a prosperous place when we learn to treat each other on this small island with mutual respect and celebrate our diversity – which is a real strength.

Violence is never the answer

It saddens me deeply that people have believed that committing acts of violence would improve their lives. The trauma that we have all suffered through violence or threats of violence over the last 100 years has to be acknowledged. Whether you call them terrorists, paramilitary groups or combatants, their illegal activity and use of physical force was wrong – it was wrong during the Border Campaign of the 1950s–60s by the IRA and it was wrong during the Loyalist Worker's Strike to cause the collapse of the Sunningdale Agreement. Violence was wrong during The Troubles and wrong during the 1912 Home Rule crisis with unionist gunrunning. The Easter Rising led to an independent Ireland but one that was incomplete, which resulted in even more death and destruction. The lives of many Irish people were lost during the War of Independence. There were failed and misguided attempts by the British government to end the rebellion, which astonishingly included a policy of officially sanctioned reprisals. None of this violence made life better for anyone across Ireland. The Irish Civil War, which followed the War of Independence, led to a division in Irish society which arguably has only begun to heal with Fianna Fáil and Fine Gael entering into a formal coalition in 2020.

I regret that there was a violent uprising in 1916. This led to further violence on both the Irish and British sides. In an ideal world, a free Ireland would have come about via solely peaceful and democratic means, but this would have involved the British government enabling full democracy by giving everyone across Ireland the right to vote for their self-determination. The granting of Home Rule would have been a start. During the Easter Rising, the rebels were originally booed and lacked widespread support, but the reaction of the UK government to put a number of them before firing squads changed the dynamics and so support for the rebellion became a retaliation against the Government's actions. This is often the case in politics – it is not the action of one party that causes change, it is the response to the original action.

If we look at the US War of Independence, no one says they are terrorists. I do not have an easy answer to the question of 'How do you compare different periods of violence?' It is a complicated issue, they are not the same circumstances. I can only look at these through the prism of growing up in Belfast in the 1980s and '90s. I appreciate that people across the political spectrum may fundamentally disagree with my view on this, but there is no glory in violence; there is only death and destruction.

While I am fortunate that I did not directly lose any family members or friends to The Troubles, there was a sense of impending doom that violence could occur at any time. Growing up as a Protestant in East Belfast during The Troubles in a staunchly pro-British and unionist household, republicanism was represented on the TV by people who took part in terrorism, who shot and killed people simply based on their religious or political beliefs. At a young age, I saw TV footage of soldiers being dragged from their car after mistakenly driving into a republican funeral; I read the detail of how they were killed and stripped of their clothing. It was instances like these that made an impression on me. But this did not make me biased – I had a similar disdain for the violence of loyalist terrorists. Violence in all forms always horrified me. As I said before, I always felt Irish – but I could never support violence and I never will.

Of course, I realised as I got older that the security services in Northern Ireland and the UK government were not blameless – it was indeed a dirty war. The war between loyalists and republicans and between each of these groups and the security services caused untold damage to the delicate fabric of society. Nobody in their right mind wants to return to that or could possibly think it was somehow a time of anything other than devastation for all. I have always believed that no matter what difficulties or challenges we face, they can only be resolved by peaceful means.

For more than 800 years England has been involved with and had an impact on Ireland. While some of this has been positive, a lot of troubling things have happened – to say the least. Prior to Brexit, Britain and Ireland, through their shared objectives and membership of the EU, enjoyed the closest relationship in the history of the two islands. Now that is in danger of being torn asunder.

Whether you are in favour of what the British Empire achieved or not, it did provide a common endeavour for people across England, Scotland, Wales and Ireland. But is there actually a British identity, or is it just an artificial construct to facilitate the expectation that everyone rows in behind England? People will sometimes seek to explain the desire for Brexit by referring to English exceptionalism, but what have they to be exceptional about? An island mentality and refusal to embrace fully their European neighbours is not in itself justification for this divisive approach.

United Irishmen

Arguably the most interesting campaign in Irish history was that of the United Irishmen. When I found out about the United Irishmen – a group founded by liberal Presbyterians – and their desire to unite Protestant, Catholic and Dissenters, I was amazed. Their actions opened my eyes to new possibilities. If such a campaign was possible in 1791, it was definitely possible in the 1990s and especially now as we move through the third decade of the 21st century. You can only wonder how different Ireland would be today if the United Irishmen succeeded in their aims in the 1790s. While violence is never the answer, it must have been incredibly difficult for the United Irishmen to pursue their desires through purely democratic means, given the difficulty in obtaining the right to vote or become an MP as a Presbyterian or Catholic, as that franchise was restricted to those who were part of the established Anglican church. The radical Presbyterian liberal tradition, which played a key role within the United Irishmen, was forgotten or ignored for many years. This lesson from our past can help guide our future.

There was enlightenment in Belfast in the 1790s as evidenced through the calls for an end to religious discrimination and equal representation for Catholics in Ireland, or the harp festival in 1792 which celebrated Gaelic poetry, music, art and language. Belfast has always been the home of radical ideas on this island – for example, members of the United Irishmen successfully campaigned to prevent slave ships from docking in Belfast at the height of the slave trade.

One of the reasons why the United Irishmen and their embrace of Irish culture and equality for all resonates is because I believe that Ulster is beginning to undergo an economic and cultural renaissance: Belfast is widely considered to be a Tech city of the future; the interest in Irish and the GAA in historically and overwhelmingly unionist East Belfast which, since partition, had shown little interest in Irish culture; Derry is growing and its role as capital of the north-west provides further opportunities; Bangor has just been named a city and planned investment will help to restore its waterfront; the North Coast has been rediscovered as a place of wellness, a century after it last provided that role; Newcastle has reclaimed its status as a desirable seaside holiday location. However, Ulster will only fully see the benefits of its renaissance when Irish unity has been secured as the border counties will only then be able to undo the damage of partition.

The Ulster-Scots tradition

The Ulster-Scots or the Scots-Irish tradition have always been radical against the establishment – when these people moved to North America, they often came out in force against British colonial rule. The Ulster Plantation of 1604 by the Scottish King James VI, who was also James I of England, was a conscious effort by a British king to take over part of Ireland. Indeed, Ulster traditionally was the most radical and rebellious of all parts of Ireland, which is why the King focused his plantation on that part of the island. He aimed to use this approach to secure control of Ireland. Consider the definition of a colony: 'a country or area under the full or partial political control of another country and occupied by settlers from that country'.[78] But while referring to someone as a planter may be historically accurate, it should not be used as an insult. Indeed, Peter Robinson, the former DUP leader said back in 2004:

> When I speak of 'our people', I speak of those who
> share my unionist philosophy and those who do not.
> I speak of both the Planter and the Gael.[79]

The United Irishmen were made up of many Presbyterians who had moved across to Ulster from Scotland. Like their brethren in Britain, Ulster-Scots were not part of the establishment, they did not have the benefit of a feudal system which was stacked against them. Ulster-Scots or Scots-Irish people are known for being strong-willed and adventurous. I think that as Ulster-Scots people increasingly see the lack of interest in and understanding of Northern Ireland, they will realise the benefits of Irish unity. Westminster is a distant place and ultimately, I believe those from the Ulster-Scots tradition will embrace the better opportunities available within a New Ireland, rather than put up with being a forgotten part of an archaic and outdated system.

We want Ulster to be reunited and fully integrated into the wider fabric of Ireland. While a lot of time and effort is spent talking about bringing the people of Ireland together, I do not think that enough emphasis is put on reuniting the historic province of Ulster. While many people, predominately within Northern Ireland, but also to an extent in Great Britain, refer to the region of Northern Ireland as Ulster, this is not exactly correct. The historic province consists of nine counties, whereas Northern Ireland only has six. Reuniting Ulster will help the Ulster-Scots of Donegal to link up with Ulster-Scots of Northern Ireland. Just as Donegal has flourished in the Irish Republic, so can everyone within Irish unity.

The failure of partition

The fractured nation caused by partition was a failure on both sides. It was always intended to be a temporary measure and not a long-term solution. The Irish Parliamentary Party thought that the proposed exclusion of the six north-eastern counties from the implementation of the 1914 Home Rule Act, by British Prime Minister Lloyd George in 1916, was a temporary initiative that would be revisited after the end of the First World War.[80]

Northern Ireland is the ultimate example of gerrymandering – it was created to ensure a permanent Protestant and unionist majority in the six counties of Northern Ireland. I passionately believe that we will not be able to achieve our full potential as an island until we get rid of partition.

Northern Ireland has served its purpose. Protestants will be safe after Irish unity has been delivered – no rational person can claim that the Irish Republic is a country dominated malevolently by Catholicism. There have been many progressive initiatives implemented – equal marriage, divorce and abortion rights, for example. One can justifiably claim that the Irish Republic is a much more progressive place than Northern Ireland.

After partition in 1921, the two parts of Ireland were separated and, particularly during the 30 years of The Troubles while terrorist campaigns were ongoing, physical and mental barriers were put up. People from Donegal who travelled to Derry for shopping found the roads blocked off and manned by soldiers. The greatest irony of Irish republican terrorism is that it too created physical barriers within Ireland and discouraged people from the Irish Republic from visiting Northern Ireland and vice versa. Republican terrorism copper-fastened partition – it allowed Unionists in Northern Ireland to focus on a limited narrative of 'no to Irish unity' by pointing to the violence.

There has been a stunted political system on both sides of the border, stuck in the framework of the early 1900s. We need an economic, left-right-and-liberal debate to enable an informed discussion amongst our political representatives about how we can best deliver for society. The Government of Ireland's formal coalition in June 2020 between the former sworn enemy civil war parties of Fianna Fáil and Fine Gael, along with the Greens, perhaps offers the space for the political debate to be widened beyond historic divisions. While there are different interpretations of what took place in the past and what it meant, we need to build an agile and constructive coalition for the future, just as the Republic did.

Calling a Border Poll/ Securing a Unity Referendum

'Thought is an infection. In the case of certain thoughts, it becomes an epidemic.'[81]

Wallace Stevens

THE DATE SHOULD be set for a unity referendum now, to focus minds and ensure that momentum on preparation picks up pace. Otherwise, we risk endless discussions with no real endpoint. Former Taoiseach Bertie Ahern stated that there should be a vote in 2028 on the 30th anniversary of the Good Friday Agreement, which he helped negotiate. But should Scotland leave the UK before then, it may be preferable to bring the date forward.

The Good Friday Agreement recognises that Northern Ireland remains part of the UK due to the consent of the people living there. It also provides for the people of the island of Ireland to exercise their right of self-determination by agreement between North and South.

The Good Friday Agreement states:

> It is for the people of Ireland alone, by agreement between the two parts respectively and without external impediment, to exercise their right of self-determination on the basis of consent, freely and concurrently given, North and South, to bring about a United Ireland, accepting that this right must be achieved and exercised with and subject to the agreement and consent of a majority of the people of Northern Ireland.[82]

Despite what some unionist commentators have stated, the border poll will be decided by a straight majority of the votes which are cast in the referendum, as set out in Article 1 (ii) of the Agreement quoted above. There is no requirement for a majority of unionists to vote in favour of Irish unity. Cross-community consent, whereby a weighted majority of votes by those who designate as unionist and nationalist is required, only applies in certain circumstances to legislation within Northern Ireland that falls under the remit of the Northern Ireland Assembly.[83] This does not include democratic votes such as for Brexit or a border poll.

In the Good Friday Agreement, it is also written that the Secretary of State for Northern Ireland can call for a border poll 'when he believes that there is a clear majority in favour of a United Ireland', but there are no specifics given on how such a majority will be measured, or what criteria will be used to justify the calling of a border poll. A recent court case taken by Raymond McCord that asked the High Court in Belfast to set out what criteria should be used was inconclusive.[84] The High Court stated that however desirable it may be to have certainty on the factors that would trigger a border poll, there was no legal justification to require the Secretary of State to set out this detail. Therefore, we are still in the dark.

However, the Secretary of State for Northern Ireland has the discretion to call a border poll at other times.[85] An opinion poll in *The Sunday Times* in January 2021 showed a majority of Northern Ireland voters wanted there to be a border poll within the next five years.[86] But the criteria for calling a border poll must include looking at a series of opinion polls, the make-up of Northern Ireland elected representatives in the Northern Ireland Assembly and those elected to Westminster. Those suggesting that there is a need for parallel consent – majorities in both unionist and nationalist voters – to achieve Irish unity are essentially indicating that they believe in a unionist veto. The Good Friday Agreement states that a vote for unity can be won by a simple majority – this is democracy.

The UK government does not have to wait simply until there is clear evidence of a majority in favour of Irish unity to decide to hold a referendum, but we can reasonably expect that any such decision from the UK government would have to be taken after consultation with the Irish government. Under Article Three Section One of the Irish Constitution, a referendum must be held in the Irish Republic before the creation of Irish unity.

University College London published research on the criteria for calling a poll and key factors which need to be considered:

> In assessing public opinion, the Secretary of State might draw on six possible sources of evidence: votes cast in elections; the results of surveys and opinion polls; qualitative evidence; a vote within the Assembly; the seats

won at elections; or demographic data. The Secretary
of State must take all relevant evidence into account.[87]

If we look at Scotland as an example, a majority of MSPs elected to
the Scottish Parliament in 2021 were explicitly in favour of Scottish Independence; a majority of MPs elected to the UK Parliament
in 2019 from Scotland also favoured independence. Therefore, they
have a larger mandate for an independence referendum than the UK
Conservatives did following the 2015 election for an EU referendum.
As stated elsewhere, there have been several opinion polls showing
majority support for Scottish independence. The UK government
refused to state how Scotland can legally leave the UK and refused
to set out the criteria that would trigger a border poll in Northern
Ireland. Under these circumstances, it does not feel like we live in a
voluntary union of equals.

While the Good Friday Agreement stipulates that it is for the
Secretary of State to set a date for a border poll, it will be the UK
prime minister who will determine this. It is unlikely that the British
government will set out the criteria for the calling of a border poll
in advance. Rather, they will only call a unity referendum when it is
in their strategic interest to do so. The need for a US trade deal may
provide the context for this – the UK left the EU at a time when the US
administration under President Trump became ever more isolationist
and increasingly engaged in protectionist measures against America's
traditional allies in Canada, Mexico and the EU, as well as China.
The current US Administration is led by a president who is proud of
his Irish roots and favours Irish unity – granting a unity referendum
would, therefore, stand the UK government in good stead with the US
regarding hopes for future trade deals.

However, the British government will also be mindful of the
fact that if they allow a unity referendum in Northern Ireland, they
would likely be compelled to allow another Scottish independence
referendum and vice versa. If unity is called for before Scottish independence, it may be more difficult to achieve, but if Scottish independence is called for before unity, achieving unity may be much easier.

Another possibility is that grassroots campaigning could be used
to show majority support for Irish unity, to such an extent that the
Secretary of State feels obligated to call a border poll. There are
learning points that could be taken from how citizens get initiatives
on the ballot in places like California and then win the vote. This is

done through engaging with voters at a local level and grassroots campaigning to seek their support for particular policies.

A democratic vote will determine where our new path lies – violence may have defined our past, but it will not decide our future. The choice is between a supposedly United Kingdom that is fracturing before our eyes, or the world's largest economic bloc; it is between being part of a union where the Government announces they will intentionally break international law and all the consequences that emerge as a result or being part of a union that is the world's most successful peace process, where rights are safeguarded in law and international treaties are respected.

We must prepare unionism and loyalism for the border poll – it will, no doubt, be a shock to them when it is called. South Africa had Harry Oppenheimer, a prominent local businessman, to help the white Afrikaners move towards accepting the need for the end of Apartheid – Unionism in Northern Ireland will need a similar figure. FW de Klerk was the political leader who helped to ease South Africa's path towards ending apartheid and he agreed to be 1st deputy president when Nelson Mandela was elected president. Similarly, there should be a senior role for Unionist politicians in the first government after reunification to help ease the transition into a blended, New Ireland.

The Government of Ireland's support for unity

There needs to be Irish government support for a unity referendum as they are co-guarantors of the Good Friday Agreement. The Taoiseach Micheál Martin stated in 2020 that there would not be a border poll for at least five years, which coincides with the planned duration of the current coalition government. Instead, he has set up a Shared Island unit designed to build links between both parts of Ireland and within Northern Ireland. This Shared Island Unit is to be welcomed as it focuses attention on sharing resources and understanding across the island; it is an opportunity to develop links between Unionism and the rest of Ireland. However, it must not be used to distract from the unity conversation – it cannot be used to attempt to slow the momentum for reunification.

Northern Ireland will remain a point of friction, with wider ramifications for the rest of Ireland, despite the Ireland/Northern Ireland Protocol, because of Brexit. This friction can only be removed in one of two ways: either the UK re-joins the EU, as no British prime minister is likely to re-join a Customs Union with the EU without also re-joining the EU, which is incredibly unlikely; or we seek Irish unity. The irony is that a new Customs Union for the UK with the EU was possible – an indicative vote on this option in 2019 was defeated by three votes in the House of Commons with the DUP MPs voting against it.

Fine Gael takes pride in their belief that they helped to establish the Irish Free State and end lawlessness after partition. As the Brexit friction increases, the question is: will the Fine Gael Taoiseach seize the opportunity to lead the building of Irish unity, or seek to sit on the sidelines? If they choose the latter option, we can assume that history will instead be made by Sinn Féin and others who will publish a green paper when they invariably get into government. This will enable the Irish government to drive the discussion forward with all citizens on Irish unity.

In his opening address to his party's Ard Fheis in 2021, Leo Varadkar – leader of Fine Gael – announced that he believed Irish unity would happen in his lifetime and stated his desire for it to do so, through the creation of a new state. He also wants to see his party establish a Northern Ireland branch to build their presence in the region and engage with others on the unity question.

Northern Ireland local government elections are due to take place in 2023. This will be another opportunity for the public to show their preference for Nationalist and non-aligned parties, as opposed to Unionist ones. UK Parliament elections are due to take place by 2024 at the latest, although they could be sooner. It is likely that if Labour wins the next UK elections, the only way they can form a government is with tacit support from the SNP, which will be dependent on allowing a second independence referendum – unless Scotland has voted for independence by then.

The next Dáil elections are currently due to take place on or before 20 February 2025. This could return Sinn Féin, who are in favour of Irish unity and are likely to make a border poll/unity referendum a prerequisite for government formation as the largest party. The other main parties in the Dáil may no longer be able to postpone active support for unity by then. Momentum is already building (Jim O'Callaghan and Neale Richmond, senior TDs for Fianna Fáil and Fine Gael have both recently published plans for Irish unity) and now that the Brexit trade deal negotiations are over, this can no longer be used as a reason to stall preparing and calling for unity.

The Irish government must not be allowed to hide behind the fig leaf that now is not the time and a border poll would be 'too divisive'. Anyone who claims that a border poll is divisive is right in the sense that we will be giving people the opportunity to vote for or against something – there will be two options and so, yes, the results will be divided to some degree. However, we are already divided by the alternative to unity – the border on the island of Ireland literally divides the island into two parts. The border poll will be giving people the chance to remove that border and by doing so remove that divide.

Scottish Independence and its effect on unity

Scotland will continue to be a significant factor in the debate around Irish unity for the foreseeable future. The independence referendum in 2014 tugged at the mooring ropes of the UK; the result of 55–45 against independence was significantly closer than anyone, including the UK government, expected. At the start of the process, the British government hoped to win by a solid 2:1 margin to put the issue to rest for at least a generation. Since the vote to leave the European Union, the issue of Scottish independence has been reinvigorated, although it must be acknowledged that those within the independence movement never showed any signs of giving up.

After the Scottish independence referendum in 2014, it appeared that many people voted reluctantly with their wallet rather than their heart, in effect creating economic captives. Now, the Conservatives are seeking to thwart the people of Scotland from having their say on whether they want to become part of the hard Brexit process or take control of their destiny. The Conservatives either seek to ignore demands for another Scottish independence referendum or just threaten to point blank refuse this democratic right. In August 2022, when asked how she would get Scotland's support for the union back, Liz Truss claimed that 'the best thing to do is to ignore [Sturgeon]', branding her an 'attention-seeker' as her audience of Conservative activists applauded her. [88] Deputy First Minister John Swinney hit the nail on the head with his response when he spoke to BBC Scotland:

People in Scotland, whatever their politics, will be absolutely horrified by the obnoxious remarks that Liz Truss has made... Unionist campaigners suggest that Scotland should be at the heart of the United Kingdom and somehow Scotland can be expected to be at the heart of the United Kingdom when the democratically elected leader of our country is, in the view of the person most likely to be the next prime minister of the UK, somebody that should be ignored is completely and utterly unacceptable.[89]

Swinney went on to say that, by her poor choice of words, Truss 'fundamentally undermined' the argument that 'Scotland, somehow, can be fairly and well treated at the heart of the United Kingdom'.

Just imagine the uproar from England if the EU had said to the UK, 'You had a referendum in 1975 so we don't think another one is justified.' The UK would have cried that this was a denial of democracy and that every country must be free to decide its future.

This harsh reality grates against the honeyed words of Boris Johnson that the UK is a union of equals. If the UK government viewed Scottish leaders as equal, they would show them respect – not dismiss their quest for political autonomy as 'moaning'.[90] Surely then, for the people of Northern Ireland, nobody who values democracy would want to stand by such a government or supposed union considering this blatant disregard for our Scottish neighbours?

The UK government says that because of the COVID-19 pandemic, now is not the time to have an independence referendum; however, this is hard to accept when the same government decided to end the transition period with the EU during the same pandemic, despite the EU offering a further extension.

It is deeply ironic that the same Brexiters who demanded an EU referendum are now refusing Scotland the same right to such self-determination – a union of countries can only exist with consent. These were the same right-wing Tories who warned Scotland back in 2014, before the first Scottish independence referendum, that if they voted to leave the UK, they would automatically leave the EU as well. Now that the SNP and others are pointing out that independence is the way back into the EU, the same Brexiters are refusing them their right to a democratic choice. Once again, this shows that the Brexiters' talk of the UK being a union of equals is simply not true.

Scotland has a separate legal system to England. Scotland's Lord Advocate submitted a reference to the UK Supreme Court, to seek a determination on the legislative competence of the question which was proposed in the Scottish Independence Referendum Bill. The SNP has submitted an application to intervene in this case. The SNP's application focuses on the inalienable right of all nations to self-determination. This is enshrined in the United Nations Charter. (At the time of writing the case was due to be heard in October 2022.) We could, therefore, quickly become witnesses to a significant political and constitutional crisis, depending on the outcome of this case and the responses of the UK and Scottish governments.

It should be remembered that the EU referendum was itself only ever advisory, so Scotland could ultimately choose to go down that route, too. If the UK government refuses to allow a referendum, the Scottish Government could put in place an advisory referendum. Indeed both the SNP and the Greens campaigned for the Scottish elections, expressly seeking a mandate for another referendum. A pro-independence majority was returned in the elections, a Section 30 order was requested from the UK government and this was refused. Once the legal route through the Supreme Court has been exhausted, if that does not provide a pathway for a referendum, the SNP government could seek to hold an advisory referendum. The pro-UK side may choose to boycott such a referendum, but after they had lost a Scottish Parliament election fought on independence, would this have credibility? The fact that former prime minister Boris Johnson refused to contemplate holding a referendum gives a clear indication that he believed the UK would lose. However, the first preference of the SNP is for the UK government to accept the legitimacy of the Scottish Parliament to hold another independence referendum. In June 2022, Nicola Sturgeon indicated that she intended to hold the referendum in the first half of the parliamentary mandate, by the end of 2023.

If the Supreme Court does provide a ruling in favour of the ability of the Scottish Government to hold another referendum, this could also in turn provide the trigger for unity advocates in Ireland to seek a court ruling that the Northern Ireland Secretary of State should call a border poll.

A clean Brexit may lead to Irish unity and an independent Scotland. There will be a significant impact on Ireland from the potential for Scottish independence following Brexit. As someone who lived and worked in Scotland for more than eight years, I do not take for granted the presumption that the Scottish voter will always fall into line with the arguments of those who seek to maintain the link with the rest of Britain. Opinion polls since the start of the COVID-19 pandemic have regularly seen a majority in favour of Scottish independence.[91]

Scottish people are by nature straight talkers who think and act independently. Now that there is a widespread debate about the potential impact of a further vote for independence, there is growing momentum for it to be seen as a natural development and progression from devolution. The question is, will the current Scottish Government, led by the SNP, be able to maintain that momentum?

The SNP have drawn a comparison with how the first Dáil came into being in 1918 after a majority of Irish MPs elected to Westminster set up a new parliament in Dublin, as a potential template to follow for independence. The British political establishment does not have the energy or desire to focus on distant parts of the UK. From a practical point of view, the British government is already consumed by the need to deliver Brexit. The EU–UK trade deal agreed upon at the end of 2020 does not signify the end of the negotiations – rather, they are only just beginning. The EU–UK trade agreement itself will be reviewed in five-year cycles starting in 2026.

There are strong cultural links between Northern Ireland and Scotland. As stated previously, many within the unionist community define their Britishness by their association with Scotland through a sense of shared values and community. Should Scotland wish to secede from the rest of the UK, this will present an interesting conundrum for these unionist voters. Do they stick to their concept of Britishness? Is there an association solely with Scotland or do they feel a similar bond to the English and the Welsh? It is interesting to note that Carwyn Jones, former First Minister of Wales, has already stated publicly his view that should Scotland cease to be part of the UK, there should be a new constitutional set-up, with equal representation in a Senate for England, Wales and Northern Ireland.

The links with Scotland are arguably much stronger for unionists within Northern Ireland than those with any other part of the UK. Scottish nationalists both before and after Scottish independence must be encouraged to meet with unionists and loyalists to discuss the importance of and benefits associated with taking control of your destiny.

Scotland will, undoubtedly, continue to work closely with Ireland post-reunification. The Irish and Scottish governments published the

Ireland–Scotland Bilateral Review in 2021.[92] This sets out a series of recommendations across several areas, on how Ireland and Scotland can work together over the next five years. It is laying the groundwork for future cooperation between Ireland and Scotland after Scottish independence. There is a good chance that they could end up working closely in the EU institutions. This cultural link will provide support. It should also be emphasised that a beefed-up British Irish Council,[93] previously referred to occassionaly as the Council of Isles, will continue to exist after Irish unity and indeed will provide a much more useful and meaningful means of communication and negotiation over shared interests. It should perhaps officially be renamed the Council of the Isles, to take account of the changing status of the states on these two islands. It could operate in much the same way as the Nordic Council does (which consists of countries within and outside the EU who meet to ensure co-operation on matters of mutual interest).

Criteria for a poll

If we look at the grounds for a Scottish independence referendum, we can perhaps get a better idea of the likely requirements for our own. A majority of MSPs elected in 2011 were in favour of Scottish independence, so the UK government negotiated with the Scottish Government to enable Scotland to hold its referendum. In Northern Ireland at the time of the Assembly elections in 2016, Unionism lost its majority for the first time. This was confirmed by the Assembly elections of 2017, where Unionism only managed to win 40 out of 90 seats. However, Nationalism did not hold a majority of seats either, with 39 seats out of 90 and the rest were unaligned under Stormont's designation system. In the UK Parliament elections of 2019, Unionism returned a minority of MPs for Northern Ireland for the first time. We have discussed how the Northern Ireland Assembly elections in May 2022 showed a further decline in unionist voters – this is due to be followed by a Northern Ireland Assembly vote on extending the Northern Ireland Protocol in 2024. Any one of these events could lead to the circumstances in which a vote for unity is announced.

We can imagine the Irish government calling for a Yes vote. Equally, the UK government will still be dealing with the wreckage of Brexit and it will not officially be calling for a vote for the union of Great Britain and Northern Ireland. The allowing of the border poll will be an explicit admission that the UK government believes a majority of citizens within Northern Ireland want to leave the UK and therefore it will be hard for them to argue against this.

I think people are right to talk about a unity referendum rather than a border poll. It is much more positive and much less divisive. Also, I think it is worth using lines such as:

> People across Ireland North and South voted to get rid of the border by voting for the Good Friday Agreement in 1998 so that we could move and trade freely across the island.

Or:

> The people of Northern Ireland voted against Brexit in June 2016 and again in the 2017 and 2022 Assembly elections and 2019 European and Westminster elections. If our clear mandate for remaining within the EU is not respected by the British government, we must be allowed to secure our own future through a unity referendum. This is about bringing people together and ensuring there can be no return to a disastrous hard border on this island.

The opinion poll conducted by LucidTalk for *The Detail* in February 2020 showed 46.8 per cent in favour of remaining as part of the UK and 45.4 per cent in favour of Irish unity.[94] This was before the full extent of the Brexit difficulties were even recognised. More recently, opinion polls have shown a majority in favour of Irish unity in the event of a hard Brexit. LucidTalk is a reputable polling company (they predicted the EU referendum results, 2017 Northern Ireland Assembly and 2019 Westminster election results within the margin of error) but for some reason, these findings have not received a lot of coverage.

The Good Friday Agreement states that any referendum on Irish unity must be held concurrently in both states on the island of Ireland. The question should be the same across both jurisdictions, although different questions were asked to get both states to endorse the Good Friday Agreement due to different constitutional structures.

Scotland's independence referendum question was: 'Should Scotland be an independent country?' The Edinburgh Agreement between the UK and Scottish governments set out that the Scottish Parliament would decide on the wording of the question and that this would be tested by the Electoral Commission for intelligibility.[95] On the island of Ireland, there is a logic that the question should simply be: 'Should there be Irish unity?'

There may be a requirement for different questions due to the different constitutional structures which currently exist for the two states on the island of Ireland. Even if the question is the same in both jurisdictions, the campaigns will likely have a different focus. For the Republic, we can assume that the calling of a referendum will have a galvanising effect as all the major parties are supportive of the principle of Irish unity. While some are hesitant to call for a border poll now, once a poll is called, they will rightly see this as a once-in-a-generation opportunity. The Good Friday Agreement stipulates that there cannot be another border poll for seven years, so we want to see a successful vote on the first occasion.

The Secretary of State for Northern Ireland will look at several factors when deciding when to call a border poll. These include Northern Ireland election results, for both the Northern Ireland Assembly and UK Parliament; trends in opinion polls over some time; and changing demographics, including the publication of the 2021 census results in late 2022. If these three factors show that there is likely a majority in favour of Irish unity in a border poll, then the Secretary of State will be obliged to call one. There are also unspecified political circumstances under which a Secretary of State may choose to call a border poll, even if these criteria are not met, but this would not happen without the approval of the UK prime minister and the endorsement of the Cabinet. As Professor Colin Harvey of Queen's University Belfast has suggested, the British Irish Intergovernmental Conference should be used to set the question, franchise and date of the vote.[96] Just as the Scottish independence referendum in 2014 enabled EU citizens to vote, so they should on the unity referendum – 16-year-olds should be allowed to vote, too.

Setting a date now would create more certainty than the current situation where we do not know when it will take place. As Britain negotiates trade deals with other countries, the divergence between Northern Ireland and the rest of the UK will increase.

Securing the vote to decide on unity will be difficult, but easier than for Scotland as the right to self-determination is written into the Good Friday Agreement. No Conservative prime minister is going to want to facilitate this after the trauma of the Scottish independence referendum in 2014 and the EU referendum in 2016.

The Northern Ireland Assembly could pass a motion backed by the majority of MLAs that calls for a border poll, after a substantial period of preparation. This is most likely in the context of seeing the negative impact of the hard Brexit which has been negotiated by the UK government. It is assumed that Alliance and Green MLAs may not come out in favour of unity; however, Alliance representatives have stated publicly that they will decide at the time of the referendum whether to campaign for Irish unity. The former Northern Ireland leader of the Greens previously mused on the merits of Irish unity post-Brexit. In short, I do not believe that Irish unity is a pipe dream any longer, thanks to Brexit.

There is likely to be a Judicial Review on the calling of a border poll. If a border poll is called, Unionists are likely to challenge this in the courts as well. The mere fact of calling the unity referendum will seriously destabilise Unionism. Unionists often state simply that there will not be a border poll, thereby ensuring that as soon as there is one, Unionism will have suffered a psychological defeat.

Gone are the days when successive Unionist leaders called for border polls. David Trimble, who served as first minister, called for this in the past; former First Minister Peter Robinson said that Union- ism should prepare for the holding of a border poll – the Unionist parties did not take this opportunity to engage in a debate but sim- ply criticised his comments and claimed that a border poll would never happen.

Arlene Foster, the former first minister of Northern Ireland and leader of the DUP, was on record in 2013 saying that the DUP may agree to a border poll request by Sinn Féin:

> If we have the border poll then that instability goes
> away and, in actual fact, what we have is a very clear
> validation of the union and that's something we're
> looking at at the moment.[97]

So, the question is, what has changed since then? Any time Unionists or Conservatives say that a border poll or independence referendum is reckless and divisive, let's remind them that we did not ask for an EU referendum. Brexit has been delivered despite our opposition and that is why we need to prepare for unity now so that, unlike Brexit, it will not be reckless. The decision by the UK government to leave the EU during an already destabilising pandemic and implement new trade frictions is reckless. The travel chaos in Dover in the summer of 2022 as UK holidaymakers faced long delays to enter France, is another example of how being outside the EU leads to greater restrictions in any interaction with Europe.

To those who say that now is not the time for a unity referendum, I say 2016 was not the time for a Brexit referendum, but we must deal with the outcome. The sense of the UK as a stabilising force for Northern Ireland has gone forever. Across the island of Ireland, we cannot allow this instability to continue, so a unity referendum must be held in the next few years after preparations have been made.

Political Unionists were largely opposed to a second Brexit referendum, even though Northern Ireland did not vote for Brexit. Now, they are opposed to a democratic vote on Irish unity. Is it just democracy that they are opposed to unless they are certain the outcome will go their way? They want to enforce the outcome of a UK vote despite the majority of people in Northern Ireland voting to remain within the EU. There has never been a democratic mandate in any part of the island of Ireland to leave the EU.

Calling for and holding a unity referendum is giving people a democratic choice. Those opposed to a border poll are opposed to democracy and therefore freedom. No true democrat can argue against people being given their say. Let both sides put forward detailed plans and let the voters decide. That way everyone wins.

Escape hatch

Irish unity is the escape hatch from the worst aspects of Brexit for the island of Ireland. You do not go through an escape hatch when everything is sweetness and light. You may prefer to wait to go through it another day when there is no unbearable heat and the room is not covered in smoke, but then there would be no need to use it. We have only a limited window of opportunity to use it and we must take that chance.

Regardless of what the end outcome is with Brexit, the Irish government needs to start planning now for what Irish unity will look like. We need to set out a clear path towards unity – the utter chaos following the Brexit vote shows the importance of being prepared for constitutional change.

Our politics is done mostly via proportional representation and that leads more towards a conciliatory approach. As a small island, we need unity of purpose and unity of delivery and the only way that we can ensure this is through unification. This will be the best and shared future for us all who call this island home.

The pro-unity campaign needs to frame the debate about Northern Ireland having the option to progress with Ireland united in the EU or to fall backwards as part of a disunited UK. Unionist leaders have had 100 years to make everyone welcome as a part of Northern Ireland and have failed to do so. Unionism has also had a century to construct a meaningful vision of what being 'Northern Irish' is but has failed to achieve this either.

Politics across Ireland is changing. The UCUNF (Ulster Conservative and Unionist – New Force) arrangements put in place for the 2010 UK election did not work for several reasons, primarily the lack of full commitment by the UUP towards joint policies and an eventual merger. This failed political experiment showed that half measures will not work. Political parties based in the Irish Republic should move north, too. Fine Gael has established their first branch at Queen's University Belfast and their party leader Leo Varadkar has established a Northern Ireland group to engage with local political parties and develop policies. All Irish political parties have a role to play in building toward Irish unity – it must not be seen as the agenda of one party.

As the disastrous Brexit negotiations have shown, the mainland UK political parties have failed in Northern Ireland. Of the major parties, only the Conservatives stand here and they have failed to win a single seat in the Northern Ireland Assembly or at Westminster from Northern Ireland; Labour and the Liberal Democrats do not stand as candidates.

The riddle of how to keep the border open between the Irish Republic and Northern Ireland while enabling Britain to restrict freedom of movement and exit the Single Market is not one with an easy solution. Or is it? Occam's Razor is the principle that the simplest solution tends to be the correct one. In this case, the simplest solution for keeping the border open on the island of Ireland permanently is to remove it altogether through reunification.

The Irish government may stick to their plan to not consider the possibility of a border poll before 2025; however, if the dynamics towards unity accelerate due to the border down the Irish Sea, the breaking of international law by the UK government and the likely vote for Scottish independence, we must be ready for an earlier unity vote – we must be ready to open the escape hatch.

Routes to a unity referendum

There are several ways a unity referendum could come about. Nationalism could secure the majority of seats in an Assembly or Westminster election; Unionists could demand a border poll to show confidence in Unionism; the UK government could call for a border poll to put the issue to bed, or to actively encourage unity to make Brexit simpler or because it can no longer provide subvention; or perhaps another unknown reason, for example, it forms part of US–UK trade deal as the UK cannot secure the border with EU via the Irish republic.

As a leader of the 'Republican Party', the Fianna Fáil Taoiseach's 2020 statement regarding a border boll being too divisive to consider for at least five years shows that there is plenty of work to be done to secure a referendum and a vote for unity. However, his party has dropped significantly in the opinion polls since the February 2020 election and has been overtaken by both Fine Gael and Sinn Féin in popularity. It is not inconceivable that the party will rediscover their core mission to reunite Ireland soon, partly as a means to reinvigorate their popularity.

The question of transitional funding post-reunification is key. Frankly, would the Irish government wish to take on responsibility for Northern Ireland, when it is already facing the unprecedented challenge of Brexit and rebuilding its economy after the COVID-19 pandemic? This is one of the many reasons why the unity campaign needs to set out a package of investments to stimulate the reunification process. This should be a two-part process showing the funding provided by the UK government and the EU (including the Irish government). The second part will show how inward investment will be secured from North America, Europe and elsewhere.

As part of building the foundation for a unity referendum to take place, a secular unity campaign (one not affiliated with any party) should ask elected representatives in both the Northern Ireland

Assembly and the Oireachtas to call for a unity referendum. At the time of the next elections to both legislatures, candidates should be invited to sign a pledge supporting Irish unity. This pledge would call for a citizens' assembly to be established immediately after the election and for a referendum to be held within the next five years. All politicians who claim to be in favour of Irish unity should be willing to sign this.

Human rights and equality are a delicate part of Northern Ireland's fragile stability – they will be crucial pillars in building a stable and agreed Irish unity. The EU can point to its record as an honest broker in the peace process; it has supported the island of Ireland through reconciliation and supported equality through implementing effective legislation. Imagine the impact it would have if the EU agreed, as part of its transitional funding support for reunification, to be committed to relocating an EU agency to Belfast.

No love for Stormont

The unity campaign must not fall into the elephant trap of offering some form of confederation with the continuation of the Northern Ireland Assembly and Executive – the full benefits of unity will only be unlocked by complete integration at a political level. Continuing with the Assembly is providing an answer to a question that is not being asked. What would be the point of continuing with devolution, other than to keep things different from the rest of the island? Unionists would certainly try and create a firewall against the current Republic, but the days of Unionist majorities are gone and so is any hope for, or attachment to, Stormont, if there ever was any. The majority of people in Northern Ireland will not grieve the end of Stormont and its various scandals such as NAMA, Red Sky and RHI which between them have cost billions at a time of government austerity and individual financial constraints.

Assembly can push for a referendum

In Northern Ireland, the Alliance party and the Greens do not designate as Unionists or Nationalists, but the lazy assumption until now has been that they favour the status quo and therefore are de facto Unionists. However, Brexit means that the status quo is no longer available. Now that we know the UK government will not advocate special status for Northern Ireland within the EU, the position of these two centrist parties may evolve further. In other words, there may then be a motion tabled for a vote in the assembly chamber calling on Irish unity to secure Northern Ireland's position within the EU and to ensure that there continues to be free movement of people, goods, services and capital across the island. Just as Nicola Sturgeon may well do the same for Scotland, we could argue that as the UK EU referendum was technically only advisory and non-binding, the Northern Ireland Assembly could hold a similar vote. A motion calling for a unity referendum could be held while the formation of a new Northern Ireland Executive remains blocked by the DUP.

Often parties will use the threat of change to encourage voters to reject any proposal for changing policy. However, the negotiations between the EU and UK will continue in some shape or form, even though a threadbare trade deal has been agreed upon, with the impact lasting over a much longer period. Northern Ireland cannot suffer this length of uncertainty – unity will solve this.

The point needs to be reinforced that no one should have anything to fear by asking the people to confirm how they want to live on this small island. At no point has a majority of voters in Ireland expressed a desire to leave the EU. We all realise that the European Union is not perfect – no organisation that works across so many areas in an ever-changing world is going to be. But the alternative of chaos and going alone is not the way to deal with the hugely challenging issues we face such as growing our economy, dealing with climate change and a pandemic, an energy crisis, a cost-of-living crisis and addressing international crime and terrorism.

Part Two: Winning the Referendum

Gaming the Campaign

'No matter what people tell you, words and ideas can change the world.'[98]

Tom Schulman

A CAMPAIGN IS a conversation with society. It needs to appeal to emotion, whereas policy development and technical expertise are logical endeavours. Through a campaign, we want to secure change for the public good. The point is that the unity debate is not some abstract discussion of concepts of sovereignty – it is about how we live each day, the environment for our children, our relationships with others across this island, across Europe and beyond; it is about how we grow our economy, gaining the skilled workers from across the world who want to be here for our public services and to share in our innovation; it is about how we deal with public health emergencies like COVID-19, using the best advice by world experts such as the WHO on flattening the curve. Essentially, it is about enabling prosperity and protecting our people. We have been waiting more than 100 years for Irish unity – the need is stronger now than ever.

But we need more than empty slogans to make Irish unity work – we need proof of action. For example, housing is a foundation stone of society. Virtue signalling and identity politics are not going to solve our housing crisis. These tactics will not help kids who suffer from educational under attainment; they will not grow the economy to provide jobs so that people can provide for their families, or so that we can invest in public services or infrastructure.

A broad coalition to win the unity referendum is both necessary and desirable – it will be needed to build Irish unity. Ideological purity is not the right approach; targeting, data analytics and digital are key. Even though there will not be the same amount of money as in a US presidential campaign, for example, the principles still apply.

We want the unity campaign to win based on facts. If we look at the Brexit campaign, it was won by Leave through a series of lies and so people voted for a scenario that was never really achievable: £350 million was not being sent to the EU every week; the UK does not hold all the cards; Turkey was not about to join the EU – as a member of the EU, the UK always had a veto on the accession of a potential new member.

Ireland has regular experience of holding referendums – marriage equality, repealing the 8th amendment – and doing so in a way that is not disruptive to the effective operation of government. This will be crucial for the unity referendum.

The centre ground is key

We cannot simply rely on a Catholic majority in Northern Ireland appearing in the next few years who will instinctively outvote Protestants and deliver Irish unity. The centre ground continues to grow across Northern Ireland; young people, in particular, are turning away from organised religion. For Northern Ireland, religion has contributed to so much civil unrest that many of our citizens want nothing to do with it, on either 'side'. Irish unity must be a liberal endeavour in the broadest sense and we need to secure a majority regardless of any religious affiliation – we can win the argument for Irish unity without resorting to this approach.

The gap between unionist and nationalist voters in Northern Ireland is minimal – according to the analysis by Daithi McKay, a former MLA, it is only 5,000 votes.[99] LucidTalk undertook an analysis of the second preferences of Alliance and Green voters and 56.8 per cent of Alliance voters indicated that their second preferences would go to Nationalist or Republican parties (as would 32.2 per cent of Green voters);[100] significantly less than this would give a second preference to Unionist parties.[101] Furthermore, the Deputy Leader of Alliance has publicly acknowledged that the views of their party membership on Irish unity are shifting in the context of Brexit. As a party, they will take a position when a referendum has been called and there is a proposal on the table.

Unity for a more liberal future

On either side of the debate on Irish unity, there will be references to patriotism. Whether it be patriotic nationalists yearning to reunite with the rest of Ireland or patriotic unionists who want to cling to the idea of Britain. But patriotism for me is about ensuring the best possible living conditions for my family and wider society in a country whose ideals, principles and actions I can proudly get behind. It is not about stopping people from expressing their democratic views or excluding others because they are different. Therefore, I believe the patriotic choice for all who live on the island of Ireland is to favour Irish unity and reclaim our EU membership. The framework of the EU provides safeguards – being a citizen of the EU allows me to travel, work, live and trade freely with no barriers across the European bloc. I am a Liberal and that is the epitome of individual freedom – a Liberal ideal.

Framing Irish unity as a way to embed and expand upon liberalism is the key to unlocking a majority of votes across the island. We need to emphasise that a cross-party approach is necessary to attain a majority in favour of it at the referendum. A July 2022 poll showed that nearly 20 per cent of voters supported centrist, pro-EU parties (16.38 per cent for Alliance and three per cent for the Greens).[102] They will be decisive in a unity referendum.

The campaign for Irish unity is a noble ambition. However, certain Unionists will seek to drag these noble ideals down. They will say that there will never be a poll, that it can never be won, that violence will break out, that we cannot afford Irish unity and that too many people have died in The Troubles to give up now.

In response, the unity campaign must be evidence-based, grounded in reality and sober, but aspiring to a more prosperous and more progressive future. It is obvious that there is a growing demand for an outward, socially liberal approach from citizens across the island of Ireland, therefore we need to first unite the people and then the country. Irish unity needs to be a cohesive offering – there was no coherent vision for Brexit, which is part of the reason why the process has been such a disaster. People projected what they wanted onto it. There *must* be a clear unity plan, to be implemented after a successful vote, which the campaign will emphasise.

Northern Ireland remains a divided society for too many of its citizens, a quarter century on from the Good Friday Agreement. So called 'peace walls' which were set up during The Troubles remain in place. These are walls that stand up to 20 feet high which keep republican/nationalist communities apart from unionist/loyalist ones. Indeed, there are now more peace walls than there were at the time of the signing of the Good Friday Agreement.[103]

We know that the overall majority of people in Northern Ireland want to live in mixed-religion neighbourhoods (76 per cent according to the Northern Ireland Life and Times Survey in 2019.[104] The majority of people in Northern Ireland also want integrated education which enables those of all religious denominations and none to learn together, to be the primary means of educating children across the region (71 per cent according to a LucidTalk opinion poll in 2021 for the Northern Ireland Council for Integrated Education).[105]

Such separation at local community level did not develop overnight and so it will take time to break down these barriers. There needs to be political leadership to bring people together, as well as integrated education and a shared housing approach. Community workers need to help citizens who are affected by peace walls to tear down both the physical and mental barriers that keep our society divided. Getting people to live and study together from an early age will be a start. Naturally, people can be fearful of change. We have to reassure our citizens that change can be positive – one way to do this is to provide a pathway to prosperity. A key part of the unity plan must include a detailed package of proposals on how these opportunities will be realised for everyone, regardless of background or political outlook.

Those of us who favour Irish unity should not be apologetic or defensive about it – Irish unity is a legitimate aspiration; it is factored into the Good Friday Agreement that upholds our nation. While a larger vote for unity is desirable, it is wrong to suggest that a super majority needs to be secured to deliver Irish unity. This is a question of democracy – all votes must maintain equal weight.

Citizens' assembly

In advance of the unity referendum, the Irish government should form a citizens' assembly and then publish a White Paper informed by its recommendations, setting out plans for Irish unity (as happened with the equal marriage referendum) which can then form the basis of the debate during the unity referendum. This citizens' assembly should be open to all – political representatives, businesses and wider society. While it is likely that Unionist representatives will boycott this there can be hope that businesspeople and civil society representatives from Northern Ireland would get involved. The aim would be to develop a range of options about the future structure of Irish unity and how it would operate. Setting out detailed, tangible plans on paper will enable the unity campaign to sell its vision and build momentum for unity; it will allow people to have a clear idea of what they are voting for. A citizens' assembly will be part of important preparatory work to ensure that reunification is a success and begins with certainty. The more we talk about what Irish unity will look like, the more people will consider its benefits.

The unity campaign must also challenge Unionist leaders to do likewise. What are they going to do to show the potential swing voters that it is desirable to stay in the UK?

Need for an all-Ireland referendum commission

We want to avoid the vote for unity being influenced by external interference such as the Russian hacking and disinformation that was allegedly used in the Brexit referendum and the 2016 US presidential election. There is an Electoral Commission for Northern Ireland and one has been mooted for some time for Ireland. As there are currently two states on the island, there will need to be two organisations undertaking a role to ensure that the campaigns operate legally and without undue influence. Ideally, there would be an all-Ireland referendum commission which would decide the rules around the unity referendum. It would set out the parameters around issues such as funding, broadcasting rules and how the question would be worded in the referendum itself. It should also confirm that the referendum voting would take place on one day, as happened with the referendums in both Northern Ireland and the Irish Republic for the Good Friday Agreement.

The pro-unity campaign must set out a positive narrative

There is likely to be a febrile atmosphere when the unity referendum takes place. Brexit is a disaster and the external environment will be unstable, anxious and highly emotive. It would be wonderful if the referendum could take place within a positive stable environment; however, people will be deciding between a terrible reality (post-Brexit Britain) and what they perceive to be an uncertain future as part of a new state created through Irish unity.

To achieve a vote for unity, the pro-unity campaign must ensure that its message is a positive one. The unity campaign must focus on offering a more prosperous, liberal and outward-looking New Ireland. Voters will decide based on their quality of life and future opportunities for them and their families. Those who favour unity must set out a positive vision so that there can be a proper debate. The campaign needs to embrace the future while remembering and respecting the past.

The unity campaign must not fall into the trap of the Yes campaign for Scottish independence in 2014, where it appeared at times the campaign was claiming that everything would be easier after independence. There will be significant effort required to make a success of Irish unity; however, leading Brexiter Jacob Rees-Mogg stated that it could take up to fifty years to see the benefits of Brexit whereas when we vote for Irish unity, the benefits will be clear from day one. There will be no hard border, guaranteed by a democratic vote of the people across Ireland; EU membership and all the associated benefits and security will be confirmed for the entire island. We need to emphasise that a vote for unity is the safe option – not the uncertain one.

Throughout the Brexit debate, pro-Brexit supporters talked about various 'unicorns'. These are impossible benefits arising from Brexit that do not exist – for example, the claim that UK citizens could continue to have freedom of movement around the EU while stopping EU citizens from moving to the UK.

The UK government tried belatedly to kill off these unicorns to get MPs to agree to the withdrawal deal, negotiated by Theresa May. However, politicians then tried to revive them even after they were proven to be unworkable or unavailable. We could, instead, call them 'zombiecorns' – unicorns that have been killed off, but then resurrected by disingenuous and misguided politicians and other Brexiters. During Boris Johnson's time as prime minister, he interchangeably referred to the loss of certain benefits, before brazenly misrepresenting the facts on the ground. For example, telling a small group of Northern Ireland Conservatives that there would be no paperwork for them to trade with Britain after the end of the transition period. This was wrong. By comparison, to maintain the trust of its supporters, the unity campaign must only represent the truth to the people of Ireland – there can be no outlandish claims that cannot be supported in reality.

The pro-unity campaign must hold its discipline and take the high road; it must not get dragged down into negativity that will likely come its way. If we are not able to have a rational discussion during the referendum campaign, everyone will lose. Securing a true mandate for unity means acknowledging the challenges in advance of the vote so that there is democratic support for implementing the necessary change.

A wide range of businesspeople should be asked to speak about how they would be willing to invest in a New Ireland, how it is a country that offers more opportunities and security of investment for inward investors as part of the European Union than a fragmented and unstable UK which has an uncertain future on the world stage with no clear relationship with the EU. There should be a detailed presentation on how infrastructure investment would be implemented across the island of Ireland, from pension funds and others who would seek to invest for emotional and sound business reasons. A detailed investment campaign should be highlighted by the unity campaign. This should set out how the all-Ireland economy will be rebuilt for the post-pandemic world.

Cultural representatives from across the creative industries and others should be invited to talk about how Irish unity would signify and help to stimulate a cultural awakening which would be accessible to all people across Ireland. This would also be a magnet for attracting tourists and inward investment.

The unity campaign should emphasise that Ireland has substantial soft power and cultural influencers, 'a friend in every port' whereas the UK post-Brexit has a more limited number of friends. Leading figures from around the world should be asked to speak on the cause for unity and encourage Ireland to become reunited. This will be much more constructive than the use of international figures to spread harsh messages about the dangers of Brexit, which ultimately fell on deaf ears.

It should also be noted that Britain will not be able to rely on the support of other European countries now that it has left the European Union. If Scotland votes for independence there is a real question mark over whether the remainder of the UK (rUK) will be able to house its nuclear deterrent. If this is not possible then the rUK may be under pressure to concede its permanent seat on the UN Security Council. There is a real prospect that Ireland, through its membership of the EU, will have a greater voice in various global decision-making bodies than rUK would have as a standalone country of around 60 million people. The UK government will be preoccupied with Brexit for decades to come, attempting to build trade links while at the same time restricting inward migration. This is never a good way to approach negotiations. The unity referendum must continually insist that Ireland can get better trade deals as part of the EU than the UK will be able to get on its own.

It is a hackneyed phrase that a winning campaign needs to build a wide-ranging coalition – this is no less true for a border poll. It is said that we live in a post-truth environment; nevertheless, the campaign for unity must set out a positive vision. This must focus on securing the support of the widest possible group of people. The pro-union campaign is likely to be unrelentingly negative, and this will be exposed by a positive vision that appeals to a wide section of society. We will be able to build Irish unity from this vision, after the vote for unity. Some positive messages backed up with facts must be selected at the start of the campaign and the focus must remain on these throughout. Irish unity is about building something together whereas Brexit is about dismantling links with the continent of Europe and putting up barriers.

Hope will always triumph over fear if it is pursued with vigour and determination. The unity campaign, unlike many campaigns for independence, cannot be painted as a negative drive for separation. It is about reuniting all the people on this small island; it is the best way of ensuring equality and protection of human rights for all.

Targeting negative ads and 'fake news'

While those of us who favour Irish unity believe in the prospect of a more hopeful future, we must acknowledge that the campaign is likely to be tough and bitter, particularly on the Unionist side.

It will be interesting to see whether the pro-UK side of the campaign decides to adopt positive campaigning, or whether Unionist representatives will dominate with negativity and fearmongering. If we look at the Brexit referendum, the Leave side put forward a positive campaign setting out the benefits of leaving the EU (albeit none of the supposed benefits were grounded in reality). The Remain side, by comparison, focused on the dangers and the negativity of leaving the EU. In hindsight, 'Project Fear' has proven to be 'Project Reality'; however, one of the main challenges for the Remain side must have been combating the question that if leaving the EU was going to be so damaging, why would any rational government allow people to vote on such an option? There was also an assumption that the UK government must have created a plan in the event of Leave winning. They did not and there was chaos as a result, which we are still experiencing more than six years after the vote.

The unity campaign cannot just ignore all the attacks that will inevitably come from Unionist leaders. Rick Wilson, the US political consultant and co-founder of the Lincoln Project addressed the need to challenge negative ads head-on in his book *Running against the Devil*.[106] But you must also push your agenda, not just simply refute claims made by the opposing side.

The techniques for political communications are changing all the time. However, several important rules need to be adhered to for a successful unity referendum. Message discipline and quick responses to negative attacks are key. In the EU referendum, the pro-Brexit campaign deployed Tory MPs as flying monkeys to attack the Remain campaign. When they, on occasion went too far, the Leave campaign was able to disown their actions, after they had caused disruption. The unity campaign must know when they can ignore these attacks and when there will be a need to refute them directly.

We must be aware that misinformation and 'fake news' – one particularly ridiculous and unfortunate consequence of a post-Trump world – will likely be used during the referendum campaign. We must deal with the challenge by ensuring message discipline. Both the official pro-unity campaign and the official pro-UK campaign should have rapid response units to address and nullify said fake news. We cannot allow this phenomenon of lies to be used to influence the referendum result. There should perhaps be an independent organisation, such as the ESRI (Economic and Social Research Institute) that can adjudicate whether controversial claims are factually correct.

If Unionists do decide to go down the route of negative ads and alternative facts, they may end up shooting themselves in the foot, so to speak. Experts have expressed concern about the long-term impact of negative campaigning:

> [it has the] potential to do damage to the political system as it tends to reduce feelings of political efficacy, trust in government, and perhaps even satisfaction with government itself (Lau et al 2007).[107]

This would be a win for pro-unity but damning for Unionism. If the unity campaign can create a positive, concise and robust narrative then it will win.

Escaping from Brexit and protecting the Good Friday Agreement will be key issues within the unity campaign. To reiterate, the DUP are the only major party in Northern Ireland to oppose the Good Friday Agreement. The only time that the DUP talks in support of this peace accord is when they think they will be bypassed for Irish unity. They have undertaken a hugely negative and disruptive role in UK politics at a crucial time – this will not be forgotten. If they apply this same disruption to the pro-UK campaign, their reputation will be even more disreputable.

The pro-unity campaign should compare the political environments between Ireland and the UK. In Ireland, there is a cross-party consensus on Brexit, whereas there is no agreement within the UK on what kind of Brexit should be pursued. This shows the difference between a mature approach that focuses on the national interest and an immature, self-obsessed view of the world being taken by the UK – often one based on lies.

We need to prepare for the media storm that will surround the unity campaign; we need to be aware that the British media is a powerful force that can aid the spread of misinformation.

In terms of the campaign itself, it will be important to ensure that it is data-informed as opposed to data-driven.[108] Data can inform a campaign, but it must not be the sole driver of strategy. The best, most successful political campaigns are ones that make a connection with the voters; ones that inspire people to go out and vote. The excellent book *Shattered: Inside Hillary Clinton's Doomed Campaign* by Jonathan Allen and Amie Parnes sets out how the campaign had an over-reliance on data and ignored the emotional factors that contributed to Hillary Clinton's surprise loss to Donald Trump in the 2016 US presidential election.[109]

A successful campaign must engage the people. There could be three strands of engagement: business, community/voluntary, and the general public (further sub-divided into age groups, socio-economic background etc). The messages for each of these strands will have to be tailored for specific audiences. While the unity campaign will have the same overall objectives, this targeting by segment will enable different points to be emphasised depending on whom the engagement is targeted.

Unionism has no positive vision to share

Invariably, when Unionist politicians talk about the union with Britain and overcoming the challenges presented by Brexit, they will refer to the past: 'The UK has overcome worse'; 'We have too much shared history to have circumstances undermine the union now'. There is rarely, if ever, a constructive vision set out for the future. An ideology that is based on a narrow interpretation of the past is not fit for the future, especially in times of rapid change.

At its core, Unionism relies on being against something more than standing for something – after all these years, the attitude still seems to be, 'Ulster says NO'. One example is Unionist leaders' opposition to holding a border poll while not being willing to set out a positive vision for Northern Ireland remaining part of the UK. Perhaps providing such a positive vision for Northern Ireland's future in the UK is too difficult a task – particularly if it is to include a long-term, credible viewpoint in a rapidly changing, complex and interdependent world.

The paradox for Unionists is that only by accepting that Northern Ireland is different from the rest of the UK, can they hope to remain part of it – special status for Northern Ireland post-Brexit could potentially have put off reunification for several generations. During the referendum campaign, Unionists will focus on terrorist atrocities in the past and how those who sacrificed their lives to protect Northern Ireland must not be let down, but the fact that Unionists wanted the same rubbish Brexit deal as Hull did more to harm the union between Britain and Northern Ireland than any IRA campaign ever did.

The Unionists will focus on two key things: economic uncertainty and patriotic/cultural issues. The unity campaign needs to address each of these issues to neuter their emotional effectiveness. If the unity campaign manages to get a lead the Unionists will likely try to deliver a vow similar to the one made by the three Unionist parties in the first Scottish independence referendum to try and stop momentum and swing back to the status quo. But what can they offer that would be effective? The unity campaign needs to say that remaining with the UK is not the status quo, it is a jump into the dark outside the certainty and security of the EU. Will they offer a federal UK which has been discussed numerous times but has never been delivered? The UK government has shown by its actions that it cannot be trusted to deliver more powers to the Northern Ireland Assembly and Northern Ireland Executive. It is stuck in an imperial time warp, focused on maintaining an outdated, unitary state.

The Health Service

One of the key areas that Unionism will seek to focus on is the NHS and how it played a crucial role in fighting the COVID-19 pandemic. They will talk about how the health service will suffer after Irish unity has been achieved. People do not want to pay for what they see as expensive healthcare in the Irish Republic. While everyone has access to the public healthcare system, some people do have to pay for visits to doctors or hospitals. The costs are €100 for a visit to A&E, if you have not been referred by your family doctor. A visit to a doctor usually costs €45–75, although it can be lower. Inpatient costs (charges for hospital stays) are a flat €80 per day up to a maximum of €800 in any twelve-month period, regardless of actual costs incurred. Around a third of people are entitled to a Medical Card due to their income levels and therefore do not have to pay for any services.[110] However, merging with the Republic does not mean that we must adopt their current healthcare system. Furthermore, the Irish government announced their intention to move away from their current two-tiered healthcare system through the introduction of Sláintecare, a reform programme with the aim of delivering universal healthcare. All the main political parties in the Irish Republic are committed to the implementation of Sláintecare: Sinn Féin has publicly stated that there needs to be an all-Ireland health service, which is free at the point of access;[111] Fine Gael[112] and the Social Democrats[113] have called for an Irish health service, too. Admittedly, Sláintecare which was due to be fully implemented by 2028 has been criticised for slow progress (not helped by the pandemic), but it is at least a step in the right direction, away from an over-reliance onprivatised healthcare. According to the Irish government:

> Working towards universal healthcare for all, Sláintecare reform is creating a health and social care service where people can access the right services, closer to home, and based on need and not ability to pay.[114]

We have all lived through a public health emergency for more than two years and I believe that people have an increased understanding of the importance of investment in universal healthcare, which is free at the point of use and funded through general taxation. Irish unity provides the opportunity to renew our public services and commit to this approach, so that there can be a truly National Health Service for all of Ireland, one that could even improve upon the current NHS.

The UK Conservative government has undermined our current health service by creating a hostile environment for EU health workers since Brexit who have left the UK in significant numbers as a result. The Health and Care Act 2022 confirms the right of NHS Digital to share patients' private data with third parties.[115] The EU provides safeguards through the GDPR (General Data Protection Regulations)[116] but the UK government has stated that they intend to diverge from GDPR.[117] This opens the possibility that patient data will be sold off to private companies for profit. There is also no barrier to private companies sitting on the new Integrated Care Systems which are being set up and will have oversight on the delivery of healthcare services across England.[118] There is a real fear that these changes and the increasingly ideological approach of the Conservative government will lead to the effective dismantling of the NHS and selling off to private companies.

While, in theory, the delivery of healthcare is largely under the control of legislatures in Scotland, Wales and Northern Ireland, the level of funding is determined in Whitehall and Westminster. The funding that goes to each of these legislatures, to be allocated by their governments, is determined through the Barnett formula.[119] Therefore if Whitehall allocates less funding to the health service in England because services are for example sold off or outsourced to the private sector and as a result patients have to pay directly, this will have a knock-on effect on the funding allocated to the rest of the UK. We know already that the UK government has not provided sufficient investment for services and has been unwilling to provide sufficient pay increases for overworked staff.

Moreover, Northern Ireland has the longest hospital waiting lists in the UK.[120] At one stage in 2021, one in seven of the population of Northern Ireland were on a waiting list for more than one year; in the Irish Republic, one in four of the population are on health waiting lists.[121] While some of this can be attributed to dealing with the unprecedented impact of the COVID-19 pandemic, by bringing the two health services into one integrated system, Irish unity will provide the opportunity to renew our public services. Full health service integration across the island makes sense and will save money.

The unity campaign must focus on how being part of the EU provides access to a large workforce of highly skilled health workers and rapid developments in digital health. The European digital health market was valued at $39.3 billion in 2021 and is predicted to grow significantly over the next decade.[122] Healthcare is increasingly provided by digital means and this will only become more important in the future; prevention and treatment of illness will increasingly rely on the use of digital health in a community care setting. This will relieve pressure on hospitals and bring healthcare closer to people, as will be provided in the comfort of their own homes. The EU protects and safely allows the usage of anonymised data for its 450 million citizens to create better outcomes. The UK will not be able to tap into this expertise and we do not know if British citizens can have confidence that their data will not be sold off by the UK government to external commercial companies in the USA and elsewhere.

There has been an increased use of Telehealth and digital health across Ireland. Mainstreaming this provides an opportunity to reset the health service for unity. We will not be going back to the way things were before the pandemic – the increased use of digital health will be key and this can build on Ireland's success in attracting high-tech and pharmaceutical investments. The Magee Medical School is key for the development of the north-west of Ireland to ensure we have a fully staffed health service and can secure the benefits of digital health – it will also help to ensure that we can train and retain medical professionals across Ireland.

We are in a climate crisis and as humans destroy more of our habitat, there is a greater potential for more pandemics. This is due to destruction of wildland, loss of biodiversity and rising temperatures which enable diseases to thrive. There is an advantage to being a small island in these circumstances, as we could approach an eradication policy, as New Zealand initially did. Northern Ireland outside the EU will find access to qualified EU health professionals more difficult. This is because the UK government that controls the borders and sets the policy for immigration has an explicit aim to reduce foreign workers coming into the country.

We can also expect to hear many emotive stories from pro-union campaigners – they are likely, based on past campaigns, to rely on third parties to deliver the hysterical message of fear of unity. In the past, survivors of terrorist atrocities have been used to attack those standing on a non-Unionist platform. Unionists will refer to these terrorist attacks from the past and how so many people fought and died for our freedom to remain part of the UK. There were many innocent citizens who were injured or killed. It is terrible that people died as a result of terrorist activity and this is to be deeply regretted. However, their deaths were not to stop the democratic process. One can argue that the deaths of members of the security services, politicians and others were about defending law and order and the right of the people of Northern Ireland to make their own decisions on a democratic basis. If the people of Northern Ireland decide, by peaceful democratic means, to embrace the opportunity of reunification this must be respected and welcomed as a legitimate aspiration achieved via democracy. Besides, Unionism used violence and the threat of violence to stop Home Rule from being implemented in 1912 and to bring down the Sunningdale Power-sharing executive in 1974. They must engage in constructive debate when both parts of Ireland vote for unity and all who campaign for or against unity must be invited to pledge their commitment to non-violence and solely peaceful pursuit of their aims.

The key priority for the unity campaign will be to stick to its core message and not be distracted from this by Unionist political attacks. The campaign must emphasise that this is a referendum about the future, not an argument about the past. We all want to move on, to provide a positive future for our children and grandchildren. If future generations do not have hope, we will continue to see our brightest and best leave these shores and never return. Of course, if people want to explore the world, that is great. However, it is extremely sad to think of people being forced for any reason to leave their homes, to split up families and circles of friends. If young people do not have hope, they have nothing. There must always be an unremitting focus on the positive future that awaits through Irish unity and how that will deliver peace and prosperity.

In American presidential politics, they often talk about 'the October surprise' – in US elections, which take place in November, one political campaign may seek to increase its momentum by releasing damaging information about the opponent close to the election. What will that be in the border poll campaign? Will Unionists suddenly offer up a more inclusive, understanding philosophy? More likely is that Unionism may seek to circle the wagons and make this a referendum on terrorism. Unionist representatives may hope that they will be able to uncover video footage during the campaign of a hard-line republican group expressing hatred of all things English or Protestant; they are likely to resort to character attacks on prominent republicans who are part of the unity campaign. If negative footage is not available from the campaign, they would seek to use old footage to claim that these same people will be running the country after unity.

Hard-line unionists will try to make the claim that as a result of Irish unity, Sinn Féin will be a permanent fixture in government. Some unionists still view Sinn Féin through their historic relationship with the Provisional IRA as some of their elected representatives were directly involved in the conflict.

The unity campaign leaders should respond to any such 'October surprise' type attacks by emphasising that those who express any form of hatred for their fellow citizens do not represent the unity campaign; that the people will decide who will represent their interests in government through a democratic vote, they will not have any leader thrust upon them without having their say; and that Sinn Féin are continuing to evolve as a party and their younger elected representatives do not have this same direct connection to violence.

Ultimately, it will be for the voters to decide themselves if they want to continue to vote for parties that are refusing to represent their interests in government. The unity campaign does not have to guarantee that Unionists will serve in government after reunification, it merely needs to show a firm commitment that Unionists will be invited to join the government after unity has been secured. Unionist leaders will face the impossible task of explaining that they will not take up a position in government post-unity. It will be hard to defend because by ruling out participation in government post-unity they will be signifying their intention to refuse the opportunity to represent the interests of their voters in government.

The pro-union campaign will become redundant if it sticks to its message of negativity. There appears to be no positive vision from Unionism, certainly not one that Unionist parties in Northern Ireland are willing and able to embrace. Our Unionist politicians are considered an embarrassment to British politicians due to their regressive and outdated views, so much so that, during the Scottish independence referendum in 2014, Northern Ireland Unionists were discouraged from featuring in the No campaign.

Stages of support for unity

Sceptics refer to a lack of support for Irish unity, despite clear results from opinion polls such as those by LucidTalk in December 2018, which showed 55 per cent support for Irish unity in the event of a no-deal Brexit;[123] the University of Liverpool opinion poll in July 2022 which showed that 43.2 per cent would vote for Irish unity tomorrow, while 39.5 per cent would vote against;[124] or the Lucid-Talk poll for *The Sunday Times* in August 2022 which showed that every age group in Northern Ireland under 45 supported Irish unity by clear majorities.[125]

Those sceptical of public support neglect to mention that there has been no clear consensus or even agreed set of options for what Irish unity would look like. People are not going to say they are in favour of something they cannot visualise.

There are a number of stages to changing political opinion on a significant issue. It starts with the status quo. There may not be a consensus actively in favour of this position, but there is at least a begrudging acceptance that it is the current position – in this case, that Northern Ireland is part of the UK.

Then there has to be an event, or series of events, that gives people the opportunity to reconsider the status quo or look at it from a different perspective. The economic, social and political benefits of the peace process, which were solidified by the Good Friday Agreement, allowed people to develop their thinking and attitude toward cooperation across Ireland. This gradual process received a significant jolt when the UK (England and Wales) voted for Brexit. As we have seen, Brexit has created a perfect storm for unity. This was compounded by the COVID-19 pandemic as we had two governments, adopting at times contradictory approaches, with those of us in the North forced to abide by rules set by an incompetent Conservative government.

After the event, or series of events, the wider population begins to consider that the status quo is not inevitable or desirable. This is the stage at which people start to discuss whether Irish unity is a viable option. A majority of people (63 per cent) in a Queen's University Belfast opinion poll in May 2022 stated that they believe Brexit has made Irish unity more likely.[126] A Lord Ashcroft poll in

December 2021 found that by a margin of 51–34 per cent, a majority thought that a border poll in ten years' time would lead to Irish unity.[127]

The next step is that people begin to consider how they move to a new position or situation. In this case, the voters across Ireland begin to think through how Irish unity would be achieved and what it would look like. This is why it is so important that there are detailed plans for unity. There does not need to be one agreed position on what Irish unity would look like, but there should certainly be a range of options.

By this stage, voters are aware of the change of circumstances, that there is an alternative option, that they understand how the alternative option can be achieved and have decided that they want to adopt this new position.

It cannot be reiterated enough that any unity referendum will be about the use of peaceful means to deliver political change. Brexit is a nightmare for all of Ireland – we need to wake up and take control of our destiny, not with violence but with democracy.

Wanting Irish unity is not a narrow form of nationalism; wanting Irish unity is a desire to be progressive, liberal and engaged in global issues (such as protecting our environment) as part of the EU. It is a desire to have frictionless trade with the largest economic bloc in the world. Irish unity is a story about hope, about bringing people together for a better and shared future.

Setting out the vision for unity

Technology plays an ever more important role in political campaigning and evolves rapidly. It will be crucial for the unity campaign to use all tools available to get a positive message across to all the key target audiences. For example, connecting with the younger voters using aspirational messages – just as President Biden's administration has briefed Gen Z TikTok stars about the war in Ukraine, so the unity campaign should seek to harness Gen Z to engage with the younger generation on the benefits of Irish unity.[128] Regardless of how social media changes, analysing and predicting voter habits, certain principles will remain.

While we may be living through the first truly global pandemic in more than 100 years, which stopped people from travelling or meeting in person for long periods of time, the US Democratic convention of August 2020 and the subsequent presidential campaign has shown that technology can be utilized for effective online campaigning and virtual events, even on the biggest issues. We should hold a series of in person and virtual town halls to debate the merits of unity, building on Ireland's Future events. We need to organise local campaigns across all 32 counties to convince people to vote for unity. There should be representatives of the campaign organised for each county to speak with voters. While we now have more face-to-face events, a blended approach of in-person and virtual meetings should be used to facilitate the widest possible engagement.

Any campaign has to have a clear understanding of what it is for. What is the vision that the campaign wants to drive voters towards? If the campaign is confused or divided on the desired destination or why people should want to reach that location, it makes the electioneering much more difficult.

When we look at the Brexit campaign, there were competing visions on the Leave side. Yet, once the referendum date was set this was put to one side – the various campaign groups who wanted to pull the UK out of the EU put aside their differences and there was a unity of purpose. Although there continued to be multiple campaigns, they did not directly contradict or undermine each other. However, the confused response since the vote conveys the difficulty in not having an agreed endpoint beyond merely winning the referendum.

The unity campaign must embody a sense of coming together by selecting well-respected, independent spokespeople for the unity campaign. A range of political parties should get involved and encourage their members and activists, but it must also include those who are not part of any political party. It needs to look and feel like a movement, but one based on rational facts. In the USA, there is a political action committee called 'Run For Something', to encourage young people to get involved with the political process and become a candidate at all levels of government. There should be an apolitical organisation, perhaps called 'Run For Unity', which would encourage young people to run for office across Ireland, for different parties, while focusing on building unity.

I certainly do not agree with everything Gerry Adams, former president of Sinn Féin, has said or done. However, I do agree with his statement that 'we all need to challenge ourselves', which was made in reference to the peace process. We will struggle to secure Irish unity if republicanism seeks to continue to justify and celebrate their violent actions during The Troubles. This will only turn off unionists and the non-aligned, as well as some parts of nationalism, from the potential of Irish unity. We must provide unionists with a sense of inclusion and safety for their future – this needs to be a respectful campaign.

Grassroots campaigning is key

Grassroots will be key to a successful unity campaign. While you can have the best data targeting team and field campaign, the key component is having a product, idea or person that people believe in and feel passionate enough about to vote for. You need something that can cut through both the noise and inbuilt apathy.

The us can provide examples of the power of a grassroots initiative through the community organising as seen in the Obama 2008 and 2012 campaigns. Just as the En Marche campaign learned about how to build a grassroots movement and identify voters from the Obama campaign, so can the unity campaign. However, as Sophie Pedder set out in her excellent book *Revolution Française*,[129] the En Marche campaign team realised they needed to adapt the Obama approach and develop some of their own initiatives. Similarly, the Irish unity campaign must create a campaign that works across Ireland, not just transport a rigid template from elsewhere.

The pro-unity campaign should seek to make Irish unity a key policy pledge for both us Democrats and Republicans. There has been much negativity in recent years directed towards the usa for the Iraq and Afghanistan wars and the election of President Trump that revealed the nation's far-right, angry underbelly. Embracing a progressive cause through the peaceful reunification of Ireland and being seen to help build prosperity there would be a major foreign policy win for America. The United States played such a crucial role in the development of the Good Friday Agreement. It can be argued that this was America's greatest foreign policy success of the last three decades.

The pro-unity campaign should seek to set up an Irish equivalent of Crooked Media, a media network which showcases voices and opinions on progressive and liberal issues, to create a platform for sharing a wide range of pro-unity voices across different platforms. The question is how can this be funded? It must be a grassroots initiative to have authenticity and to properly engage with voters who tend to think, first and foremost, at a local level. Therefore grassroots funding will be key.

The #Think32 initiative, which promotes the desirability of Irish unity on Twitter and podcasts, will also continue to play an important role, as will the Ireland's Future campaign group. Every single person who believes in Irish unity can be an effective campaigner using the tools already at their disposal – digital grassroots campaigning is key. Former Senior Advisor to President Obama for Strategy and Communications Dan Pfeiffer stated in an email to his Message Box subscribers:

> For the last several years, I have been obsessing over a version of politics that leverages every supporter with a smart phone and a social presence and turns them into messengers who persuade voters and shift the political conversation... This can only be accomplished if we treat our volunteers like political pros and offer them sophisticated political analysis, strategic advice, and specific guidance on how to communicate with the people in their personal networks.[130]

The unity campaign should set up local clubs or digital hubs for unity which are peaceful and inclusive and celebrate Irishness. There is always going to be a wide spectrum of views amongst those who now support Irish unity and that is a good thing, as a reunified Ireland will therefore be diverse. The key thing is to make sure that they campaign cohesively and do not undercut or undermine each other.

As part of a truly grassroots campaign for unity, an independent think tank should be set up – based on the model of the Center for American Progress which undertakes research and promotes a liberal approach to social and economic issues – perhaps called the Centre for Irish Unity. The think tank needs to set out how we prepare for a unity referendum, how we win the campaign and how we build unity after the vote for it. The work will truly begin after the vote for unity. We need to address the long term consequences of the public health emergency arising from the COVID-19 pandemic, the climate crisis and rebuild the economy; we will need to have strong links with Washington, Brussels and Dublin.

The think tank could be linked to one prominent Irish university, as several universities already have constitution units. However, there would be benefits in being independent of these as well, as it would allow for collaboration with multiple universities. It may also be desirable to establish a think tank for Irish unity in the United States, perhaps in New York City as it is an epicentre of the diaspora, which could provide likely economic support for Irish unity and will continue to have significant political relevance.

The unity campaign could seek to engage with Max Stier who established the Partnership for Public Service. This is a non-profit and non-partisan organisation, focused on seeking to ensure that government works as effectively as possible.[131] Ireland could tap into this expertise and seek to set up a similar organisation for reunification. This organisation could be used to help identify, for example, where shared services can be used, post-reunification.[132]

The Sunrise Movement has been an influential grassroots campaign in the United States, focused on addressing the climate emergency.[133] This is a key concern for young people across the globe and if the unity campaign can link up with this group, or perhaps even create its own group focused on the environmental benefits of unity, it could help to attract young people in the North and the Republic to the unity campaign by tying unity to dealing with the climate crisis. Brexit and leaving EU environmental safeguards – whether on car pollution or chlorinated chicken – will not help to address the climate emergency.

Those sceptical of the urgent need for unification may say that the climate crisis is the most pressing issue we face, so why should we pursue the quest for unity? But we do not have to choose between addressing the climate crisis and addressing Irish unity. In fact, it is only through reunification and membership of the EU that we can ensure environmental standards that will tackle the climate crisis. The EU is leading the way on addressing the climate emergency with multiple initiatives, including the European Green Deal.[134] As part of this, the European Commission adopted a set of proposals to structure the EU's climate, energy, transport and taxation policies in such a way that they will lead to a minimum 55 per cent reduction of net greenhouse gas emissions by 2030, compared to 1990 levels. The EU sets a framework for addressing the climate crisis, encourages investment in renewables and other behaviour change to reduce the carbon emissions we all create. Therefore, climate-conscious citizens of the current Republic should view unity as a way to safeguard nearly two million people in the North from falling victim to UK-imposed changes to environmental standards and therefore contributing further to climate change. Climate issues do not stop at political borders, so unity will help to preserve the entire island of Ireland's environment. Through Irish unity all of us who live across the island can work together in a fully integrated way, to address the climate crisis which is the greatest challenge of our time.

Governance options

The unity campaign must not allow itself to be distracted by issues such as the final shape of Irish unity or arguing over the past; it must either agree in advance what the structure for Irish unity must be or set out a clear process for how an agreement will be reached after the vote to reunite Ireland has been achieved. In other words, the unity campaign does not necessarily need to agree on whether the Northern Ireland Assembly will disappear immediately after reunification, after a set period of time or continue indefinitely. The actual governance structure can be decided after the referendum has been won – the key requirement is that the campaign for unity provides a positive vision and a clear plan before the referendum. This should include a sensible range of options and it should be explained clearly that the actual decision on governance structures will be agreed upon by the Irish government via a process of negotiation, in consultation with civil society and through a constitutional convention. An official mapping exercise as part of the UK government's preparations for delivering on the Brexit vote, identified 142 policy areas of North–South cooperation, 51 relating to the operation of the North–South Ministerial Council established under the Good Friday Agreement.[135]

Presidential role

Successive presidents of Ireland have done an excellent job in reaching out to Unionists over recent years; however, the time has come when the president should no longer be neutral on the question of Irish unity. He or she should acknowledge that there are those on the island who may hold a different view, but the president should lead the aspiration for Irish unity. They should use their office as head of state to offer support to all minorities and seek to assure all citizens of the island that they will be protected and cherished within a reunited Ireland.

If the forthcoming referendum to allow Irish citizens who live outside the Irish Republic to vote in presidential campaigns is passed, it will have a transformative effect on the island of Ireland. Since 1918, there has only been one occasion when all the registered voters across the island of Ireland voted on the same day, for the same thing. That was in 1998 to endorse the Good Friday Agreement. If we do not have Irish unity by the time of the next Irish presidential election in 2025, we could still have Irish citizens across the island voting for the next president of Ireland. For the first time, this could mean Irish citizens in Northern Ireland will get to vote for their head of state.

Former unionists with post-Brexit Irish passports would be able to vote and would therefore feel they have an increased stake in the Irish state. Indeed, by law anyone born in Northern Ireland is automatically entitled to Irish citizenship, regardless of whether they have applied for an Irish passport. All of these small steps make the journey towards Irish unity a little more straightforward.

This means candidates will need to campaign and canvas for votes in Northern Ireland, as well as the Irish Republic. The question of Northern Ireland's constitutional position, if it has not been resolved by then, will likely be a key feature and candidates who overtly support reunification will garner more votes in Northern Ireland. While the role of president is largely symbolic, candidates will be able to set out how they would help to achieve Irish unity, using the structures of the Irish government.

In the longer term, after Irish unity has been achieved, it would be necessary that local councils in Northern Ireland have the right to nominate candidates for president in the same way that a minimum of four from the Irish Republic are currently required as one of the routes to securing a nomination to contest the presidential elections. The presidential candidates would be wise to emphasise to this newly empowered constituency that they can make their voices heard.

Do unionists and loyalists in Northern Ireland believe their rights will be respected in a post-Brexit Britain run by a right-wing Tory government? A new, written constitution would be passed after unity which would safeguard diversity and the success of the Good Friday Agreement for all who live on the island. Ireland would be able to position itself as a launching pad to Europe and beyond for American and Asian businesses. Unionists would have real power at a national level for the first time in more than a hundred years. In deciding on Irish unity, all voters will be able to choose at every sub-sequent all-Ireland general election whether the nation is a 32-county, socialist republic; a low tax, small state country; or something else. If Northern Ireland remains part of the UK, it will not matter what we think – the voters of England will continue to decide our future. Through Irish unity, by comparison, unionist voters will have significant influence. They are irrelevant at Westminster (a small number of backbench MPs, not part of the UK Cabinet or shadow cabinet) and Westminster politics is increasingly irrelevant in any part of Ireland.

Imagine if Irish citizens in Northern Ireland proved to be the swing vote in the presidential elections. Having Irish citizenship, living on the island, supporting the all-island economy and remaining in the EU and then voting in the presidential elections are all steps towards an Irish unity mindset. Whereas England is increasingly a foreign land, the rest of Ireland is ever more familiar.

Lessons from other referendums

There are many lessons we can learn from other referendums including that of the Good Friday Agreement, the first Scottish Independence Referendum, the AV referendum in the UK and other referendums outside of the UK and Ireland. The fear factor to maintain the status quo worked for the No campaign in Scotland in 2014, despite the irony of many subsequent Brexiters warning that Scottish independence would mean automatically leaving the EU. In the Scottish referendum in 2014, the independence campaign took the lead within the last two weeks, before ultimately losing. The unity campaign must build a lead and ensure that the momentum can be maintained when it counts.

The AV (Alternative Vote) referendum was lost due to a highly negative attack on the leaders campaigning for change and the use of claims about the supposedly significant cost of change and the money that would be diverted away from public services.

The equal marriage referendum and the woman's right to choose referendums in the Irish Republic are both examples of progressive campaigns that advocated positive change and delivered this result at the ballot box.

We should also look to Quebec as an example of what not to do. Quebec lost its referendum for separation in 1995 in part because it was portrayed as a vote to break up a nation; Irish unity is about coming together as one – this must be the clear message. Both the Canadian and US administrations made clear that as a sovereign nation, Quebec would struggle to benefit from the NAFTA trade agreement, which had recently been agreed upon. Irish unity is different in this regard, as it is the UK government that has chosen to break away from its membership of the European Single Market, the Customs Union and the EU.

Voting groups

If we focus predominately on Northern Ireland, it is possible to break the voting public into six groups: hard-line republicans/nationalists, moderate republicans/nationalists, agnostic/don't know, moderate unionists/loyalists, hard-line unionists/loyalists, post-unionists.

Please note that when I refer to hard-line unionists or republicans, it is not meant as a pejorative term. It reflects their fixed views, which are less likely to change on the constitutional question. To secure the support for Irish unity any campaign needs to secure the support of both hard-line republicans and moderate nationalists. One of the issues is that Northern Ireland has developed a large public sector and many nationalists and unionists may fear the loss of this if Irish unity is achieved. These include cultural nationalists who are comfortable being part of the UK, as they rely on the highly paid public sector jobs provided by HM Treasury. These people need to be convinced that post-Brexit their future and their careers lie within Irish unity. In a transition period, there will be a gradual adjustment where functions and therefore jobs (eg healthcare workers, teachers and other public services such as the Police and Fire Service) move from being part of the UK state to being part of a reunited Irish state.

The section of people that we can call post-unionists have come from unionist backgrounds and historically would have identified as British. However, they have become jaded with the UK political environment as it moves to the extremes on the right and left. They rarely, if ever, identified with the local politics in Northern Ireland, as espoused by Unionist leaders. These Northern Ireland politicians who, as Unionists, claim to be pro-British, are seen as tribalists by the moderate centre ground. Just as Richard Nixon talked about the silent majority in the USA, I believe that in Northern Ireland there are a significant number of moderate voters who have not been near a ballot box in years and could be convinced to come out and vote for change. They do not take part in opinion polls, they do not vote for Nationalist parties, but they may be persuaded to vote for Irish unity.

Case studies

Case studies should be prepared and then deployed throughout the campaign. For example, the unity campaign should show how the eastern corridor could be packaged for infrastructure investment after a vote for unity. It is encouraging to see the launch of the Dublin–Belfast Economic Corridor initiative, something that the Irish government has already committed to undertaking a feasibility study into.

Another case study could show the significant savings that would be achieved by integrating the public services on the island (one health service, one planning service and one economic development agency) which would help to reduce duplication and create a more strategic offering for the entire island.

Hopefully, senior representatives of the European Commission, European Council and European Parliament could be persuaded to say, during the campaign, that they would support the reunification of Ireland and contribute to a transitional fund. The unity campaign should put together a package of how this transitional fund would be structured.

Getting the Irish Republic to Vote for Unity

'Everything is theoretically impossible, until it is done.'[136]

-Robert A Heinlein

I RECOGNISE THAT there may be a sense of fatigue across Ireland, a desire to ignore the momentum towards a border poll. The Republic has been through a lot, even in the last decade from dealing with the troika following their bailout, Brexit and then the COVID-19 pandemic. I understand that people are emotionally tired and want a break from disruption, but unity cannot wait. For those who say that now is not the time due to the complications of Brexit and COVID-19 and the climate crisis, that we should pause any debate on Irish unity, I would say that all of these issues would be far simpler if we had one jurisdiction and one government on the island of Ireland rather than two, particularly as inflation increases and the cost-of-living crisis worsens.

Unity will begin to heal our divisions – it will not miraculously cure all of our problems, but it is part of the solution. It may take a generation, but once unity has been secured following a democratic vote, we can begin to grow beyond tribal and constitutional politics across the island.

I hope that the current batch of politicians across Ireland can step up and respond to the pressing need for preparation for and then implementation of unity. One or both of the two civil war parties have been in government in the South continually from 1932, almost since the state's foundation and there is a view that these parties do not want the change that would be brought about by unity, as their power base would be undermined. The full names of their parties are Fianna Fáil - The Republican party and Fine Gael (United Ireland). If they are not able to embrace unity for whatever reason, then we will need a new generation to take up the mantle.

We need to embrace progress and positive change in whatever form it takes. The Black Lives Matter movement – including the protests and action taken on our island – has shown how important diversity and inclusion are, in Ireland and across the world. It is right that we show respect for each other and value our diversity as a society. A New Ireland must be progressive and committed to this; it needs to be a space where everyone feels welcome, safe and valued, regardless of race, gender or sexuality. When it comes to the important discussions on our island's future, inclusivity also makes for better decisions – boards lacking diversity are at greater risk of groupthink, which means that there is less innovative, individual thinking. In the same way, as an island, we will be better and stronger if we embrace our diversity and see it as a strength.

In 2017 Leo Varadkar, as Taoiseach, told Irish citizens in Northern Ireland that they will not be left behind by an Irish government; now, we are beginning to find out what this means, as the Irish government is making a financial commitment to ensure that citizens in Northern Ireland can continue to access the Erasmus+ student exchange scheme and to be able to use the EHIC (European Health Insurance Card).

Irish unity is about East and West, as well as North and South. I do not mean the Sinn Féin Éire Nua concept but the need for unity to focus on all parts of Ireland and not just be seen as a negotiation between Belfast and Dublin.

All of the parties in the Dáil have shown that they can put the national interest first in agreeing a cross-party approach to dealing with the fallout from the Brexit vote and so they must do the same for unity.

We cannot afford to accept casual partitionism, before the vote for unity, for example where people object to Northern Ireland-based members of an all-Ireland party voting on whether that party should join the Government. We are a small island – we have to work together.

Addressing negativity towards Irish unity in the Irish Republic

There are likely to be several negative angles to the anti-unity campaign in the Irish Republic. There will be a focus on the backward nature of Northern Ireland on social issues, but a liberal future for Northern Ireland is only being held back by a small number of elected politicians, not wider society. There will likely be concern about loyalist violence in the event of a vote for Irish unity. Republican violence, or threats of it, could not force Northern Ireland into Irish unity against the will of the majority of its citizens. While we hope that it is not even a remote possibility in the same way, loyalist violence, or threats thereof, cannot stop Irish unity from happening if it is the desire of the majority across the island.

There will be a focus on the cost of reunification and a claim that large tax rises would be necessary to incorporate Northern Ireland into a new unified Irish State. Opinion polls consistently point to a healthy majority in favour of Irish unity in the Irish Republic; however, there are often caveats when tax rises are included.[137] Yet Northern Ireland will, through reunification, be re-joining the EU and securing full unrestricted access to the European Single Market. This will lead to further economic growth, for all of Ireland and there should be a single integrated economic development agency focused on attracting FDI across the entire island.

There is also a tendency of people in the South to respond that they favour unity in the next ten years, rather than the immediate future. The Good Friday Agreement stipulates that the Secretary of State will order a border poll 'when he believes that there is a majority for a United Ireland'. When this happens, the key will be making the point to the Irish Republic that this is a decision that needs to be acted upon now.

In times past, it was often presumed that only if those in Northern Ireland could be persuaded of the benefits of Irish unity, it could come to pass. However, decades of partition have had a lasting effect on both sides of the border – the malaise of a partitionist or protectionist attitude to others is not restricted to those in Northern Ireland. Some across the rest of Ireland have become comfortable with a 26-county state and are openly hostile to the idea of reunification. Particularly during difficult economic times, there are those in the South who may have little or no interest in pursuing Irish unity at this time. This negativity towards unity pervades all sections of society. Of course, the more sinister problem is sectarianism – a poison that seeped through Ireland. If we are to move forward as a society across the island, we need an antidote. This small-minded and backwards approach must be eradicated.

Leadership is key

Political leadership by southern parties can make a difference – Leo Varadkar and Simon Coveney as leader and deputy leader of Fine

Gael are ambitious young politicians who want to leave a positive legacy behind them. What better legacy to leave than to be involved in reuniting a nation that has been divided for 100 years? And will there ever be a more pressing time to do it?

To achieve this historic opportunity now, we need to see leaders across all political parties in the Irish Republic publicly endorsing the call for Irish unity. This needs to be more than honeyed words – there needs to be concrete actions taken to prepare for contesting and winning the inevitable border poll. Let's put forward a positive case and address concerns, in advance of the campaign.

There should be an aspiration of equal representation in the Seanad (Irish Senate) from the four provinces, through majority direct election with a small number retained for the Taoiseach to nominate. Currently, Seanad Éireann consists of 60 senators who are not directly elected. Instead, eleven are appointed directly by the Taoiseach and the rest are voted for by graduates of two universities or small electorates for a number of vocational panels.[138] This could help to create a balanced legislature so that the Oireachtas is not overly dominated by the Belfast to Dublin corridor. The Government must be for all of Ireland, East and West, as well as North and South. Such a change may require an amended or new constitution, which could mean an additional referendum after the vote in favour of unity. Clarity on constitutional issues such as this, is one of the many issues which should be worked out in advance of a border poll being held.

Fianna Fáil and Fine Gael may be concerned about the influence of Sinn Féin after Irish unity. Sinn Féin, who have been most active in arguing for Irish unity, have seen their support surge in Northern Ireland and they can now argue that they have the largest support of any party across the island of Ireland. They will automatically be part of any government in Northern Ireland under the Good Friday Agreement and may well feature in government in the Irish Republic after the next election, whenever that may take place.

However, the Sinn Féin party, particularly the Northern branch, may well fracture post-reunification, as it is a broad coalition with a binding focus on securing unity. Once this has been achieved, it may well disintegrate into a wider range of political views. Furthermore, should Unionists stand in an all-Ireland government and should mainstream southern parties, Fianna Gael, Fianna Fáil, Irish Labour and the Green party make it clear that they are willing to go into government with Unionists, they could, in fact, lock Sinn Féin out of government.

The Southern parties could organise in Northern Ireland or develop formal relationships with an existing party, as Fianna Fáil did in their partnership with the SDLP. However, this needs to move from a dormant state to a dynamic partnership – they should take the political fight to Sinn Féin and map out an alternative path for unity.

At one stage it could be said that the SDLP was the representative party of the Irish government in Northern Ireland. It played a leading role under its former leader John Hume in the peace process. However, circumstances have changed. The SDLP has been an amalgam of different political views, so it can be expected that its membership and supporters may split between Fianna Fáil, Fine Gael and Irish Labour after Irish unity has been secured.

Whatever their feelings towards each other may be, there needs to be a cross-party consensus of Southern parties showing their commitment to Irish unity. In ordinary circumstances, none of us may have chosen to push for reunification now. It would arguably have been much better to let the outworking of the Good Friday Agreement develop over the course of several decades – reunification could have evolved gradually. However, events outside our control have overtaken us – stability through reunification is our only option.

We must ensure that the message is clear that we are not intending for the South to be dragged down by the North. This will be a coming together of both parts of the island, to build something even better than we have now. There must be a hard-headed focus on ensuring economic success for all of Ireland and it is up to our nations' leaders to communicate this to the people, north and south of the border.

It may seem, at first, counterintuitive to suggest it but emphasising the economic benefits for Northern Ireland following on from reunification can help to sell unity to the Irish Republic. As previously stated, Northern Ireland – Belfast in particular – can provide much-needed skilled workers, less expensive housing, education and urban infrastructure which will help to take the pressure off Dublin. All of Ireland will benefit from a balanced economy where investment can be planned and encouraged in different urban and rural areas across the island.

Key initiatives

There are several key initiatives that will help to reassure voters in the Irish Republic that Irish unity can be achieved successfully.

Firstly, the European Union needs to reiterate that there will be a seamless re-joining process for the North of Ireland post-reunification, in other words, an acknowledgement that Northern Ireland would be reuniting with an existing European Union member state and therefore would not need to re-apply for membership. This has already been confirmed at a European Council meeting in April 2017, but it would not hurt to refresh the memory of any unity sceptics.[139]

Secondly, the European Union would need to confirm that all the previous grants and funding Northern Ireland received will still be made available post-reunification (alongside the hoped-for and certainly achievable structural funds for reunification). After all, the European Commission has stated that the EU is committed to the continuation of peace, as well as regional development funding.[140] Similarly, the UK government must be asked to provide assurances about financial payments continuing for a specified amount of time to aid the reunification process.

Next, a detailed plan should be provided by the unity campaign to show that investment tours and activity will be used to secure foreign direct investment at an early stage in the event of a vote for Irish unity. There should also be someone, most likely from Northern Ireland, who will commit to working with the Protestant/Unionist/Loyalist (PUL) community to convince them of the benefits of Irish unity. This is an area where the European Commission can excel by putting together a task force which could have a particular focus on helping to ensure a smooth transition to reunification. As part of this, they would be able to provide assurances that members of the PUL community would be respected and safeguarded after Irish unity – they are currently ignored within the UK. It should be evident that they will receive much more safeguarding and grant funding than would be possible as part of Brexit Britain. Post-Brexit the UK, or what remains of it, will be seeking to cut funding and only invest in those parts of the UK where there is a genuine chance of securing votes and seats in parliament. Ultimately the PUL community want to be able to celebrate their culture in a safe environment. Once this package of assurances is provided, voters in the Irish Republic will have less concern about the potential for loyalist violence.

Then, the unity campaign needs to reach out to a series of Irish American businesspeople and/or politicians representing the Irish diaspora who will stand up during the campaign to indicate their support for Irish reunification and commit to helping to secure funding or investment for the reunification process. The unity campaign needs to pitch this as an opportunity for Irish America to be part of history, but it is also crucial that investments are offered based on providing real financial benefits for investors. They must make financial sense.

At the same time, the benefits of streamlining of governance (an all-island planning system and full integration of the health service as well as the economic benefits) need to be reinforced to Southern voters. They must be reassured that they would be offered an economic dividend by voting for reunification and that there will be significant investment in an all-Ireland health service.

It should also be highlighted that, in the wider European context, Ireland post-unity would become a bigger, more powerful, country within the EU by growing from a population of circa five million to one of around seven million. There would also be an increase in the overall number of MEPs and voting strength in the European Council.

Appealing to Unionism

'After the final no there comes a yes and on that yes the future of the world hangs.'[141]

Wallace Stevens

I AM PROUD of my unionist background and when I was growing up, I firmly believed Northern Ireland's existence as part of the UK was what was best for our nation. I know how dejected and upset I felt once I found out that the UK had voted to leave the EU – I felt like part of my own identity had been stripped away, but I was grateful that I had the option to maintain my European citizenship as an Irish citizen. Therefore, I empathise with those unionists who may feel the same towards Northern Ireland leaving the UK – I can see how they may feel as though they will lose a big part of their identity. But unionists will be able to maintain their British citizenship post-unity. All those who are currently eligible for British citizenship will still be eligible after reunification.

King Charles III has talked about his love of the island of Ireland, about how he has personally suffered the loss of a close relative during The Troubles and about his investment in reconciliation between the peoples of this island and between the islands of Ireland and Britain. We must recognise that as we move forward as an island, we need to bring all our people with us. There will continue to be close links between the royal family and a reunited Ireland, just as there are between the royal family and the Irish Republic now. We will not be part of the same country after unity, but we can remain close friends and partners in addressing many of the mutual challenges we face.

There is a bigger question of what happens if the remaining parts of the UK break up. Unfortunately for Unionism, successive Tory leaders – despite what they may claim – have been more focused on keeping their party together than on keeping the UK together.

I have lived and worked in London, Edinburgh and Cardiff, as well as my home city of Belfast. Unlike most political representatives, other than Northern Ireland Westminster MPs I have spent a significant amount of time outside Northern Ireland, so I understand how both Unionism and the region are viewed by the rest of the UK. My eldest brother was born in England, and my other brother lives in London with an English-born wife and kids. Changing my beliefs from unionism does not mean I want nothing to do with the UK whatsoever – I want Ireland to be close friends and partners with the different constituent parts of Britain.

Unionism has been in a difficult place since they did not win enough seats and votes to nominate a first minister. Instead Sinn Féin earned the right to do so following the May 2022 Assembly election. Even though early indications are that the Northern Ireland Protocol is leading to increased trade for Northern Ireland, all the Unionist parties have set themselves the impossible task of securing its removal. This cannot happen.

The Loyalist Communities Council, which is a legal organisation, represents the UVF, UDA and Red Hand Commandos. Their spokespeople have openly talked about how they might have to fight physically for their right to remain part of the UK, in a radio interview about the Northern Ireland Protocol being introduced,[142] and in giving evidence to a UK parliamentary committee.[143]

Loyalist paramilitaries have even threatened Unionists who go against their wishes – the UDA threatened the UUP to stop them from standing in North Belfast in the December 2019 Westminster election;[144] the Loyalist Communities Council wrote to Boris Johnson when he was the UK prime minister withdrawing their support for the Good Friday Agreement because of the Northern Ireland Protocol. Loyalist paramilitary groups have no right to seek to dictate to those making political decisions. Their actions show that within unionism there is an out-of-touch group, struggling to deal with the reality that Unionism no longer holds a majority of votes in the region. We need to guide unionism and loyalism along a peaceful path, towards recognition and acceptance of Irish unity.

One of the things that will repel unionists and loyalists from the idea of unity is referring to a 'United Ireland', as this phrase was used by Provisional IRA and Sinn Féin prior to the 1994 ceasefire. A phrase with such negative connotations will not appeal to those who otherwise, especially in the context of Brexit, would be open to Irish unity.

We should acknowledge that unionists have, until now, looked to the rest of the UK for guidance and protection. Brexit changes all of that. The UK is no longer a stable country, it is deeply divided and its economic future is uncertain. With respect and patience, we need to explain to unionists that the comfort blanket they previously relied on has gone. Irish unity, being part of the EU, offers the only way to stability and prosperity. The former UK Health Secretary claimed that the vaccine roll-out across the UK was quicker than the EU because of Brexit.[145] Whereas the EU exported millions of vaccine doses to the UK, at the start of the rollout the UK focused on vaccinating its own citizens. The UK has not helped its neighbours. Yet again, Brexit has shown itself to be something that creates barriers and enflames narrow self-interest, which actually inflicts self-harm in the long term. So many of the issues which we face in the world today, such as fighting pandemics, addressing the climate crisis or dealing with a global economic slowdown, require partnership working across the world. Additionally, COVID-19 deaths per capita across the UK have been some of the highest in the world – it is difficult, surely even for unionists, to see this as any less than a government failing its people.[146]

The unity campaign needs to be conciliatory towards Unionism but there are also some harsh truths that it needs to accept. Brexit does not have the consent of Northern Ireland – Unionists who say that Unionism did not consent to the Northern Ireland Protocol must realise that this is a consequence of Brexit. The UK government was offered a customs union and a commons SPS (sanitary and phytosanitary) area, which they rejected, which would have significantly reduced friction between Britain and Northern Ireland. The UK Conservatives won an election on the basis of implementing something that risked peace in Northern Ireland – a border down the Irish Sea. Loyalists withdrawing their support for the Good Friday Agreement or Unionists refusing to nominate ministers to a new Northern Ireland Executive will not change this reality. I will say this until it sinks in for all unionists on our island – the UK government does not care about Northern Ireland, that is the sad reality.

In our public discourse we must demand the truth. We must listen to others, this is important. In the campaign for unity, we need to talk about issues in terms of the audience not as individuals. As part of this, we need to engage with those with opposing views and persuade them. The Carson Project, which will be discussed in this section, is one way to engage with Unionism, but every approach must be grounded in respect and seeking understanding of others' perspectives.

In some ways, it will be more a case of managing Unionism than appealing to it. There will be some Unionist politicians who will refuse to engage constructively in the creation of a renewed Irish nation, regardless of the democratic will. For too long, the Unionist mindset has been about saying no, about digging in and counting on superior numbers. There has been little evolution of thought.

The Democratic Unionist Party is currently the largest party in a fragmented Unionist political structure. However, it is simply not possible to build a political philosophy around saying 'NO' to delivering progress of any kind.

Many of these Unionists have never actually lived or worked in the rest of the union and the reality is that, despite their best efforts, Northern Ireland Unionists are seen as Irish by the vast majority of people and there is little actual support for them. The Hari Kari politics of blindly following the UK government's view is not sustainable. When the former leader of the DUP said that the vote to leave the EU made the UK stronger, it simply showed her lack of understanding.

The DUP voted against a trade deal while also seeking to proclaim the opportunities it will provide. This is not leadership. While there are mixed views about the accuracy of the Kubler Ross model, which sets out the five stages of grief, we can hope that after emotions of shock and anger we can get to acceptance with Unionists. People like Peter Robinson have called for a Council for the Union to be set up. It is interesting that Unionism has recently announced several groups including We Make NI and Uniting the UK. Time will tell whether they can agree on positive messaging that sets out a constructive case for Northern Ireland to remain part of the UK, but I am confident that when we have a measured, evidence-based discussion about what is best for all the people of Ireland, Irish unity within the EU will be the only viable answer.

The role of Canada and the USA

Unionists who favour maintaining Northern Ireland's link with Britain hold a particular affinity for Canada, due to the deep ancestral links that go back many generations. The fact that Canada is also a member of the Commonwealth is a further commonality the country shares with unionists in Northern Ireland – arguably even stronger than unionists' link with the USA.

In many ways, Canada can be an honest broker for Northern Ireland's future. Just as Canadian General John de Chastelain led the verification of decommissioning as part of the Good Friday Agreement, so Canada can lead again now. Similarly, a retired Supreme Court of Canada Judge Peter Cory led an inquiry into allegations of collusion by both British and Irish security services with paramilitaries. In both instances, Canadians were key to helping Northern Ireland move forward through some difficult steps.

Canada is renowned around the world for its peacekeeping role. This is not just charitable action – it is in the country's selfish economic interests to maintain good relations with the European Union, as well as with the UK. CETA (Comprehensive Economic and Trade Agreement, between Canada and the EU) is an important agreement for Canada and Ireland is a key gateway for Canadian businesses to trade into Europe. According to the Canada Census of 2016, more than four million residents of Canada claim Irish ancestry.[147]

Canada is a multicultural country that has often been described as a cultural mosaic compared to the melting pot of the USA; it will be able to play a key role in guiding Unionism towards a feeling of security within a New Ireland. It is a nation that has shown that there is a template where religious and cultural diversity can be respected, while still creating a cohesive and well-respected country. This is shown through their ready acceptance of significant numbers of immigrants from all over the world.[148] The Canadian government continues to set ambitious targets and operate innovative schemes to attract more people to move to their country, as they recognise the economic and societal benefits of doing so, especially for underpopulated provinces.

Canada has already stated its intention to increase immigration to help the recovery process from the COVID-19 pandemic. There could be a targeted program much like the former Atlantic Immigration Pilot Program, which welcomes people from the island of Ireland – the Walsh and Morrison visa programs in the United States enabled citizens from across the island of Ireland to move to the USA for work visas in the run-up to and immediately after the passage of the Good Friday Agreement. I know from my own experience in living and working outside of the island of Ireland, that opportunities to experience life elsewhere can help people to develop their skills and bring fresh perspectives back to Ireland when they return.

There is a route to Irish unity for unionists via Irish America. There are more than 31 million residents in the USA with Irish ancestry.[149] It is often said that going abroad makes unionists feel more Irish – particularly when visiting America, a place where the Irish are adored, if only just for our accent. They are identified as such by others and often will proclaim themselves to be Irish – or at least Northern Irish – as opposed to British.

The USA played a key role in the peace process, by encouraging Irish republicans to seek their goals via purely peaceful means. President Bill Clinton went against the advice of his own administration and the UK government at the time to grant Gerry Adams, then president of Sinn Féin, a visa. Now, the US government can help unionists to contribute to building the new constitution which will be required for Irish unity.

The role of the Commonwealth

An obvious step to consider, which would appeal to unionists, would be for Ireland to re-join the Commonwealth, as South Africa has done. Unionists need to be assured that their cultural expression will not be stymied after reunification. However, it must be recognised that Ireland is an independent Republic and that will not change after reunification. The Commonwealth did go through a process whereby it appeared to be moving away from the British monarch being made its head automatically, although King Charles III, has been confirmed as its next head. Ireland will not be re-joining the UK or leaving the EU, so any consideration of re-joining the Commonwealth needs to be carefully thought through and would require democratic consent across Ireland. It should be noted that the passing of Queen Elizabeth II may accelerate the transition to republics, of some countries which currently have the British Monarch as Head of State. It remains to be seen whether there will be a wider change in the structure of the Commonwealth as well.

Commonwealth links could be developed with Canada, Australia and New Zealand where advisors could help the PUL community feel part of a greater network that they feel comfortable with and connected to. However, this could be achieved regardless of whether Ireland re-joined the Commonwealth after unity or not. These Commonwealth networks could help with regeneration and the upskilling of young people.

We must address the fear that some unionists may feel and work with them to create a narrative that points a way forward to a brighter future. The Royal Irish Academy could help with this, as this body advocated re-joining the Commonwealth, as did former Taoiseach Bertie Ahern.

Westminster dysfunction

It is clear to see that there is a growing dysfunction in Westminster politics, where the parties will be increasingly focused on navel-gazing and dealing with the outcomes of their self-inflicted wounds from leaving the EU. There is a distrust of the Conservative government, particularly as a result of the ineffective management of the COVID-19 pandemic; the Labour opposition has provided little hope and a lack of inspiration.

The UK government never intended to stick to the commitments it signed up to in the Northern Ireland Protocol. Boris Johnson said that he did not think the EU would fully implement what was agreed; other Brexiters have said that they only saw the Protocol as a necessary step to 'getting Brexit done' and that once they were out, they could renegotiate it. This is a fundamental problem as the UK government is led by people who have no intention to stick to an international agreement which they negotiated and then passed legislation on.

The Institute for Government has outlined the procedure, should Article 16 be invoked:

> Before undertaking such measures, however, the parties should follow the process set out in Annex 7 of the Protocol. First, if either party is 'considering' unilateral action, it must notify the other party as soon as possible through the UK–EU Joint Committee, the body established by the Withdrawal Agreement to oversee its implementation. At this point, both parties should enter negotiations to find a solution – though no measures can be implemented during the initial one-month negotiating period. If negotiations fail and either party adopts unilateral measures, the other may take 'proportionate rebalancing measures'. All measures are

subject to review every three months, although each
party can also request a review at any point.[150]

While it may temporarily please the DUP and perhaps the UUP, Sinn
Fein, the SDLP and Alliance will be extremely unhappy with this
course of action. Similarly, a wide range of business and civil groups
that have expressed their support for the Protocol have called for
negotiation through dialogue. They will rightly be frustrated that
their voices are being ignored and concerned that instability caused
through the triggering of Article 16 will damage the economic potential of the Protocol, which had just begun to be realised by Northern
Ireland. It could also lead to civil unrest, which no right-minded person wants to see.

The UK's lack of a written constitution means that it depends
on convention and leaders adhering to acceptable standards of
behaviour instead, but the problem with having a constitution based
on convention is that when you have a leader who ignores said convention, it creates chaos. This was evidenced by the reaction of the
public to behaviour in 10 Downing Street during the pandemic,
namely in the Partygate scandal that finished Boris Johnson's career
as prime minister.

Boris Johnson was often rightly compared to Donald Trump,
but the difference is that at least there is a written constitution in
the USA which should act as a guardrail against unconstitutional
behaviour. With a written constitution there are limits on what any
individual or party could do to change constitutional norms. In
the UK, an unwritten constitution provides fewer clear safeguards –
the politician who was the UK Justice Secretary said in 2022 that
he wanted the Government to have the power to 'correct' wrong
legal decisions.

Ideology takes priority over practical considerations for those
who lead the UK government. There will not be the same funding
available to support Northern Ireland as there has been previously;
EU funding has been taken away from Scotland, Wales and Northern Ireland. Instead, the UK government is controlling the budgets at
Westminster for its UK Shared Prosperity Fund. This undermines the
devolution settlements endorsed by referendums across the UK.

Invest Northern Ireland, the economic development agency for
Northern Ireland, is going to see a significant amount of its budget
cut through the loss of EU grants because of the Brexit being pursued

by the UK government.[151] Unionism needs to be shown that this loss of funding and opportunities can be reversed through Irish unity.

When we step back from the morass of Brexit and look at the overall focus of the current UK government, it should be a wake-up call for us all. There is a coordinated approach to stripping our freedoms. Instead of dealing with the everyday challenges that people are facing, the UK government is increasingly focused on removing rights. For example, they have sought to criminalise peaceful protest through the Policing Bill; take control of the Independent Electoral Commission through the Elections Bill; make it easier to strip nationality through the Nationality and Borders Bill; to reduce government accountability in law through the Judicial Review Bill; and to remove the Human Rights Act through the Brexit Freedoms Bill.

Over time, Unionists will find their attention orientates itself away from Westminster and towards Dublin. It is increasingly clear that the UK government is in essence, on bread-and-butter issues, mostly a government for England alone. The very fact that the UK Prime Minister at the time considered it to be acceptable to call a UK General Election in 2019 during a period of political crisis in Northern Ireland when there was no functioning Assembly or regional government, confirms that the region is not a priority. Rather it is a minor consideration at best. The destiny of all on the island of Ireland will be decided by those within Ireland and this future needs to be embraced.

A unity campaign does not have to win over all unionists, it only has to win over a certain percentage. If unionists believe that there will be a white knight who comes riding over the horizon to rescue Northern Ireland's position in the UK, the way the three main UK parties did in the Scottish referendum in 2014 with 'The Vow' for more powers, they will be sorely disappointed. There is simply not the same interest in Northern Ireland or desire to hold onto it. In fact, I can confidently say that should Westminster ever have to choose between holding onto Scotland or Northern Ireland, they would choose Scotland every time. English independence is still a possibility, especially if they do not get the Brexit they want, or it proves to be disastrous. But they are less likely to claim that Brexit is the problem, rather they need to shake off the Celtic parts of the UK which are supposedly making Brexit more complicated than it would otherwise be.

Conservative history of betrayal

Unionists cried betrayal when Brexit did not work in their favour – betrayal by Tory politicians they supported, as though the party does not have a history of sacrificing Northern Ireland (unionists included) for Britain's gain. The harsh reality is that this has been a regular occurrence throughout the existence of Northern Ireland: Churchill during World War II was willing to give up Northern Ireland to the Irish Free State, in return for access to their ports and the ending of Ireland's neutrality;[152] his father invited unrest in Ireland and boasted about playing the Orange card; the UK Conservatives ended the old Stormont Parliament in 1972, signed the Anglo-Irish Agreement in 1985, agreed a Northern Ireland Protocol in 2019 and then in 2020 agreed on a trade deal with the EU that created the Irish Sea border. On each of these occasions, they went against the expressed wishes of Unionism.

There are customs barriers between Northern Ireland and Britain for the first time since the Act of Union in 1801. (Unionist politicians were warned by the business sector and civil society but chose to ignore both.) This shows that the UK government would rather be free to pursue a hard Brexit than focus on keeping the cohesiveness of the UK internal market. Time and time again, the DUP and wider Unionism puts their faith in the UK government only to have their wishes ignored or overruled. Surely it would be better for Unionism to embrace its destiny in Ireland and play a role in shaping a New Ireland, where it will have a much bigger say in its future?

UK sovereignty

There has been much discussion about sovereignty in the context of Brexit and Irish unity. That by voting for Brexit, the UK would 'take back control', yet we have seen that the reverse is true. Instead, it is the EU that has taken back control. British citizens now have fewer rights when they travel to the EU, including restrictions on the amount of time they can spend in EU countries; their ability to work in the EU is no longer automatic.

I believe sovereignty is, first and foremost, about putting food on the table and a roof over your head. We have seen increased barriers to trade between Britain and the EU. Supply chains have struggled to cope, including those for food[153] and construction materials required to build housing.[154] While the pandemic has played a part, these problems have been exacerbated by Brexit. The divide and conquer approach by the UK government that has turned Brexit into a culture war is not one we want or need in Northern Ireland anymore.

We need to encourage all of those who live within Northern Ireland to consider and compare Northern Ireland's treatment by the UK and Irish governments. The UK government continues to appoint more life peers to the House of Lords, the unelected second chamber of the UK Parliament. There are now over 830 of them. This is not a sign of a healthy, well-balanced democracy – only China has a larger legislative chamber and that is a country with a population of one billion. The UK government has ruled out a Swiss-style deal which would have reduced friction on the Irish Sea border by significantly reducing the required number of veterinary checks because it would impinge on the UK's sovereignty. A Swiss-style deal would avoid Sanitary and Phytosanitary (SPS) checks for agri-food products – live animals, fresh meat and plant products. The agreement with Switzerland removes nearly all the physical checks, but not documentary ones. This would be achieved through a dynamic regulatory mechanism to avoid divergence between the EU and UK on agri-food, through the creation of a Common Veterinary Area.

It is a damning indictment of the UK government that the Secretary of State for Northern Ireland claimed publicly at the start of January 2021 that there was no Irish Sea border, even though the same UK government insisted on new customs infrastructure being built in Northern Ireland ports, to make sure that the requirements of the Northern Ireland Protocol were followed. The UK government is putting in said infrastructure in Northern Ireland for trade from Britain at the same time as the Irish government is ensuring the continuation of EU-funded programmes. The British government is putting up barriers to trade between Britain and Northern Ireland; the Irish government is, by comparison, putting financial investment into Northern Ireland.

Whereas Britain has decided to pursue a policy of isolation the Irish government, throughout the Brexit process, has shown itself to be the defender of Northern Ireland's interests in the EU. Through such comparisons, we can hope that unionists see that unifying with a government that cares about their homeland is the best decision and the right one.

While the Irish government was successful in securing safeguards for the island of Ireland, there is more that can be done. For example, Northern Ireland has the highest concentration of EU citizens in a region outside the EU. For this reason – alongside its unique geography – the Irish government should lobby for Northern Ireland to access EIB (European Investment Bank) funding post-Brexit and pre-reunification.

Welsh independence

We are all aware by now of the growing independence movement in Scotland, but the final piece of the UK puzzle may be coming loose, too, as we are beginning to see a political decoupling of Wales from England. Support for Welsh independence within the EU has reached 41 per cent whereas it was seven per cent just a few years ago, according to a BBC poll in February 2019.[155] This is significant, as Wales has been perceived to be highly integrated with England economically and historically there have always been low levels of support for Welsh independence.

Governing priorities should be determined by what needs to be done depending on circumstance – it is not about making governing priories fit within a specific ideology. We can argue about to what degree we should have liberalism, or we can focus on the key issue of whether we want to live in an open or closed society. Now the only way for those in Scotland, Wales and Northern Ireland to live in a truly open society is through independence and unity.

The border must go somewhere

The Brexit conundrum that the UK faced was that it had three choices: an economic border between Northern Ireland and the rest of Ireland; an economic border between Northern Ireland and the rest of the UK; or agreeing to maintain full alignment between the UK and the EU.

This issue would have been much simpler for the UK government if a reunified Ireland was integrated within the EU, as Emmanuel Macron has previously stated on a visit to Ireland.[156] After Irish unity, no part of the island of Ireland will suffer directly the consequences of English hostility to the European project.

It is unfortunate that during a time of great change, unionists have been represented by the DUP who have shown an inflexibility and intransigence towards resolving the Brexit conundrum. The fact that the DUP have not been willing or able to bring forward detailed proposals on how to make Brexit work, without creating a border either within the UK or within the island of Ireland, shows that they did not fully think through the consequences of a UK vote to leave the EU. Despite being in favour of Brexit, they have repeatedly voted against its various proposed forms in the UK Parliament, but Brexit means putting up borders and they must go somewhere.

Unionist politicians' entrenched resistance to change is not a sign of strength, it is a sign that Unionism is brittle and in an increasingly weak position. It will do unionists a disservice if their leaders and elected representatives continue to bury their heads in the sand.

Civic unionism

The campaign for unity should be focused on winning over unionist voters, not Unionist politicians, as political Unionism will be the last to engage with Irish unity. The latter mentioned continue to complain about the position they find themselves in, without acknowledging their role in getting there or providing constructive suggestions for improving the situation. Unionist politicians have collapsed the Northern Ireland Assembly in an attempt to force the UK government to abandon the Northern Ireland Protocol. As referenced previously, David Campbell, the Chair of the Loyalist Communities Council stated on local radio that, for some loyalists, 'if it comes to the bit where we have to fight physically to maintain our freedoms within the United Kingdom then so be it'.[157]

Former First Minister and leader of the DUP Peter Robinson wrote in a newspaper column:

> There are forces using the exigencies of Brexit to advance
> a programme of constitutional change through stealth
> and propaganda. My advice to those who are driving this
> agenda forward is as short as it is restrained. Take care.[158]

Unionist leaders could have decided to campaign against Brexit as they knew that leaving the EU would be unsettling for Northern Ireland. They could have used their position of influence between 2017 and 2019 to secure a soft Brexit, with no borders between the UK and EU, which would have meant no border between Northern Ireland

and Britain. They could, even now, seek to set out a positive vision for Northern Ireland remaining part of the UK.

I recognise that the reality of the Northern Ireland Protocol and the barriers it has created between Britain and Northern Ireland has deeply unsettled Unionists. Reality has slowly dawned on them that the British government negotiated a deal with the EU, implemented into international law, that places Northern Ireland apart from the rest of the UK.

Understanding unionist/loyalist hostility and fear

Unionism's brittle confidence is highlighted by the actions of senior Unionist politicians putting a Queen's University Professor of Human Rights under pressure by writing to the Vice Chancellor to complain about his actions, simply because he was publicly advocating the benefits of Irish unity and had published a paper about the challenges that Brexit poses for Northern Ireland.[159] This is a legitimate aspiration as recognised by the Good Friday Agreement. The desire for the peaceful reunification of Ireland is a political viewpoint that should not offend anyone. As mentioned previously, many in Northern Ireland were already happy to let things progress naturally, before the calamity of Brexit.

Unionism has a genuine fear of being controlled by Sinn Féin – they remember the atrocities they suffered at the hands of republican terrorists. There is a belief that the Irish government were complicit in this, as they did not often extradite known terrorists and some such as Charles Haughey were alleged to have sometimes turned a blind eye to gunrunning. When loyalists burn the Irish Tricolour on bonfires, it is because they associate that flag with the IRA – although this does not excuse such an act.

We also need to understand and address PUL concerns around Brexit. Fine Gael, of all Dáil parties, has a unique opportunity to assuage concerns and convince unionists that they respect their identity and that it will be welcome within Irish unity. It is often said that in a coalition government the smaller party acts as a mudguard and suffers electoral decline as a result. In Ireland it appears that Fine Gael has both a windscreen (Fianna Fáil) and a mudguard (Greens). While Fine Gael lost seats in the 2020 election and Fianna Fáil gained them, it is Fine Gael that now has the highest level of support in opinion polls of any of the three parties in the coalition government. The Greens are already an all-Ireland party. I hope that Fianna Fáil and Fine Gael and their historic pragmatism will mean that they embrace the push for unity. Fine Gael have a strong history of supporting law and order, as well as hostility to Sinn Féin. They are likely to be most sympathetic to unionist concerns in this context.

I understand the desire of Sinn Féin to avoid splits within their party. However, Sinn Féin and the wider republican movement need to realise that if they continue to be seen to justify past violence,[160] it will be harder to build the necessary coalition required for unity to be a success.

We must acknowledge that, within loyalist communities, there is a genuine fear of change; of their communities being 'taken over' or eradicated by any culture that does not fit with their concept of Britishness. As is often the case, all too often this fear wrongly materialises as hate and is exploited by those in power to consolidate their own control. *The Detail* reported one such incident which saw Somalian immigrant Sahra Mahamuud being forced to leave her home in the Village – a predominantly loyalist part of Belfast, still under the influence of paramilitaries – due to targeted abuse and discrimination she and her young children were subjected to.[161] Sadly, this was not an isolated incident – the Village is in South Belfast, an area in which the PSNI reported 'a higher number of racist crimes than any other part of Northern Ireland' between 2014 and 2019.[162] However, this is not to say that only or all loyalist communities are inherently dangerous for newcomers – according to Executive Director of the Northern Ireland Commission for Ethnic Minorities Patrick Yu, there have also been racially motivated attacks in Catholic West Belfast areas, although these are 'less prevalent'; Yu explained that it just so happens that 'most of the available housing stock for private rental happens to be in loyalist areas where there is already a wariness of outsiders'.[163]

Former leader of the Progressive Unionist Party (PUP) Dr John Kyle explained the problem to *The Detail*:

> The Village is an area of social disadvantage. You've got families and community groups there who are grappling with welfare reform, poverty, poor housing, lack of employment opportunities and educational underachievement.

> Then you will get individuals who, for reasons
> of personal gain or animosity, stir up fear and racial
> resentment of newcomers. They end up exploiting peo-
> ple's pre-existing sense of grievance.[164]

This abuse of power mirrors the sad reality of Trump's America and Nigel Farage's Little England: people who are hit the hardest are fed stories about who is responsible for their hardships and they turn against them. Those in positions of power, legitimate or otherwise – whether politicians or paramilitaries – prey on the fear of their hard-done-by, and therefore easily riled and manipulated communities, for their own selfish gain. They distract from their own failings by pinning the blame on an easy target: the outsider. Take the current state of the UK, for example. At a time when energy costs are skyrocketing, the health service is under severe strain and we face a climate crisis, the UK government continues to talk about wanting to send a greater number of migrants to Rwanda whilst struggling to deal with the real, pressing issues their people face.

There must be a positive narrative provided which gives hope for these loyalist communities to embrace; we cannot allow for their fears to be heightened by unreasonable leaders who simply want their support. If we consider the flag protest in 2012 when Belfast City Council decided to fly the Union Flag on designated days like most other cities across the UK, rather than every day of the year, this caused a great deal of damage to local businesses, particularly in East Belfast.[165] But loyalists were encouraged to create disorder by paramilitary groups, even though it was damaging their own communities.[166] The CBI (Confederation of British Businesses) estimated that the flag protests cost Belfast businesses £15 million. In addition, the Chief Constable of the PSNI said that policing the flag protests cost more than £15 million.[167]

Minimising the risk of loyalist violence

One of the areas of concern regarding unity is the increased risk of violence erupting especially from people living in economically disadvantaged loyalist areas during the unity campaign or after a successful vote for unity. If we look at how certain cities in America are undertaking steps to combat gun violence in deprived areas, we could consider similar tactics, for example the use of so-called 'violence interrupters', who are trusted members of the community that work to diffuse tensions that lead to violence in their own areas – they 'can do what the police can't'.[168]

There needs to be an early focus on addressing the deprivation suffered in loyalist working-class areas in advance of a unity referendum – disadvantaged communities need to be provided with opportunities, such as community outreach programmes, that will allow them to flourish in a New Ireland. These areas need economic investment and stability; there needs to be a package of proposals that set out how loyalist culture will be protected and how local communities will be facilitated to help develop learning and entrepreneurial culture, which could perhaps be achieved with tax breaks for firms who are willing to set up in areas of deprivation, for example.

The reality is that there will be no place for working-class loyalists in Brexit Britain – the primary focus of any UK government will be to protect the City of London, the manufacturing base and where possible increase investment in public services.

Loyalists and unionists must not be allowed to believe that threatening or undertaking violence to frustrate a democratic desire for Irish unity would work. They must be reassured that a positive future will be available through Irish unity.

It has been said that unionists in Northern Ireland are more loyal to the half-crown than the crown,[169] meaning that they are motivated by financial reward rather than a sense of loyalty to the monarchy. Therefore, I believe, fundamentally, that unionists in Northern Ireland will be pragmatic when they realise that the UK is ending and that there is a more prosperous future available through Irish unity, but they need to be reassured that their rights will be protected.

Culture is not a threat

When we look at how there are increasing levels of Irish being spoken within the working-class unionist population such as in the previously mentioned Turas initiative and the first Irish medium primary school being established in East Belfast, it shows that there is an awareness of Irish culture and that desire for it is increasing amongst the unionist community.

Most of the Establishment in Britain do not understand Irish culture, particularly loyalist and unionist culture. In a reunified Ireland this culture would be understood, preserved and celebrated.

There are those within the unionist community who will try to exploit fears of cultural encroachment through the Irish language. They will seek to play off of the fear of the erosion of unionist identity. However, the Irish language should be emphasised as a shared cultural asset by the pro-unity campaign. The campaign must continue to emphasise that the Irish language is a native, not a foreign, language – it has been part of Ireland for longer than the English language. Historically there have been strong links between the Protestant community and the Irish language: Presbyterianism had a key role in preserving and promoting the Irish language in the 18th and 19th centuries;[170] in the 1911 census, 20 per cent of Protestants who lived on the Shankill Road spoke Irish;[171] Orange Lodges used to display signs in the Irish language. Many of Northern Ireland's towns and cities have names which are directly derived from their original Irish names. While there has been increasing interest in the Irish language within Protestant communities, when unity succeeds there will not be an expectation that all people will be compelled to learn Irish, unlike the current requirements in the Irish Republic where most students have to learn the language at school.

In addition to making it clear that the Irish language will not be forced upon Unionists post-reunification, there are two other key points that should be made: firstly, Irish should be given the same status as Welsh and Scots Gaelic are given in Scotland and Wales; secondly, Irish is a culture for all, it is not a language solely for republicanism. Everyone across Northern Ireland should be free to savour their rich cultural heritage – culture should not be seen as a zero-sum game, which has to be seen through a prism of total victory or defeat. Instead we should accommodate, respect and appreciate many cultures. The reunified state should also continue to facilitate the learning and celebration of Ulster-Scots culture and language, for those who wish to do so.

We live in a complex world and within our small island, we should be able to enjoy different aspects of our multi-layered culture. This strengthens our own citizenship; it does not weaken it. Unionism's past hostility towards and ignoring of the Irish language resulted in a hollowing out of identity and this was lessening their experience of living on this island. Let's embrace all peaceful parts of our culture.

It is also important to make clear that Irish unity will not mean that everyone will suddenly have to become a Catholic or send their children to Catholic schools – this may seem obvious, but it is a genuine concern for some unionists. All state schools across a New Ireland should provide integrated education by default. People should be able to specifically opt-in to faith-based schools if they so wish, but integrated education should be the mainstream option. Nor will everyone have to attend GAA games, although the East Belfast GAA team set up in early 2020 has proven to be popular and, despite threats to it, has also shown a strong desire for embracing Irish culture. The message needs to be reinforced to unionists and loyalists that a sense of Britishness can still be safeguarded through Irish unity, just as nationalists have been able to maintain a sense of Irishness for all their years as part of the UK. There is no desire for a homogenous cultural identity where everyone is expected to think and act in the same way in terms of cultural affinity. There will be a recognition of cultural diversity enshrined in the new constitution after Irish unity has been secured, just as there is recognition and safeguards in the Good Friday Agreement.

Carson Project

Just as the Lincoln Project in the United States built a campaign to appeal to conservative voters to vote against Donald Trump, so the unity campaign should develop a Carson Project run by former unionists to reach out to those from a unionist background who are now open to Irish unity.

Edward Carson, a Dublin barrister who campaigned against Home Rule for Ireland, is often seen by some within unionism as a founding father of Northern Ireland, but he abhorred the partition of Ireland and turned down the offer of becoming Northern Ireland's first prime minister. Indeed, in 1921 he said:

> What a fool I was. I was only a puppet, and so was
> Ulster, and so was Ireland, in the political game that
> was to get the Conservative Party into power.[172]

This is the harsh reality of what the DUP and wider Unionism faced, when Boris Johnson agreed to an Irish Sea Border against their wishes. While there have been some good, rational people in the Conservative Party, including those who genuinely cared for the UK union, they have been overtaken by a hard-right group who are obsessed with the notion of breaking all links with the EU. The Conservatives are not now and never have been popular in Northern Ireland – we must not let them ruin our island again.

A successful Carson Project should make clear that rights and equality are key to Irish unity. These rights must be for unionism, nationalism and the non-aligned – unity cannot be seen as nationalism's way to undermine unionism.

A focus on constitutional rights will be key for this project. A bill of rights was promised in the Good Friday Agreement but never delivered. A new written constitution for Ireland building on 1937 should include a bill of rights which will explicitly provide safeguards for people from all backgrounds and identities. This can be used to provide reassurance to the PUL community.

Justice John Murray said a constitutional court may be necessary to protect minority rights:

> You could have a special constitutional court, its composition could be, maybe, a UK judge, maybe a mixture of judges from this island. But these are all things we need to think and speak of.[173]

So, there could be a UK judge sitting in Ireland as part of a package of measures to assure unionists, who would technically be a minority in a unified nation, of their rights. (Although unionists and British people will be a minority after Irish unity, in no way do they – as predominately WASPs – experience the same plight as other ethnic minorities.) As part of this, the British Irish Council should continue after unity.

Unionism is an ideology that has been based on a sense of triumphalism and a siege mentality. Objectively, it can appear a contradiction to both claim superiority and feel under siege. The unity campaign will not win by trying to claim that previous terrorist campaigns were justified. In a similar way, harking back to the glory of the Easter Rising will not work. The events of 1916 have taken on, for some sections of nationalism, an almost legendary status. Those who fought and died in the GPO and surrounding streets were heroes who have become icons of the Irish Republic. There are different views about this – it is, without a doubt, the case that the heavy-handed approach and response taken by the UK government led people who previously were opposed to the Rising to embrace its objectives. There was much bloody fighting for years afterwards – the violence and the partition of the country should not be celebrated or used as a means of campaigning for Irish unity.

One national Parliament

I can understand why people might think that maintaining the Northern Ireland Assembly would be a good idea, that it would help to make Unionists in particular, feel more welcome after Irish unity has been secured. However, I want to see all parts of Northern Ireland brought into the new state fully. I do not want Unionism or Northern Ireland separated from the rest of Ireland. That is why we need one national Parliament and greater power devolved down to local councils. The best way to safeguard unionists is to fully integrate them into the operation of the new state.

On current voting patterns Unionism at best can hold 11 out of 650 seats in the UK Parliament. After the December 2019 elections, despite agreeing to several Unionist pacts, they were down to only eight seats. In a New Ireland, they are likely to hold a significantly larger proportion.

Northern Ireland currently has 18 out of 650 seats in the UK Parliament, less than three per cent of the total. In an Irish unity scenario, based on the current ratio of seats to population in the Dáil, Northern Ireland would hold approximately 58 seats in a 215 all-Ireland Parliament.

I can understand the deep affection unionists have for the royal family – I can see it in those close to me. While I do not personally feel that way, I understand and respect those who do. After Irish unity has been achieved, we must accommodate our unionist neighbours by having regular royal visits, but a British monarch will no longer be the head of state – this is important. The Irish Republic will remain that post-reunification. Any attempt to adopt two heads of state would lead to more division when we really want to unite all the peoples of this island. The presidency of Bosnia and Herzegovina consists of a three-member head of state, but I do not believe that this would work or be desirable for Ireland.[174]

The president of Ireland should use the bridge-building template of Mary McAleese who welcomed those from unionist and loyalist backgrounds into Áras an Uachtaráin. Just as there was the Downing Street Declaration in 1993 by the UK and Irish governments that the people of Ireland had the right to self-determination,[175] there should be a declaration by the Irish government confirming that they want to create an Irish nation for all, respecting the democratic mandate and diversity.

In a New Ireland, Unionism would be a permanent swing vote. We must emphasise that the people of Northern Ireland will only be able to fully take control of our affairs through Irish unity. As the EU referendum has starkly shown, while Northern Ireland remains a part of the UK, our political destiny will be controlled by the voters of England.

Leadership required

There is a desperate need for proper leadership for Unionism. We know that Unionism, as it always does at times of danger, will retreat into its own shell and hunker down. Every time Unionist leaders attempt to reach out to other people and show a vision that would enable them to build a broader coalition for their position, they are defeated. This defeat does not come at the hands of Nationalists or Republicans, rather it comes from within their own ranks. Unionism's leaders such as O'Neill, Faulkner, Trimble or Paisley were not forced out of office by Republicans and Nationalists. Unionism's own side will undermine any attempt at outreach as a sign of weakness. The siege mentality is still very much in force.

Unionism has barricaded itself into the corner by supporting Brexit which has led to constitutional uncertainty across the UK. Many commentators have discussed the lack of leadership for unionists. I feel, as someone who comes from a unionist background, that there has been a dearth of liberal, forward-looking Unionist leaders.

Whatever one thought of David Trimble, he at least had the vision and determination to negotiate with Sinn Féin and do the deal to secure the peace process, when other Unionists refused to even speak with them. Admittedly, his endorsement of a hard Brexit approach and dismissal of the potential threats to the peace process by such an approach has tarnished his legacy. Many unionists – predominantly those in politics – are opposed to evolving. Some are literally opposed to the concept of evolution as well as the practicalities of developing their thinking.

Unionists and loyalists will protest that the Union Flag should be flown more regularly or complain about a perceived loss of sovereignty because of the Northern Ireland Protocol and they will be supported by their leaders in doing so. We need to engage with working-class loyalist communities and to understand that their concerns are wider than just the Northern Ireland Protocol. Unfortunately, historically they have been used as voting fodder, as people whose support was easy to win, then taken for granted and ignored. You will rarely if ever see them protesting about the need for more housing, lack of jobs or low educational attainment, all of which are issues for unionist and loyalist communities and all of which are issues that have not been resolved by their leaders. Is there no ambition to progress?

On a practical level, the unity campaign should point to the stagnant levels of educational attainment in unionist/loyalist areas over many decades. If we look at East Belfast in particular, educational attainment is low, unemployment is high. There must be a commitment to provide investment into these working-class communities to help raise living standards and to provide education and skills training. It will only be through community organising, creating job opportunities and building new aspirations for work, that these communities will begin to have hope again. As abolitionist and former slave Fredrick Douglass once wrote in his *Blessings of Liberty and Education* (1894):

> Education means emancipation. It means light and liberty. It means the uplifting of the soul of man into the glorious light of truth, the light by which men can only be made free.[176]

Many young people from a unionist background tend to leave Northern Ireland to study and work in Britain and rarely come home – this is known as the 'brain drain'. Those with ambition and an outward-looking mindset tend to leave for Britain and never return. Those who have remained have been disappointed by successive Unionists in our government and betrayed by the UK Tory government.

Since the Brexit vote, the Irish government have clearly shown their desire to ensure the best possible outcome from the negotiations for the island of Ireland. With the help of elected politicians and senior civil servants, they prepared thoroughly for a range of options in the event of a UK vote to leave (which is more than the UK government did); they held a series of all-island Brexit Forums and sector-specific meetings. The UK government's mantra by comparison, prior to the triggering of Article 50 stating their intention to leave the EU, was 'Brexit means Brexit'.

There are significant parts of society within Northern Ireland, including those from a unionist background, who are fed up with the current state of government in the region. We Ulster Scots are proud of our stubborn, independent streak – we must not continue to meekly allow ourselves to be an afterthought, or develop Stockholm Syndrome and simply agree with whatever England decides. This does us no favours.

Blindly following the UK government's decision to pursue a herd immunity approach at the start of the COVID-19 pandemic put us all at risk. There was much talk about flattening the curve, but precious little action in the crucial early days and weeks prior to the first lockdown to do anything to achieve it. In the middle of November 2020, the Northern Ireland Executive could not agree on whether to continue with restrictions to minimise the COVID-19 infections, even though they were recommended to continue by the chief medical officer and based on scientific advice. Furthermore, the UK government chose to turn down the opportunity to be part of an EU-wide solution to the ventilator shortage during the pandemic. Instead, they decided to seek ventilators from a Brexit-supporting company with no experience in making them.[177] In the end, none were made – this is unforgivable.

The Petition of Concern (POC) was used by the DUP to block the extension of COVID-19 restrictions. This mechanism was supposed to provide community safeguards, not enable a minority to block the majority from enacting public health measures. It is a further example of a government willing to risk the health, safety and well-being of its people; it highlights the need to abolish the POC and ultimately the Northern Ireland Assembly.

Quality of life

According to the UN Development Index of 2020, Ireland was ranked second in the world for quality of life, whereas the UK was 13th.[178] Surely anyone in their right mind would see the benefits of being part of Ireland from this fact alone? For the sake of their families, surely unionists would embrace Irish unity to provide a better quality of life? Are they willing to allow stubbornness or worse, fear of change, to hold them back from a better future for themselves and their children?

The UK will gradually be overtaken by new emerging economies, whereas the EU will continue to be a significant player in the next decades. Ireland, through their member status, will therefore be more likely to assure a better quality of life for its citizens. Together, we could make it even better.

In 2022, the cost-of-living crisis in the UK reached a point where many people could not afford to heat their homes or use their ovens; food banks stopped taking potatoes in some instances, as people could no longer afford to heat the water to cook them.[179] Rishi Sunak boasted about taking public money from deprived areas and redirecting it to wealthier locations that were more likely to vote Conservative;[180] interviewed by Susanna Reid on Good Morning Britain, Boris Johnston was told about an elderly woman who could not afford to heat her home, so spent all day riding around on public buses instead – his response was to boast about his decision to provide pensioners with 24-hour free bus passes.[181] Why would anyone want to cling to a nation whose leading party only prioritises or cares about the wealthy and sacrifices the health and happiness of ordinary people?

I do believe that unionists will seek out the best future for their families when they realise that Irish unity is a real prospect. In the past, support for the union with Britain was largely about the survival of their cultural identity when it was under threat politically and physically. But they have already embraced their Irish identity to some extent by securing Irish passports – I have seen it myself in friends from unionist backgrounds. In a 2022 index, the Irish passport was ranked the third most powerful in the world, whereas the UK one was only ranked 26th.[182] In the post-Brexit world there is a strong attraction to being able to continue to travel and work freely across the European Union and this is only possible with an Irish passport. For the first time, more Irish passports were issued than British ones in Northern Ireland – applications for British passports dropped by 15 per cent between 2015 and 2020 while applications for Irish passports have doubled as moderate unionists and agnostics are desperate to maintain their EU citizenship.[183] Whether this was simply to avoid queues at airports, figures show people are recognising that there are benefits to being an Irish citizen that the UK cannot currently offer.

A DUP MP has publicly stated that just because unionists applied for Irish passports, this does not mean that they want to be citizens of the Irish Republic. This totally misses the point. Once unionists have crossed the Rubicon by applying for Irish passports, suddenly the idea of Irish unity is not so remote or undesirable. At this point the genie is out of the bottle and these former unionists are up for grabs.

Change is coming and the unionist population should decide to embrace it and help to shape it – it is surely not worth going down with a sinking ship just because you happen to be onboard.

Hard truths for Unionism

The unity campaign needs to reach out to Unionism by highlighting a number of hard truths.

ONE: the unionist community will be respected and cherished within Irish unity (safeguards will be provided in part via membership of the EU).

TWO: several current and former members of the UK Cabinet, including Michael Gove, Suella Braverman and Rishi Sunak have publicly stated their desire to remove the UK from the ECHR. This is expressly written into the Good Friday Agreement. Such actions would therefore ignore the democratic wishes of all the people of the island of Ireland. The ECHR will help to protect unionists, as well as nationalists and the non-aligned, within the New Ireland that will follow a vote for Irish unity.

THREE: Brexit can be used to frame the argument that whereas the Good Friday Agreement being applied across two states may have been seen as a permanent settlement, the vote to leave the EU means that can no longer be the case. Whereas the people of Ireland could allow relationships to evolve at their own pace, now there is an urgent requirement for all Irish people on each side of the border to take back control of their destiny.

FOUR: the generous funding from Westminster will end. The UK government are going to focus their efforts and money on mitigating the negative impacts of Brexit that will require funding and they will also invest money and effort on parts of Northern England and the Midlands that voted Leave. The parliamentary seats in these areas were won by Conservative MPs for the first time, who want to see increased investment as part of the supposed 'Brexit dividend'. There are no votes and frankly no thanks from Northern Ireland for continuing to invest there.

FIVE: whereas the EU ensured that funding went to regions of significant need such as Northern Ireland and indeed parts of the

Irish Republic, the UK government will be much more driven by the need to satisfy unhappy voters in Britain.

SIX: Northern Ireland is detached from the political environment at Westminster. There are no Northern Ireland MPs either in government or the official opposition. While Westminster is not irrelevant to Northern Ireland, the Northern Ireland MPs are irrelevant at Westminster. The DUP confidence and supply agreement with the Conservatives between 2017 and 2019 showed itself to be ineffective. The DUP were not able to draw down the money as quickly as they wanted. The views of the DUP were ignored in the withdrawal agreement and the trade deal the Conservatives agreed with the EU, including the Protocol.

SEVEN: Boris Johnson was focused on securing the best trading conditions for Britain; Northern Ireland was not and is not a priority. Any Tory PM will be loath to use up precious political capital (of which there is little) and any leverage on Northern Ireland.

EIGHT: the Irish government has been focused on securing the best deal for the island of Ireland. Through this action, we can already see that the Irish government is providing for all the people of Ireland, whereas the UK government is not.

The pro-union campaign must be encouraged to set out a positive vision for the future – just saying no to any change will not be enough to maintain the union with the UK or rUK. There is a clear discrepancy between the socially progressive values that have been emerging across Britain and the reactionary approach of Unionism in Northern Ireland. It is fundamentally different from the perception of Britishness in Scotland, England and Wales and it must be called out as such.

While the campaign for unity will be positive and forward-thinking, the response from hard-line Unionist leaders is likely to be very negative in tone. They will see this campaign as a fight to maintain their place as citizens of the UK. They may claim that they would no longer be able to stay in Northern Ireland if there was a vote for unity.

Despair and lack of hope for the future is the thing we must fight against. Unionism needs to be given an opportunity to prosper in a New Ireland where they will have a strong voice for generations to come.

The Power of Sport

'Sport has the power to change the world. . . sport can create hope where once there was only despair'.[184]

Nelson Mandela

ONE OF THE major challenges in creating Irish unity will be ensuring that there is a shared identity for people across Ireland, to minimise a sense of loss or unfamiliarity in a 'new' country. Sport provides solid foundations for a shared identity. Across a range of sports, people regularly compete for and represent Ireland: rugby, cricket, golf, tennis, athletics, boxing, basketball, hockey and badminton to name a few. Even during the height of The Troubles nationalists and unionists from across Ireland supported the one rugby team. In light of this, 'Ireland's Call', the rugby anthem, perhaps has potential to be a fully inclusive new national anthem post-reunification. The song was written by Phil Coulter specifically to be inclusive and so should resonate with all of Ireland.[185]

George Best – 'a footballer without comparison', according to the great Pele – said that he hoped there would be one soccer team for all of Ireland before he passed away.[186] He was iconic for the Northern Ireland soccer team. As long as there are two teams, I will admit that my first preference will remain Northern Ireland – old habits die hard – but I too want to see one team.

There is perhaps nothing more boring than politics mixing with sport. The best of politics can be invigorating and sport can certainly be stimulating, but when the two are put together it brings out the worst in both. Unfortunately, there have been occasions where politics has crept in. For example, the targeting of some players from Northern Ireland by the Football Association of Ireland to entice them to declare for the Republic of Ireland team instead of the Northern Ireland team has appeared to focus only on those from a particular religious background; the disgraceful treatment of Neil Lennon (who gave his all for the Northern Ireland team) by a small number of bigoted fans for being a Catholic and playing for Glasgow Celtic is a particularly sickening example.

Despite the threat of sectarianism, the all-island approach for soccer will be sensible from a practical point of view – given the inevitably small talent pool across Ireland – and something that will prove to be positive in its outcomes. Before partition, there was one national soccer team, headquartered in Belfast – I see no reason why we cannot recreate this post-unity and have the reunified soccer association headquartered in Belfast.

There are huge opportunities for a united approach to soccer on the island. Bringing the two soccer structures into one will give soccer on the island a critical mass it currently lacks and the domestic game would benefit from one structure as the national team could represent the island as one, so we could move away from the corrosive arguments about players from one jurisdiction being poached for another. Plans are being worked on for an all-island soccer league which is a welcome development but while an all-Ireland soccer league is desirable, it must be implemented respectfully – we must discourage sectarian chanting, anywhere. This is not a problem that is unique to Ireland, Scotland has introduced legislation to tackle this scourge.

Just look at how successful the all-Ireland rugby team has become – it was ranked number one in the world for the first time in 2022 and has won championships in the Six Nations tournament multiple times. This is not just about sporting success on the pitch, these sporting teams and their fans are ambassadors for the entire country. Being a supporter of the Ireland rugby team is a shared identity for all rugby fans across the island of Ireland.

When we think of the great successes achieved by Irish teams and Irish individuals over many decades, we can project a strong sense of Irishness onto society. Consider how the British Lions team name was changed to British and Irish Lions, to recognise that some of the players are Irish – this points the way to continued engagement and positive relations with our neighbours on the next island.

When rugby moved to an All-Ireland League, it helped to improve the playing standard across the island and it proved to be a useful platform and feeder system for the four provinces and the national team of Ireland. The continuing success of the Ireland team percolates into wider society and makes us all feel that we can succeed against bigger countries.

Similarly, the women's hockey team's journey to the World Cup Final in 2018, while still competing as amateurs, shows the power of working as one state, representing Ireland on the world stage. This is the power of unity.

The power of sport can be an inspiration for building Irish unity and already we have seen unity across the border by means of good sportsmanship. For example, Leinster rugby fans sang 'Stand Up For The Ulstermen' (the Ulster Rugby chant) as a mark of respect after the tragic death of a young and highly talented Ulster Rugby player Nevin Spence;[187] the Ireland soccer fans mourned side by side with Northern Ireland fans at the Euro 2016 soccer tournament after the tragic death of a Northern Ireland fan, by clapping in the 23rd minute during the next game.

Ireland and Northern Ireland soccer fans jointly received an award in Paris for being the best fans at the Euro 2016 soccer tournament – a positive indicator of what can be achieved together on the global stage.

Fans from across Ireland can celebrate boxer Carl Frampton and golfer Rory McIlroy, who are both from Northern Ireland. Carl Frampton came from a unionist area of Belfast but represented Ireland from an early age as boxing, like many sports, is organised on an all-Ireland basis. He said that he was proud to box for Ireland because he had been looked after so well by the Irish boxing authorities.[188] Carl Frampton has shown, just like his former manager Barry McGuigan before him, that sport can transcend all socio-economic and political barriers across Ireland and unite the people of this island together in a common venture to cheer on one of their own on the world stage.

If well-respected sportspersons who are not tarnished with a political brush and who have cross-community support, such as Brian O'Driscoll or Rory McIlroy, were to come out in favour of unity, it would really help to raise awareness and consideration for the cause. In fact, Rory McIlroy has already said people need to consider the possibility of unity in light of Brexit.[189]

All too often sport is used to divide families, communities and countries. Ireland is not alone in this problem – we can see it happening in Scotland as the divide between Glasgow Rangers and Glasgow Celtic over political issues as well as being a sporting rivalry.

However, this is not always the case. If we look at the example of the Springboks rugby team immediately after the end of apartheid it served to bring the country together. President Mandela realised that white South Africans were passionately attached to the Springboks rugby team, so he resisted calls for the team to be disbanded or for the symbol of a Springbok to be changed. This was at a time when a new flag was adopted and a new anthem was introduced, alongside the existing one from the time of apartheid. Instead, he embraced the sport, the team and the symbolism. The diverse nature of the country was emphasised and this was a new beginning – the team went on to win the 1995 Rugby World Cup Final and become World Champions.

The GAA

The Gaelic Athletic Association (GAA) was founded in 1884 as a way to preserve indigenous Irish culture and sports during British rule. (These sports include Gaelic football, rounders, handball and hurling.) During a Gaelic football match at Croke Park in Dublin in 1920, players and spectators were attacked and some were killed by British soldiers (known as Black and Tans) on what has been referred to as Bloody Sunday 1920.[190] This unlawful attack on civilians was considered to be undertaken in response to the IRA assassinations of British Army intelligence officers.

There are GAA clubs across all 32 counties; however, the sports are predominantly seen to be for those from a Catholic and nationalist background. Some of the trophies are named after those who were involved in political activity by violent means and that is hard for people to accept. The organisation is evolving – in 2001 a ban on members of the police force, the British army and security services playing in any official GAA team in Northern Ireland was lifted. The President of the GAA has even said that his organisation may look at the flag and anthem used in the event of political realignment across the island of Ireland. While some commentators have criticised this stance, it is further evidence of the GAA's evolution as a body and willingness to modernise. Ultimately, it is more important that we bring the people of Ireland together in an agreed way than it is to resist change on the basis of symbols. The Irish symbols of the flag and anthem are supposed to represent the Irish nation. If, however, during a process of change, these symbols become a barrier to bringing the people of Ireland together, then of course they must change, with the support of citizens.

The GAA could usefully be deployed during a referendum on Irish unity in Northern Ireland by pointing to the changes it has made – in recent years it has made great strides to become more inclusive, not least in the way the organisation warmly welcomed Queen Elizabeth II to Croke Park during her tour of Ireland in 2011.

Croke Park in 2007 saw the England rugby team play Ireland, with their national anthem 'God Save the Queen' ringing through the stadium – years ago, this may never have happened, particularly after the tragic events of 1920. It was only in 2005 that the GAA finally allowed rugby and soccer to be played at Croke Park. This was important for both political and economic reasons, as the national stadium at Lansdowne Road was being redeveloped and therefore unavailable.[191] 'Garrison Games' such as soccer and rugby were banned from being played by members of the GAA until 1971.[192] While Unionists may wish to criticise the GAA for not doing more, the response should be quite straightforward: there have been substantial changes already and there may be more by agreement, following a vote in favour of reunification. A simple question which would stump most Unionists, particularly the narrow-minded DUP, is what compromises or changes have they undertaken? Other than those they accepted begrudgingly to get their hands on power, there is very little that they can point to. It would be a debate where they would clearly be on the back foot and on uncomfortable terrain.

For decades, hard-line Unionists castigated the Irish Republic as being backwards-looking and under the malign influence of religion. That can no longer be claimed with any credibility. Ireland now represents an open, transparent and outward-looking country. The DUP viewpoint is to hold onto what they have, refuse to support equal marriage, seek to frustrate the right to access abortion and demonstrate hostility to immigrants, as a prominent DUP MP made blatantly obvious when they were caught on microphone agreeing to 'get the ethnics out'.[193]

Part Three: Thriving After the Vote for Unity

Governance

PICTURE THE SCENE: the people of Ireland, North and Republic of, have spoken; the UK government and the Secretary of State for Northern Ireland after consultation with the Irish government have agreed to hold a unity referendum; fearmongering and negativity from hard-line Unionists is unsuccessful; vested interests in the Republic warning about the dangers of unity are rejected by voters; the unity campaign is strong, positive, far-reaching and it inspires citizens across the island of Ireland; representatives from business, community groups and wider society all set out a positive vision for Irish unity; Irish citizens from all over the world come home to have their say; we come together as a nation; influential figures from all reaches of the Irish diaspora endorse the reunification of our island; a poll is held; people vote with hope for a New Ireland; a majority of votes declare we will have Irish unity. We are successful in achieving the reunification of Ireland and, after 100 years, at last we can say that the time of division on our island is coming to an end. We have achieved our goal.

But what's next? The campaign for Irish unity will not end when we vote for it, that is just the start of the journey. We will have to alter the structure of our new nation, beginning with how our new island is governed, including how we oversee the running of our towns and cities, to provide effective public services on an all-Ireland basis.

When both the UK and Ireland were part of the EU it was feasible to consider the possibility of joint authority, where the Northern Ireland region would be under the joint custody of the Irish and British governments, on the path to Irish unity as a transitional state. However, now that Ireland is in the EU and the UK is outside of it, there can be no halfway house. Northern Ireland has been half-in, half-out of the UK since its foundation. We do not want to see it suffering the same fate within a New Ireland. History has shown that temporary solutions tend to have a long-lasting impact. Look at partition – we are still suffering its effects one hundred years later.

Structurally, we already have the Good Friday Agreement and this will continue to provide a context for shared rights within Irish unity – it provides a way forward for both the holding of a unity referendum and ensuring that East–West relations post-reunification are maintained. There is also the EU structure that will continue to provide a strong framework for Ireland, in terms of safeguarding rights and equality for all. It provides a platform for our continued health, prosperity and protection of our environment.

The UK is a unitary state. Some hoped that there would be a move to a federal UK after the Scottish independence referendum in 2014, but it did not happen. If we look at both Canada and the United States of America, they moved from a confederation to a full feder-ation of provinces and territories (Canada) and states (USA). There has been much talk about whether the Northern Ireland Assem-bly (Legislature) and Northern Ireland Executive (Government) should continue after reunification. If this is considered necessary for a limited period, to provide reassurance to the Unionist minority post-reunification then it may be acceptable. However, my clear preference is full integration. Closing Stormont is not a hostile act towards Unionism – it is a statement of intent that we want Union-ism to be brought into the Irish political mainstream.

We must move straight from being part of the UK to Irish unity, through a united structure of governance. Sadly, some Unionists have relished the potential for increased differences between North and South ever since the UK left the EU. A political philosophy that cele-brates the potential for division is a deeply flawed one.

After a vote for unity, the Irish Republic will likely have to hold a further referendum to make the necessary changes to its constitution which will cover governance structures. We must make sure that the post-referendum process is about building Irish unity, not allowing anti-Irish unity groups to block or delay this important work. We also want to bring forward a package of constitutional proposals in a way that minimises the need for multiple referendums. This is par-ticularly important as the Irish Supreme Court has made decisions to require referendums for what it perceives to be significant constitu-tional change, such as the incorporation of new EU treaties.

Local government

After reunification, the best way to build a New Ireland will be through devolving power to the local levels, to keep democracy close to the people – local councils should be empowered as much as possible. City region deals in Belfast, Derry and Newry will help to develop trade and integration on an all-Ireland basis.

Local councils have different structures and functions in the North and South. Irish unity will require balanced devolution to councils as we want citizens to experience the same type of government across the island, rather than have different powers devolved to local government based on their geographic location. The Irish Republic has consulted on introducing directly elected mayors in proposed city regions. While the results were mixed as only some places voted in favour, this is something that could be rolled out across Ireland after reunification. However, we must keep in mind that in the North, in particular, there could be a danger that locally elected mayors would lead to a sectarian headcount, which would be unhelpful. Local government, like central government, should continue to be elected through the Single Transferable Vote, a proportional representation form of government. This is the most fair way of reflecting what voters intended and makes cooperative working across political parties necessary to get things done.

Belfast City Council has successfully lobbied the UK government for a City Region Deal to enable the city and surrounding area to unlock additional spending and other powers to help continue the development of the region. Within Irish unity, additional powers such as those for transport, regeneration and citywide infrastructure as requested by the Council's Chief Executive,[194] should be given to Belfast City Council to help unleash its true potential as the second city of Ireland. As previously mentioned, Belfast was once the economic powerhouse of the island and within a streamlined, unified Ireland, it has the potential to become a key economic driver again.

An all-Ireland Civil Service

Sam McBride's excellent book *Burned* sets out some of the challenges faced in Northern Ireland in terms of political dysfunction.[195] The political discourse in Northern Ireland is all too rarely focused on making the lives of its citizens better or how to grow the economy and increase investment in public services. The Northern Ireland Civil Service is in a difficult place because there are only a small number of opportunities in any given policy area – it is rare for civil servants to be able to develop their expertise in one sector. It also has regular experience of having to run Northern Ireland without a functioning

Northern Ireland Assembly and Executive. The Northern Ireland Civil Service has a policy of requiring people to move departments on promotion, thereby ensuring that they cannot build up sustained expertise in a given area. There is an agenda to restructure Whitehall and the UK Civil Service but, on most bread-and-butter issues, this essentially only covers England. The Northern Ireland Civil Service is separate to the UK Civil Service, whereas the civil services in Scotland and Wales are not separate.

In the longer term, one civil service for the island of Ireland is logical. While it may not be possible to move towards this in the short term (before unity) it would be helpful to have increased secondments and transfers between North and South. Also, the Northern Ireland Civil Service could seek more secondments from the private and third sectors to help bring in the needed expertise temporarily in the transitional period as it integrates with the civil service in the rest of Ireland.

While re-joining the Commonwealth can be considered, the key focus should be on ensuring East–West linkages post-Brexit and after reunification. To help achieve this there should be the continuation of the British-Irish Parliamentary Assembly, and the British-Irish Council should also be strengthened. The Brookings Institution could provide independent advice on effective government after Irish unity has been secured.[196]

The Institute of Politics/School of Government at Harvard, using their expertise, could offer a template for developing structures for reunification. This institution has extensive knowledge of how government should operate effectively which could be harnessed to plan out a unified structure for Ireland. Sláintecare has set out plans for how universal healthcare can be delivered in the Irish Republic; the Bengoa report written by a panel of healthcare and social care experts set out improvements for the health and social care service in Northern Ireland.[197] We need to adopt an approach to national and local government on an all-Ireland basis which provides the best possible services while delivering efficiencies.

Unity must be all-Ireland

We must ensure that all four provinces of Ireland have the same representation in a New Ireland and there is not an asymmetric union of Ireland where Northern Ireland has a different status. We do not want it to be Dublin centric. We only have to look at how damaging it is for Britain that the UK is London centric. The best way to aid Northern Ireland is to have its political structures fully integrated into the all-Ireland framework, which is why we must absorb the Northern Ireland Assembly into the national parliament in Dublin.

Virtuous circles will be created by having TDs (Teachtaí Dála, members of the Dáil Éireann) engage on issues across Ireland. The old Northern Ireland Parliament established in 1921 was designed to entrench partition and give Unionists permanent control, therefore it has no place within Irish unity, where all will be equal. The diverse population should help as in the South it is no longer Orange versus Green. In an all-Ireland Parliament, 112 representatives would be needed to form a majority government;[198] in an all-Ireland Dáil there would potentially be around 223 TDs, so approximately 160 TDs in the 26 counties and 63 TDs in the 6 counties. The proportional representative method of voting would mean that no single party is likely to win a majority, everyone would have to work together; everyone would have a voice. This should help to assuage any fears about a Sinn Féin government having unfettered powers after unity, as the system is highly unlikely to deliver a majority for any party.

A time limit on the NI Assembly

The more layers of government there are, the more barriers we are putting in place between the people and those who are elected to represent them. Northern Ireland as a region would have a majority in favour of Irish unity after a successful referendum, so what would be the point of keeping a power structure that was designed to ensure a permanent Unionist majority within it? There have been vast periods without a functioning assembly since the Good Friday Agreement. The old Northern Ireland Parliament, which operated for the first fifty years after partition, did not have the support of the entire region. The last thing we want in a newly established nation is unwieldy, unsupported and ineffective governance that will diminish the many benefits of unity.

We can hope that Unionists will participate in the proposed new national Parliament, but there is unfortunately a history of walk-outs, strikes and protests in Unionism. This will not serve people well, as Unionism must have a voice to ensure the stability of the entire nation. However, we do not want to finally achieve unity only to create a Bantustan for Unionists within the government.[199] Therefore, stipulating that there must be a set number of Unionists in government is wrong. A new government must be built from natural coalitions resulting from negotiation between political parties, with safeguards for all minorities. The enforced mandatory coalition at Stormont, while introduced with the best intentions at an early stage of the peace process, did not create an effective government. It enabled people from different parties to take up positions as government ministers without committing to an agreement to collectively deliver on a set of priorities for its citizens.

If it proves necessary to maintain the Northern Ireland Assembly, it should be for a strictly time-limited period, for example, 10 years maximum. It should also have a clear mandate to deliver integration with the rest of Ireland and perhaps only spend money that the UK government has provided during a transition. MLAs should also sit as TDs in Dublin, so they would have a dual role during this time-limited period.

People are frustrated with the gridlock at Stormont. To those who would say that abolishing Stormont shows that unity is an anti-Unionist project, I would say that it is evidence of the opposite. We want to fully embed Unionism within the legislature of the new state, not keep it off to one side. It has been made clear that Unionism's voice will be strengthened through a single national Parliament, so we do not need to maintain the Stormont assembly indefinitely to safeguard British/unionist people and their identity. We can do this by fully integrating them into the political structures in the national Parliament.

Stormont has simply never functioned effectively, neither the 1921–72 parliament, nor the Sunningdale Assembly from 1973–74, nor the 1982–86 Assembly nor the Assembly set up in 1998 under the terms of the Good Friday Agreement. Whether it is the structure or the makeup of parties elected that has had a negative impact is open to debate.

Northern Ireland's politicians need to be integrated into a national Parliament that raises and spends taxes. A legislature that does not raise its own revenue can never be a fully mature decision-making body as it is just spending money which is allocated to it from another government.

Imagine we have voted for unity and then are faced with another economic or health crisis like COVID-19. Do we think it would be acceptable to have two different approaches on this small island again? That is what could happen if Stormont is maintained and it is why we need to have one set of government institutions and end the Northern Ireland Assembly after unity. One government equals one approach.

The Northern Ireland Executive is the only government in the UK and Ireland where a minister has not resigned due to delivery failure, despite there being many failures. The aspiration for a successful, joined-up government remains unfulfilled more than 20 years after the Good Friday Agreement.

Outdated structure of the UK

Formed during British imperialism, the United Kingdom is now an outdated, historic structure that has not evolved sufficiently enough to recognise the fact the empire no longer exists, nor that there is a need for the centre of power in London to be replaced by a structure that gives greater autonomy across the UK. The UK narrowly avoided dismantlement in 2014 after the Scottish independence referendum. There was a small window of opportunity to implement the change to its operation that may have kept the UK together by loosening its ties; however, the UK is still essentially a highly centralised state, where the majority of the control and funding resides in London.

Devolution began to address this in a tokenistic manner, by giving the impression that legislatures across the UK would be able to make decisions, but the funding was still controlled from London. Full federalism was needed to keep the UK together post-2014 – it was resisted then and will not happen now. Clearly, some within the UK government see Brexit as an opportunity to take power away from the devolved institutions in Scotland, Wales and Northern Ireland.

The Brexit vote is the first sign of a reawakened English Nationalism which is resentful at the Celtic parts of the UK for appearing to have some of the benefits of control without paying the full cost. The economics of this can be argued but the perception for many in the English areas who voted leave is that there is an urgent need to redress the balance and if that means an end to the UK union, so be it.

Legacy Issues – Dealing with the Past

'The only limit to our realization of tomorrow will be our doubts of today.'[200]

Franklin D Roosevelt

THERE ARE MANY challenging issues arising from our island's troubled past. Building Irish unity is about peace and prosperity for the future, but to achieve this we must be able to address the past in a way that allows us to move forward in an inclusive manner.

There is a lot of good work being done by cross-community groups and victims' organisations across Northern Ireland in local communities. These people are making a positive impact on a daily basis. The UK government is seeking to bring a conclusion to the legacy issue, although their latest proposals on a partial amnesty for those who have come forward to confess their part in crimes during The Troubles do not have widespread support among those who were directly impacted by the violence. Objections have been raised by republicans and loyalists. Addressing legacy issues needs to be managed in a way which helps us to heal from the past – it cannot simply be seen as a way to provide those who committed crimes possible immunity from prosecution. We must not dismiss the hurt and pain of families who have suffered during the conflict; however, we cannot postpone our future until these issues are resolved – progress must be concurrent. Let's find healing on a UK and Ireland basis, not in isolation.

In June 1995, Nelson Mandela said in the Houses of Parliament, Cape Town, that he regretted the loss of life, anywhere and under any circumstances:

> Let us, therefore, dedicate ourselves, in memory of all the lives lost in conflict, to working together to seek solutions to the problems which generate conflict. We must bring an end to violence... As long as we fail to tackle these problems, we will...undermine our capacity to improve the quality of life of our people, millions of whom still live in abject poverty.[201]

There have been suggestions in the past for a truth and reconciliation commission as operated in South Africa after the end of apartheid. However, to undertake something similar in Ireland, there would need to be clear parameters and a timescale for completion. Too often inquiries incur too great a financial cost over too long a time. Even if such a truth process was established to help to heal society, some may seek to use such a process to aggressively pursue narrow political agendas which are based on bitterness and divisiveness. We do not want to give those people fuel to further their backwards-looking, negative dogma.

It must be acknowledged that there was a great deal of hurt and anguish caused by different sides of the political conflict. Unionists had every right to feel that they were targeted because of their religion and political beliefs, just as nationalists did. It was a fact that this happened, just as mixed marriages between Catholics and Protestants were targeted. The terrorist campaigns and criminal activity by loyalists and republicans, and the apparent collusion of some in the security services, are also to be deplored. It was a dirty war where people across Ireland undertook deplorable acts against each other. People believed that the Unionist government pre-1973 gerrymandered electoral districts and blocked housing for Catholics; there was a perception that the Irish government did not pursue republican terrorists as fully as they perhaps could have done.

It is completely understandable that Unionists did not wish to engage in any discussion about Irish unity during The Troubles, but now the conditions are fundamentally different. There is full acceptance of the need for consent and support for law and order by all the main political parties.

Martin Luther King, in his speech accepting the Nobel Peace Prize in 1964, said:

> Violence as a way of achieving racial justice is both impractical and immoral. I am not unmindful of the fact that violence often brings about momentary results. Nations have frequently won their independence in battle. But despite temporary victories, violence never brings permanent peace. It solves no social problem: it merely creates new and more complicated ones.

> Violence is impractical because it is a descending spiral
> ending in destruction for all.[202]

All open-minded people would surely agree that former Deputy First Minister of Northern Ireland (and self-confessed former IRA commander) Martin McGuinness showed real leadership by standing next to the Unionist First Minister and Chief Constable of the PSNI calling out dissident republicans as 'traitors to the island of Ireland' when they murdered police officers and soldiers.[203] He also showed, by example, an ability to build an agreed Ireland by meeting with the Queen on her official visit to Ireland. There has been some positive leadership on the Unionist side when their elected representatives have attended GAA games, but this good work needs to continue.

The past will always be disputed as there are differing interpretations of events. Some people pursued their objectives peacefully, some did not. All violence must be regretted and as an island, we must commit to purely peaceful means going forward. Of course, building Irish unity is about creating a more prosperous and peaceful future for all who call this small island home. There were dark periods in our history and we need to learn our lesson to ensure we do not repeat the same mistakes.

Legacy issues need to be addressed to help everyone move on. There is the question of whether those who give evidence about their past deeds should be entitled to immunity or be at risk of imprisonment. This is a difficult and emotive issue; however, we want any truth and reconciliation process to be about moving society forward. There must be no glorification of past violence and respectful acknowledgement of victims must be achieved.

Ultimately, a truth and reconciliation process is unlikely to be effective, as there would never be full participation – people will just not be willing to publicly admit all of the wrongs they have done. The fact that there would be no justice meted out either, makes the whole process one that is riddled with problems. Some people would make it their full-time occupation to drag up every story and seek to pull us back as a people and whip up outrage. Therefore, while it is far from satisfactory, we have to realise that a commission would have the reverse effect to its stated aim of helping people to move on from The Troubles. The best way to deal with this, in a way that is not adversarial, is perhaps to invite people to record their stories and deposit writings of their experience of The Troubles in an all-island digital catalogue which would be accessible to all. A digital archive would enable all stories and experiences to be collated, so that future generations can read and hear about all sides of our history. Canada has a National Centre for Truth and Reconciliation which includes digital archives. These enable visitors to understand the history of Canada and the mistreatment of Indigenous Peoples.[204] Hopefully, if we adopt a similar approach in Ireland, this could help to ensure that we do not forget the past, but that we learn from it, while we build a future together.

Lessons from Other Countries

HISTORICALLY, IRISH REPUBLICANISM has identified and sought alliances with places such as Catalonia, the Basque Country, South Africa and Palestine, as they sympathised with their political aims and sought to place the quest for Irish unity in an international context. While no two political situations are the same, we can always learn from other nations. Each of these listed, as with Quebec and Scotland, are described as separatist campaigns by their opponents.

I know that Canada is not perfect – there is still much work to be done with the First Nations, 150 years after the founding of the country. Similarly, Irish unity will not miraculously resolve all our problems overnight. But creating a New Ireland will give us a framework to build on, so that we can address the many blights caused before and since partition.

Irish unity should seek to align with the efforts to bring together both parts of Germany and also Vietnam North and South after its war in the late 1950s to mid-'70s. The ongoing efforts to build a peaceful relationship between North and South Korea should also be a reference point and we must learn from the ongoing blockages to attempt to reunite Cyprus, too.

If we look back throughout history, we can see the problems caused by the partition of India, at the time of the British withdrawal into India and Pakistan. The ongoing tensions there are a reminder of how disputed borders and ethnic strife can have long-running negative impacts on a country and its people. In Ireland, it is not that the location of the border on the island is disputed, it is that most people on the island do not want a border at all. The prospect of a new hard border after Brexit is horrifying for all sane people across the island, regardless of political outlook.

Vietnam has been transformed since effective partition was removed. It is a country that, like Ireland, has suffered significantly at the hands of invaders and was partitioned by a foreign power. But in recent years, Vietnam has become reinvigorated and reunited. It now has a positive story to tell on tourism and the growth of its indigenous businesses. The similarity between Ireland and Vietnam was acknowledged by President Higgins of Ireland when he spoke about the two countries' common experiences dealing with colonisation and that both countries had undertaken an 'irrepressible struggle for independence' on a state visit to the country in 2016.[205] While the Irish Republic and Northern Ireland have both seen their tourism industries grow, Northern Ireland has a significant amount of growth still ahead if it is to catch up with the size of the industry for the rest of the island. Reunification is likely to lead to increased interest in Ireland from across the world with the message that Ireland has come through a difficult period, most recently The Troubles and the risk of economic vandalism by an English-driven Brexit. A reunited Ireland will be a beacon of hope for the world, one that will be able to attract new investment and people to its shores, as its liberal future is secured within the European Union.

While each scenario is different, there are lessons we can learn by looking at other countries and how they have successfully or otherwise implemented reunification processes. If we look at Germany, the East is still, in many ways, seeking to catch up to the old West Germany. This is reflected in part by the politics, with greater support for AfD (Alternative for Deutschland), a hard-right party, in the eastern part of the country. While Germany is the economic powerhouse of the European Union, the economic growth in the East still falls behind the West. Germany is still going through a process of reintegration nearly three decades after the Berlin wall came down.

Former Taoiseach Enda Kenny referenced the process of reunification in Germany shortly after the UK voted to leave the EU. This has been held up as an example and precedent for facilitating Northern Ireland to immediately re-join the EU, in the event of Irish reunification. There are important lessons for Ireland from the role the EU played in the reunification of Germany. Former Taoiseach Charles Haughey, while chairing the European Council, played a key role in securing reunification, by offering support for German unification at a special informal European Summit which he arranged. He also invited the Prime Minister of East Germany to a Dublin Summit, despite opposition from some other European leaders.[206] The West German Chancellor Helmut Kohl said that German unification would not have happened without Haughey's support.

There are few permanent alliances in geopolitics, which is why being part of the EU is so important. Look at the African Union (AU) and how it is being developed. The AU brokered the African Continental Free Trade Area (AfCFTA).[207] This was set up to create a single market for goods and services, as well as to allow for the free movement of people across continental Europe. According to the United Nations Economic Commission for Africa, this was predicted to increase intra-African trade by 52 per cent by 2022.[208] While the COVID-19 pandemic will have impacted this, it shows that, as the world we live in becomes more turbulent, there are many benefits to being part of a large economic bloc. For Ireland, the EU provides a level of geopolitical security that would otherwise not be available for such a small country.

The Sunshine policy of positive engagement by South Korea with North Korea was not successful in the sense that it did not lead to immediate reunification of the peninsula. However, it did set out an ambitious narrative that there could be a constructive dialogue between the two countries. Cyprus is an example of particular note. At the time of writing, the negotiations to bring the two parts of the island together are still ongoing – this is not the first attempt in this century to reunite the island. In a referendum held in 2004 on the Annan Plan, Northern Cyprus (the part occupied since 1973 by Turkish troops) voted to reunite with the rest of the island; the southern part of the island, however, voted against reunification.[209] We want to avoid a similar fate befalling Ireland. The Annan Plan proposed a federation of two states; Irish unity must lead to a unitary state.

Unity will take time

The reconstruction work carried out in the USA after the American Civil War was ongoing for many years. Some may even say that the effort to bring the North and South together is still a work in progress. In the USA, there were many problems with reconstruction after the end of the Civil War. Progress to ensure African Americans had the same rights as their Caucasian neighbours after initial steps forward, fell back and it was not until the 1960s that comprehensive Civil Rights legislation was passed by President Johnson. The civil rights movement in Northern Ireland was inspired by the movement in the US. John Hume referenced his admiration for Martin Luther King in his lecture after being awarded the Nobel Peace Prize.[210] As Hume rightly said in his Nobel Peace Prize speech:

> Difference is an accident of birth and it should therefore never be the source of hatred or conflict. The answer to difference is to respect it. Therein lies a most fundamental principle of peace – respect for diversity.[211]

There is a need to guard against extremes seeking to take advantage during a time of change after the vote for Irish unity. We must be prepared for the fact that creating unity successfully will take time, but that does not make it any less worthwhile. Just as the USA is still dealing with the repercussions of the Civil War, so we must acknowledge that the challenges of reunification and our own violent history will not disappear overnight, after a successful vote in favour of unity. The Federalist Papers sought to address potential division caused by religious sects in the US – there can be lessons for Ireland from there.

Where We Want to End Up

'We cannot predict the future but we can invent it'[212]

Dennis Gabor

NONE OF THIS is going to be easy. We have seen with Brexit and the first Scottish independence referendum, that promising something will be quick and easy, when it will not, undermines the project you are pursuing.

Benedict Anderson talked about a nation as being an 'imagined community'.[213] By this he meant that a nation is a socially constructed community, which is brought to life through the imagination of people who consider themselves to be part of a particular group. It may be a cliché to say it but that does not make it any less true.

It is not whether we can afford to be reunited, it is whether we can afford not to be. The great reset that we are experiencing as the worst impacts of the COVID-19 pandemic come to an end provides us with a unique opportunity to do things differently, reassess our priorities and look at what matters – a better future for us all.

I think it is important to encourage people into politics, for those who want to make a positive difference in society. For example, in the USA there is still a reverence for those who want to go into public service, as highlighted by former President Barack Obama. It should be welcomed and celebrated as a legitimate and worthy career choice.

We want to have a New Ireland where there is a complete separation of church and state – integrated education and housing should be the default; there needs to be a secular constitution, secular schools and secular architecture of the state generally. There will always be a role for faith-based schools, that is part of free choice, but there should be a presumption in favour of the schooling together of those from all faiths and none, in a neutral environment.

While the King or his successor will no longer be head of state, the British monarch will continue to be welcome in Ireland. Just as Queen Elizabeth II came to Dublin Castle in 2011 and spoke in Irish, the relations between the two islands of Ireland and Britain will remain strong. The Queen as Head of State for the UK paid her respects and laid a wreath at the Garden of Remembrance in Dublin, to all those who lost their lives in the fight for Irish freedom. There is a warmth of feeling between our two islands which will continue.

We want a peaceful and prosperous island firmly anchored within the EU, using this as a launching pad to trade with the rest of the world. Just as reunification may, with time, help to drain the tribal and sectarian nature of Northern politics, hopefully, it will help to end the civil war nature of politics in the rest of the island

In terms of an all-Ireland Dáil after reunification, there will be a negotiation to form a new government. It is highly unlikely that a single party will be able to form a government alone, which encourages consensus-style politics and guards against a single party receiving a majority of seats despite securing a minority of votes, unlike the FPTP (First Past the Post) system used in the UK Parliament. If Unionists choose not to participate in the new government, then the Irish government can focus its engagement on civic unionism instead, until such times as political representatives are willing to do so.

We want Irish unity where we continue to welcome immigrants to our island, just as we travel to all parts of the globe. Irish unity must be focused on economic growth, as a small state where decisions are taken transparently, as close to the citizens as possible, with a pro-enterprise approach. Ireland must continue to be focused on projecting its peace-keeping ethos. There can be no question of Ireland leaving the EU – Ireland is a proud European country.

If the unity campaign is handled with dignity and maturity, we should be able to come through it with an enhanced relationship with the UK. The Brexit fallout has damaged the partnership approach between Britain and Ireland which had been in place since the signing of the Good Friday Agreement; a vote for Irish unity will help to reactivate it again.

Just as Reagan famously asked voters if they were better off than four years ago during the presidential debates in 1980 (the answer was no), so the unity campaign should ask unionists in Northern Ireland if they are better off now than before partition. Before the creation of Northern Ireland, as the economist David McWilliams stated:

> If we go back to 1907, two-thirds of the industrial output of the entire island of Ireland came from the six counties that would go on to become Northern Ireland, with activity largely centred on Belfast. This was where

all Irish industry was located. Ulster was industrial and innovative; northern entrepreneurs and inventors were at the forefront of industrial innovation. By 1911, Belfast was the biggest city in Ireland with a population of 386,947 — comfortably outstripping that of Dublin at 304,802. Belfast was also growing rapidly. The northeast was by far the richest part of the island.[214]

Before the COVID-19 pandemic, the Irish Republic's industrial output was ten-times the size of Northern Ireland. Irish unity will enable us to rebuild our post-pandemic economy in a balanced and sustainable way for the long term.

Going forward now that the UK has left the EU, Ireland will have to work harder to secure alliances without the country that was formerly its closest ally. There is no reason to think that Ireland should seek a permanent alliance of specific countries – any coalition will change depending on the topic. There is a well of goodwill for Ireland within the EU, as a fully committed member which is also a net contributor. This should be leveraged to get the best deal on any issue for the country. The fact that Ireland has not been blighted significantly by irrational Euroscepticism or a deluded sense of self-importance, means that the Government can afford to take part in grown-up politics and adopt a pragmatic approach to its interactions with other European countries. One example of this has been how Ireland has signed up to several security and defence capability projects in cooperation with other EU countries, under the PESCO (Permanent Structured Cooperation) initiative.[215] The prospect of an agreement to increase Corporate Tax rates, following the suggestion by the Biden–Harris Administration, is an issue which needs to be monitored carefully.

Ireland may not be perfect, but it is on the right path. After unity, Northern Ireland will no longer feel like it is an afterthought and inconvenience, as it does currently for the rest of the UK. Gone will be the days when the island of Ireland is used to leverage better deals for the UK government, as it was during the fiasco of Brexit.

This New Ireland will be a place where all are welcome. The Irish people have been successful immigrants around the world who have ended up in powerful and important jobs, as leaders. However, they have also managed to keep a strong sense of their own identity and community. Research shows that the economy works better when highly skilled immigrants come into a country and after reunifica-tion, we must maintain this positive approach. Ireland has strug-gled when there has been a clash of cultures between unionists and nationalists and between pro-treaty and anti-treaty. The best way to overcome this is to add more diversity to society, enrich our culture and help us move away from a binary 'us or them'. Let's give every-one a shot at tapping into the Irish dream, in the way that people have talked about the American dream.

The potential shape of Irish unity will continue to evolve in the period ahead of the unity referendum. We live in a time of huge uncer-tainty and rapid change. However, one thing remains constant: the clear logic for this small, beautiful island to be reunited, to reclaim its place as a single nation, healing after centuries of division and partition, placed firmly at the centre of the European Union.

Conclusion: A Summary of My Support for Unity

MY AIM FOR this book was to outline a balanced, rational, fact-based argument of why pursuing Irish unity is the best decision for *all* who live on the island of Ireland – Catholic, Protestant, agnostic; nationalist/republican, unionist/loyalist; from North to South, East to West.

What had been a long-term aspiration of Irish unity for me, since the signing of the Good Friday Agreement, became an urgent necessity, due to the disaster of Brexit. It does not hurt to reiterate my own reasons for campaigning for a New Ireland.

I went to university in Scotland just at the time of the first ceasefire in 1994 and was able to appreciate how all of us from across Ireland have a lot in common; after the first ceasefire, I did not feel that stubborn, burning need to say 'NO!' immediately to any talk or consideration of a 'United Ireland'.

I always wanted to be Irish and realised I did not need to have a foaming-of-the-mouth hatred of the English to be Irish; I realised others agreed with my thinking, that you do not need to be a particular religion, speak a certain language or play GAA games to be Irish.

I studied Irish history a bit (which I did not get to do at school, unfortunately) and realised partition has been a disaster for both parts of the island; normal politics, without the traps of constitutional debates, will only happen after the island is reunited.

I realised it was too complicated trying to explain what being Northern Irish is, because I am and always have been Irish; I have always loved the Ulster and Ireland rugby teams and used that to help develop my sense of Irishness, which does not have to be the same as anyone else's.

I worked in Scotland and listened to the SNP talking about soft nationalism and fiscal autonomy at their conference in 2002 and realised that having control over fiscal levers (within an EU context) is very appealing.

I want to be part of an outward-looking liberal country with a positive, strong identity internationally while staying part of the EU; looking at the steady drift to the right by the Tories in England, I have been horrified as they have marched to an EU exit.

Truly, I am tired of living in a siege mentality.

Endnotes

1   Lundy was a governor at the time of the siege of Derry in 1689, who wanted to open the gates of the city to those who were laying siege as he believed that people would die otherwise. It is a pejorative phrase used by unionists to criticise those from a unionist background who now favour Irish unity.

2   Aschcroft, M, 'Brexit, the Border and the Union', lordashcroft-polls.com/2018/06/brexit-the-border-and-the-union/#more-15616 19/06/2018

3   FitzPatrick, S, 'Brits increasingly don't care whether Northern Ireland remains in the UK', YouGov, yougov.co.uk/topics/politics/articles-reports/2020/04/22/brits-increasingly-dont-care-whether-northern-irel 22/04/2020

4   '2022 State of the Union Address by President von der Leyen', European Commission, ec.europa.eu/commission/presscorner/detail/ov/speech_22_5493 14/09/2022

5   'Public support for the Protocol is edging up in Northern Ireland, yet concerns persist', Queens University Belfast, qub.ac.uk/News/All-news/2022/public-support-Protocol-increases.html 29/06/2022

6   'Northern Ireland Secretary Shailesh Vara considering MLA pay', ITV News, itv.com/news/utv/2022-08-18/remember-you-duty-ni-secretary-tells-mlas-with-people-struggling-to-eat 18/08/2022

7   'Northern Ireland Business Brexit Working Group – Written Evidence (FUI0025)', committees.parliament.uk/writtenevidence/109037/pdf, 07/06/2022

8   'Nationality and Borders Act 2022', UK Public General Acts, legislation.gov.uk/ukpga/2022/36/contents/enacted 2022

9   Simpson, C, 'New British rules for non-Irish EU citizens who want to cross the border branded "absurd"', *The Irish News*, irishnews.com/news/northernirelandnews/2022/07/22/news/new_british_rules_for_non-irish_eu_citizens_who_want_to_cross_the_border_branded_absurd_-2778183, 22/07/2022

10 Ryan, P, 'Britain may get "turned off" by Northern Ireland, warns Martin', Independent.ie, independent.ie/irish-news/politics/britain-may-get-turned-off-by-northern-ireland-warns-martin-39430120.html 28/07/2020

11 Fagan, M, 'Number of EU workers in Northern Ireland fell by 26% since Brexit vote', thedetail, thedetail.tv/articles/number-of-eu-workers-in-northern-ireland-fell-by-26-since-brexit-vote 29/06/2018

12 'Northern Ireland Protocol: UK Legal Obligations', Volume 679, UK Parliament, 08/09/2020

13 Morris, S, 'Westminster warned as poll shows record backing for Welsh Independence', *The Guardian*, theguardian.com/uk-news/2021/mar/04/westminster-warned-as-poll-shows-record-backing-for-welsh-independence 04/03/2021

14 McGowan, C, 'Emma de Souza v Home Office', McKeown's Solicitors, mckeowns.com/insights/articles/emma-de-sousa-v-home-office 09/06/2020

15 'Ian Paisley on Irish passports: It's a European document with an Irish harp stuck on posing as a passport', *Belfast Telegraph*, belfast-telegraph.co.uk/news/northern-ireland/ian-paisley-on-irish-passports-its-a-european-document-with-an-irish-harp-stuck-on-posing-as-a-passport-34949658.html 08/08/2016

16 McHugh, M, 'Brexit: Northern Ireland support to "remain" in EU soars to 69%', *Belfast Telegraph*, belfasttelegraph.co.uk/news/brexit/brexit-northern-Ireland-support-to-remain-in-EU-soars-to-69-36928116.html 21/05/2018

17 A notice signed by at least 30 MLAs that is presented to the Speaker. This usually relates to a motion before the NI Assembly and requires a vote on a cross-community basis. This means that for the motion to pass, it must obtain a majority of both designated Unionist and Nationalist MLAs, rather than a simple majority of all MLAs.

18 Beatty, C, Fothergill, S, 'The Impact of Welfare Reform on Northern Ireland', Centre for Regional Economic and Social Research, Sheffield Hallam University, 2013

19 Reported in 'Parliamentary Debates', Northern Ireland House of Commons, Vol XVI, Cols 1091–95, 24/04/1934

20 'David Trimble's Address at the Waterfront Hall, Belfast, Thursday 3 September 1998', CAIN Archive, Ulster University, cain.ulster.ac.uk/events/peace/docs/dt3998.htm 03/09/1998

21 'Quotations on the topic of Discrimination', CAIN web service, Ulster University, cain.ulster.ac.uk/issues/discrimination/quotes.htm

22 McDonald, H, Jowit, J, 'DUP stands by climate change sceptic environment minister', *The Guardian*, theguardian.com/environment/2009/feb/10/sammy-wilson-climate-change 10/02/2009

23 McDonald, H, 'Northern Ireland unionist parties alienating young protestants, study says', *The Guardian*, theguardian.com/uk-news/2017/aug/04/northern-irish-unionist-parties-alienating-young-protestants-study 04/08/2017

24 Tierney, P, 'Work to install GAA pitch at Victoria Park in East Belfast "halted" pending further discussions', BelfastLive, belfastlive.co.uk/sport/gaa/work-install-gaa-pitch-victoria-24659237 03/08/2022

25 Hutton, B, '"Hate campaign" forces Irish language pre-school in east Belfast to move', *The Irish Times*, irishtimes.com/news/education/

hate-campaign-forces-irish-language-pre-school-in-east-belfast-to-move-1.4633054 28/07/2021

26 'Systems, Not Structures – Changing Health and Social Care – Full Report', Department of Health, health-ni.gov.uk/publications/systems-not-structures-changing-health-and-social-care-full-report 25/10/2016

27 'The State of Ireland 2021, Infrastructure and a digital future', Engineers Ireland, engineersireland.ie/listings/resource/688 23/12/2021

28 'Uniting Ireland & its people in peace and prosperity Brexit & the future of Ireland' senatormarkdaly.ie/uniting-ireland--its-people-in-peace--prosperity-brexit--the-future-of-ireland.html

29 Connolly, F, United Nation: *The Case for Integrating Ireland*, Gill Books, Dublin, 2022

30 'Research into the financial cost of the Northern Ireland divide', Deloitte, 2007

31 Gore, A, 'The Climate Crisis is the Battle of our Time, and We Can Win', *New York Times*, algore.com/news/the-climate-crisis-is-the-battle-of-our-time-and-we-can-win 20/09/2019

32 'Modelling Irish Unification', 2015, KLC Consulting, www.cain.ulster.ac.uk/issues/unification/hubner_2015-08.pdf 17/11/2015

33 Ibid.

34 Emanual, R, 'Let's make sure this crisis doesn't go to waste', *The Washington Post*, washingtonpost.com/opinions/2020/03/25/lets-make-sure-this-crisis-doesnt-go-waste/ 25/03/2020

35 Goodier, M, 'UK set to grow slower than every G20 economy except Russia', *The New Statesman*, newstatesman.com/chart-of-the-day/2022/06/uk-economic-growth-slower-every-g20-russia 08/06/2022

36 'Brexit analysis', Office for Budget Responsibility, obr.uk/forecasts-in-depth/the-economy-forecast/brexit-analysis/#assumptions 03/2022

37 Barns-Graham, W, 'Trade between Great Britain, Northern Ireland and Irish Republic continues to change', Institute of Export & International Trade, export.org.uk/news/592886/Trade-between-Great-Britain-Northern-Ireland-and-Irish-Republic-continues-to-change.htm 19/01/2022

38 McCurry, C, 'Cross-border trade continues to soar, figures show', The Irish News, irishnews.com/news/republicofirelandnews/2022/07/18/news/cross-border_trade_continues_to_soar_figures_show-2775149/ 18/07/2022

39 Jordan, D, Race, M, 'Bank of England warns the UK will fall into recession this year', BBC News, bbc.com/news/business-62405037 05/08/2022

40 'Economic forecast for Ireland', European Commission, economy-finance.ec.europa.eu/economic-surveillance-eu-economies/ireland/economic-forecast-ireland_en 14/07/2022

41 'European Economic Forecast – Summer 2022', European Commission, economy-finance.ec.europa.eu/economic-forecast-and-surveys/economic-forecasts/summer-2022-economic-forecast-russias-war-worsens-outlook_en#forecast-for-countries

42 Jones, H, 'EY Brexit tracker finds 7,000 finance jobs have left London for the EU', Reuters, www.reuters.com/world/uk/ey-Brexit-tracker-finds-7000-finance-jobs-have-left-london-eu-2022-03-28/ 29/03/2022

43 'Brexit: UK–Irish relations', 6th Report of Session 2016–17, European Union Committee, House of Lords, pp24

44 Campbell, J, 'Northern Ireland economy growth "slowed in 2018"', BBC News, bbc.com/news/uk-northern-ireland-47306884 20/02/2019

45 'Average Salary and Wage in Ireland', Jobted, jobted.ie/salary 2022

46 'Employee Earnings in Northern Ireland: October 2021', Department for the Economy, economy-ni.gov.uk/news/employee-earnings-northern-ireland-october-2021 26/10/2021

47 Harker, R, 'Pensions: International Comparisons', The Commons Library, House Of Commons, 2022

48 'Exiting the European Union: Publications', HM Government, gov.uk/government/publications/exiting-the-european-union-publications 03/12/2018

49 Parker, G, Thomas, D, 'Border red tape will mean 50,000 new form-fillers after Brexit', ft.com/content/6cf7bba6-598f-11ea-abe5-8e03987b7b20 27/02/2020

50 Bermudez, J S, Cha, V, DuMond, M, 'Making Solid Tracks: North and South Korean Railway Cooperation', Beyond Parallel, beyondparallel.csis.org/making-solid-tracks-north-and-south-Korean-railway-cooperation/ 10/12/2018

51 McWilliams, D, 'Start building and don't stop until we have all-island transport', davidmcwilliams.ie/start-building-and-dont-stop-until-we-have-all-island-transport/ 08/12/2020

52 'DTTAS Quarterly Aviation Statistics Snapshot Quarter 4 2018 Report', Government of Ireland, assets.gov.ie/19082/cdf89777994642828b90e0137beb81fb.pdf 2018

53 Keep, M, 'Brexit: the financial settlement – a summary', the Commons Library, House of Commons, commonslibrary.parliament.uk/research-briefings/cbp-8822/ 29/07/2022

54 Common Agricultural Policy, an EU programme.

55 'Economic Forecast Summary (June 2022)', OECD, oecd.org/economy/ireland-economic-snapshot 2022

56 'European Convention on Human Rights', Council of Europe, 1950

57 'Negotiations and agreements', European Commission, policy.trade.ec.europa.eu/eu-trade-relationships-country-and-region/negotiations-and-agreements_en

58 'Northern Ireland for Security & Defense', Invest Northern Ireland, investni.com/international-business/americas-security

59 McGowan, A, 'We need political stability to stop being seen as a burden', *Belfast Telegraph*, belfasttelegraph.co.uk/business/analysis/we-need-political-stability-to-stop-being-seen-as-burden-31338891.html 29/06/2015

60 Bergin, A, McGuinnes, S, 2020, 'The political economy of a Northern Ireland border poll', Cambridge Journal of Economics, Vol 44, Issue 4, pp 781–812

61 'Project Ireland 2040', Government of Ireland, gov.ie/en/campaigns/09022006-project-ireland-2040/

62 Hade, E J, 'Four out of five tourists say the traditional Irish pub is Ireland's biggest tourist attraction', Independent.ie, independent.ie/irish-news/news/four-out-of-five-tourists-say-the-traditional-irish-pub-is-irelands-biggest-tourist-attraction-30521202.html 19/09/2014

63 Hade, E J, 'Four out of five tourists say the traditional Irish pub is Ireland's biggest tourist attraction', Independent.ie, independent.ie/irish-news/news/four-out-of-five-tourists-say-the-traditional-irish-pub-is-irelands-biggest-tourist-attraction-30521202.html 19/09/2014

64 Harvey, F, 'MPs reject calls by campaigners to enshrine food safety in UK law', The Guardian, theguardian.com/politics/2020/oct/12/mps-reject-calls-by-campaigners-to-enshrine-food-safety-in-uk-law 12/10/2020

65 @SkyNews: 'Work and Pensions Sec @theresecoffey says "getting rid of European regulations" that govern private investment in UK water supplies may improve the country's water infrastucture', Twitter, twitter.com/skynews/status/1557990095332024320?s=21&t=oeRFe-7kARhpoGPLIjnnMNA 12/08/2022

66 Slack A, Tagholm H, Taylor D, '2021 Water Quality Report', Surfers Against Sewage, sas.org.uk/wp-content/uploads/SAS-WaterQualityReport2021-DIGITAL.pdf 2021

67 'The Irish News 4th Attitudinal Survey July 2022', The Institute of Irish Studies, University of Liverpool, 07/2022

68 E H Mikhail, *Brendan Behan, Interviews and Recollections. Vol. 2*, p.186, 1982.

69 Baldwin J, 'Stranger in the Village', *Harpers Magazine*, October 1953 Issue, 1953

70 'The history of the national flag of Canada', Government of Canada, canada.ca/en/canadian-heritage/services/flag-canada-history.html

71 'Ireland End Summer Tour as World's Number One Ranked Team', IRFU, irishrugby.ie/2022/07/18/ireland-end-summer-tour-as-worlds-number-one-ranked-team/ 18/07/2022

72 '"Executive failed" over Irish language strategy, court rules', BBC News, bbc.co.uk/news/uk-northern-ireland-39157612 03/03/2017

73 'Global Ireland: Ireland's Global Footprint to 2025', Government of Ireland, gov.ie/en/campaigns/globalireland/

74   'Ireland's Tricolour – The 1848 legacy of Thomas Francis Meagher', meagherstricolour.com/international-connections/

75   Ní Aodha, G, 'US delegate says "it's up to London" to help find a solution on Protocol', *Belfast Telegraph,* belfasttelegraph.co.uk/news/northern-ireland/us-delegate-says-its-up-to-london-to-help-find-a-solution-on-Protocol-41684195.html 24/05/2022

76   Luxembourg, R as quoted in Freeman, I A, *Seeds of Revolution: A Collection of Axioms, Passages and Proverbs, Volume 1*, iUniverse, pp 588, 2014

77   Heany, S, 'An Open Letter', Field Day Pamphlet Number 2, 1983, Field Day, Derry

78   Google definition.

79   Lynn, B, 'Extract from Speech by Peter Robinson Marking his Reselection as the DUP's Westminster Candidate for East Belfast, 12 November 2004', CAIN Archive, Ulster University, cain.ulster.ac.uk/issues/politics/docs/dup/pr121104.htm

80   '1916 Llyod George Negotiations', Queen's University Belfast, qub.ac.uk/sites/irishhistorylive/IrishHistoryResources/Shortarticlesandencyclopaediaentries/Encyclopaedia/LengthyEntries/1916LlyodGeorge-Negotiations/

81   Milton, J B Stevens, W, *Opus Posthumous*, pp 185, Knopf, 1989,

82   'The Belfast Agreement: An Agreement Reached at the Multi-Party Talks on Northern Ireland', assets.publishing.service.gov.uk/government/uploads/system/uploads/attachment_data/file/1034123/The_Belfast_Agreement_An_Agreement_Reached_at_the_Multi-Party_Talks_on_Northern_Ireland.pdf 1998

83   'Northern Ireland Act 1998', UK Public General Acts, c 47 Part 1 Section 4, 1998

84   'Raymond McCord's Application: Border Poll', judiciaryni.uk/sites/judiciary/files/decisions/Raymond%20McCord's%20Application%20Border%20Poll.pdf 27/04/2020

85   Whysall, A, 'A Northern Ireland Border Poll', The Constitution Unit, University College London, 2019

86   Corr, J, O'Brien, S, 'Northern Irish back border within five years', The Sunday Times, thetimes.co.uk/article/northern-irish-back-border-poll-within-five-years-6ndbkz80s 24/01/2021

87   The Constitution Unit, 2020, 'Interim Report: Executive Summary', Working Group on Unification Referendums on the Island of Ireland, UCL Department of Political Science

88   Morris, S, Scott, J, 'Truss suggests she would "ignore" Nicola Sturgeon if she becomes next PM', Sky News, news.sky.com/story/liz-truss-suggests-she-would-ignore-nicola-sturgeon-if-she-becomes-next-pm-12663818 02/08/2022

89 'Tory leader contender Truss remarks obnoxious – John Swinney' BBC News Scotland, bbc.co.uk/news/av/uk-scotland-62390743 02/08/2022

90 Morris, S, Scott, J, 'Liz Truss suggests she would "ignore" Nicola Sturgeon if she becomes next *PM*', Sky News, news.sky.com/video/jacob-rees-mogg-says-nicola-sturgeon-is-very-often-wrong-and-is-always-moaning-12664006 02/08/2022

91 'Scottish Independence', YouGov, yougov.co.uk/topics/politics/explore/issue/Scottish_independence

92 Government of Ireland, Scottish Government, 'Ireland-Scotland Joint Bilateral Review – Report and Recommendations 2021-25' 2019

93 The BIC brings together the administrations of Ireland, the UK, Scotland, Wales, Northern Ireland, Channel Islands and the Isle of Man. Government representatives and officials come together to discuss issues of mutual interest on a sectoral basis.

94 Ingoldsby, S, 'Results of a future border poll on a knife edge' www.thedetail.tv/articles/a-majority-favour-a-border-poll-on-the-island-of-ireland-in-the-next-10-years 24/02/2020

95 HM Government, The Scottish Government, 'Agreement between the United Kingdom Government and the Scottish Government on a referendum on independence for Scotland', The National Archives, webarchive.nationalarchives.gov.uk/ukgwa/20130109092234/http://www.number10.gov.uk/wp-content/uploads/2012/10/Agreement-final-for-signing.pdf 15/10/2012

96 Colin Harvey (@cjhumanrights) via Twitter, www.twitter.com/cjhumanrights/status/1526973539697434625 18/05/2022

97 'Border poll considered by DUP, says Foster', BBC News, www.bbc.com/news/uk-northern-ireland-21140469 22/01/2013

98 Schulman, T, Weir, P, Dead Poets Society, Buena Vista Pictures Distribution, 1989

99 Daithi McKay via Twitter, www.twitter.com/daithimckay/status/1524094995896090625?s=21&t=D9ocI1I55HmaTzdxFD9kNg 10/05/2022

100 'The Irish News Opinion Poll April 2022', The Institute of Irish Studies, University of Liverpool, 2022,

101 White, B, 2022, 'Northern Ireland (NI) Tracker Poll Results Poll Questions Results – Main Report 28th April 2022 – Main Report – Final', LucidTalk, 024943a0-ce9e-4fe5-85a2-d9f4d3bc845d.usrfiles.com/ugd/024943_18342423111847aa81d5599aboa7dd14.pdf 28/04/2022

102 Black, R, 'Sinn Fein could take more than 30% of vote in Northern Ireland, poll suggests', Belfast Telegraph, belfasttelegraph.co.uk/news/northern-ireland/sinn-fein-could-take-more-than-30-of-vote-in-northern-ireland-poll-suggests-41864549.html 25/07/2022

103 'A history of the peace walls in Belfast', The Week, theweek.co.uk/ northern-ireland/952591/a-history-of-the-peace-walls-in-belfast 21/04/2021

100 '10 New Shared Housing Developments – T:BUC Contributes To Shared Neighbourhood Programme', Community Relations Council, 15/10/2019

104 '10 New Shared Housing Developments – T:BUC Contributes To Shared Neighbourhood Programme', Community Relations Council, 15/10/2019

105 'Lucid Talk poll finds overwhelming support for Integrated Education', Northern Ireland Council for Integrated Education, nicie. org/2021/08/lucid-talk-poll-finds-overwhelming-support-for-integrated-education/

106 Wilson, R, 2020, Running Against the Devil: A Plot to Save America from Trump – and Democrats from Themselves, Crown Forum

107 Haselmayer, M, 2019, 'Negative campaigning and its consequences: a review and a look ahead' Fr Polit 17, 355–372

108 Thanks to Benjy Messner of Precision Strategies for his input on how to run an effective campaign.

109 Allen, J, Parnes, A, 2017, Shattered: Inside Hillary Clinton's Doomed Campaign, Crown Pub INC.

110 'Beware the Irish model of healthcare!', The Lowdown, lowdownnhs. info/comment/beware-the-irish-model-of-healthcare/ 30/09/2019

111 'Mary Lou McDonald says health trumps "flags" in united Ireland debate', breakingnews.ie, breakingnews.ie/ireland/ mary-lou-mcdonald-says-health-trumps-flags-in-united-ireland-debate-1209893.html 07/11/2021

112 'Building A Better Health Service', Fine Gael, finegael.ie/our-policies/ building-a-better-health-service/

113 'Irish people deserve a high quality public health service that provides universal healthcare for all on the basis of medical need – not on the ability to pay', Social Democrats, socialdemocrats.ie/colleges/ building-an-irish-national-health-service/

114 'Sláintecare', The Government of Ireland, gov.ie/en/campaigns/ slaintecare-implementation-strategy/

115 'The Health and Care Act 2022', Patients4NHS, patients4nhs.org.uk/ the-health-and-care-bill/

116 'Regulation (EUO 2016/679 of the European Parliament and of the Council of 27 April 2016 on the protection of natural persons with regard to the processing of personal data and on the free movement of such data, and repealing Directive 95/46/EC (General Data Protection Regulation)', Official Journal of the European Union eur-lex. europa.eu/legal-content/EN/TXT/PDF/?uri=CELEX:32016R0679

117 Palmer, D, 'Data protection: UK to diverge from GDPR in post-Brexit overhaul of privacy rules', ZDNET, zdnet.com/article/data-protection-

to-diverge-from-gdpr-in-post-brexit-overhaul-of-privacy-rules/ 26/08/2021

118 'The Health and Care Act 2022', Patients4NHS, patients4nhs.org.uk/ the-health-and-care-bill/

119 'Barnett formula', Institute for Government, instituteforgovernment. org.uk/explainers/barnett-formula

120 'Connolly, ML, 'NI waiting lists: Health service in court over hospital waits', BBC News Northern Ireland, bbc.com/news/uk-northern-ireland-61569239 24/05/2022

121 Cullen, P, 'One-quarter of State's population on health waiting lists', iThe irish Times, irishtimes.com/health/2022/06/06/one-quarter-of-states-population-on-health-waiting-lists/ 06/07/2022

122 'Europe Digital Health Market Size, Share & Trends Analysis Report By Technology (Tele-healthcare, mHealth, Healthcare Analytics, Digital Health Systems), By Component, By Region, And Segment Forecasts, 2022 – 2030', Grand View Research, grandviewresearch. com/industry-analysis/europe-digital-health-market-report

123 White, B, 'Northern Ireland (NI) Tracker Poll Results Report: Winter (December) 2018 TRACKER POLL QUESTIONS RESULTS - GENERAL REPORT 6th December 2018 – Version 1 – Full Report', LucidTalk, docs.wixstatic.com/ugd/024943_ b89b42d32364461298ba5fe7867d82e1.pdf

124 'The Irish News, 4th Attitudinal Survey July 2022' The Institute of Irish Studies, University of Liverpool, 2022

125 Breen, S, 'How Brexit and a blundering DUP have ensured the Union's days may well be numbered', Belfast Telegraph, belfasttelegraph. co.uk/sunday-life/comment/how-brexit-and-a-blundering-dup-have-ensured-the-unions-days-may-well-be-numbered-41925789.html 21/08/2021

126 'A growing majority in Northern Ireland think Brexit has increased the likelihood of a united Ireland', Queen's University Belfast, 26/05/2022, qub.ac.uk/News/Allnews/2022/majority-northern-ireland-brexit-united-ireland.html

127 Ashcroft, M, 'Northern Ireland: Unification, or the Union?', lordashcroftpolls.com/2021/12/northern-ireland-unification-or-the-union/ 13/12/2021

128 Lorenz, T, 'The White House is briefing TikTok stars about the war in Ukraine', washingtonpost.com/technology/2022/03/11/tik-tok-ukraine-white-house/ 11/05/2022

129 Pedder, S, Revolution Française: Emmanuel Macron and the quest to reinvent a nation, Bloomsbury Continuum, 2018

130 Pfeiffer, D, email entitled 'An Update on Message Box', 09/09/2020

131 Partnership for Public Service, ourpublicservice.org

132 'GETTING READY FOR SHARED SERVICES, FIRST STEPS FOR FEDERAL AGENCIES: ASSESSMENT', Partnership for Public

Service, ourpublicservice.org/wp-content/uploads/2018/09/Getting_
Ready_for_Shared_Services__First_Steps_for_Federal_Agencies__
Assessment-2015.07.08.pdf

133 sunrisemovement.org

134 'A European Green Deal, Striving to be the first climate-neutral continent', European Commission, ec.europa.eu/info/strategy/priorities-
2019-2024/european-green-deal_en

135 'Technical Explanatory Note: North-South Cooperation Mapping
Exercise', Department for Exiting the European Union, HM Government, 07/12/2018

136 Heinlein, R A, Between Planets, Charles Scribner's Sons, New
York, 1951

137 Sheehan, F, 'Majority favour a united Ireland, but just 22pc would
pay for it', Independent.ie, independent.ie/irish-news/centenaries/
centenarypoll/majority-favour-a-united-ireland-but-just-22pc-would-
pay-for-it-40375875.html

138 'Seanad Éireann', House of the Oireachtas, oireachtas.ie/en/visit-and-
learn/how-parliament-works/role-of-the-oireachtas/seanad-eireann

139 Beesley, A, 'EY leaders back membership plan for a post-Brexit united
Ireland', Financial Times, 29/04/2017

140 'Northern Ireland: PEACE PLUS programme will support peace
and prosperity across Northern Ireland and the border counties of
Ireland', European Commission, ec.europa.eu/regional_policy/en/
newsroom/news/2022/07/13-07-2022-northern-ireland-peace-plus-
programme-will-support-peace-and-prosperity-across-northern-
ireland-and-the-border-counties-of-ireland

141 Stevens, W, 'The Well Dressed Man With A Beard' as quoted by
Bloom, H, in Wallace Stevens: The Poems of Our Climate, Cornell
University Press, pp 158, 1980

142 "If it comes to the bit where we have to fight physically to maintain
our freedoms within the UK, so be it" – Loyalist Communities Council Chair', The Nolan Show, BBC, @BBCNolan on Twitter twitter.
com/bbcnolan/status/1356957494476759042

143 Manley, J, 'Widespread concern at LLC warning that violence is "not
off the table"', The Irish News, irishnews.com/news/northernireland-
news/2021/05/20/news/widespread-concern-at-lcc-warning-that-vio-
lence-is-not-off-the-table--2328374/ 20/05/2021

144 'PSNI called in as UDA tells UUP to step aside', News Letter, news-
letter.co.uk/news/politics/psni-called-uda-tells-uup-step-aside-927375
02/11/2019

145 Woodcock, A, 'Coronavirus: Regulator rejects Matt Hancock's
claim that UK got vaccine first because of Brexit', Independent,
independent.co.uk/news/uk/politics/coronavirus-vaccine-matt-han-
cock-mhra-brexit-b1765005.html 02/12/2020

146 Raleigh, V, 'Deaths from Covid-19 (coronavirus): how are they coun-
ted and what do they show?', *The Kings Fund*, kingsfund.org.uk/
publications/deaths-covid-19 23/08/2022

147 'Census in Brief: Ethnic and cultural origins of Canadians: Portraits
of a rich heritage', Statistics Canada, www12.statcan.gc.ca/census-
recensement/2016/as-sa/98-200-x/2016016/98-200-x2016016-eng.
cfm, 25/10/2017

148 'Canada sets record-breaking new immigration targets with international graduates a priority', ICEF Monitor, monitor.icef.com/2022/03/
canada-sets-record-breaking-new-immigration-targets-with-
international-graduates-a-priority/ 02/03/2022

149 Dolan, R, Moore, D, Vasquez, G, 'Residents With Irish Ancestry Are
in All 3,142 U.S. Counties and make up 20% of the Population in
Some', census.gov/library/stories/2021/03/happy-saint-patricks-day-
to-one-of-ten-americans-who-claim-irish-ancestry.html 16/03/2021

150 'Northern Ireland Protocol: Article 16', Institute for Government,
instituteforgovernment.org.uk/explainers/northern-ireland-Protocol-
article-16

151 Campbell, J, 'Brexit: Invest NI to be hit by loss of EU grants',
BBC News Northern Ireland, bbc.co.uk/news/uk-northern-
ireland-55339227 17/12/2020

152 Tallant, N, 'Claim Dev torpedoed unity twice in WWII', Belfast Telegraph, belfasttelegraph.co.uk/sunday-life/news/claim-dev-torpedoed-
unity-twice-in-wwii-28455123.html 12/07/2008

153 Henley, J, 'Food shortages hitting Britons more than many in the EU,
poll finds', *The Guardian*, theguardian.com/business/2021/dec/22/
food-shortages-hitting-britons-more-than-many-in-eu-poll-finds
22/12/2021

154 Ward, B, 'Construction materials: the current state of play', Construction Journal, RICS, ww3.rics.org/uk/en/journals/construction-journal/
construction-materials--the-current-state-of-play.html 21/12/2021

155 Shipton, M, 'Support for Welsh independence soars in new poll by
YouGov for Plaid Cymru', Wales Online, walesonline.co.uk/news/
wales-news/support-welsh-independence-soars-new-16911177
13/09/2019

156 'Macron: Irish reunification will solve Brexit problem', ANF News,
anfenglishmobile.com/news/macron-irish-reunification-will-solve-
brexit-problem-37165 25/08/2019

157 "If it comes to the bit where we have to fight physically to maintain
our freedoms within the UK, so be it" – Loyalist Communities Council Chair', *The Nolan Show*, BBC, @BBCNolan on *Twitter* twitter.
com/bbcnolan/status/1356957494476759042 1

158 Robinson, P, 'Peter Robinson: Unionists are more alienated than
I have ever seen at any time in my 50 years in politics', *News Letter*,
newsletter.co.uk/news/opinion/columnists/peter-robinson-Unionists-

are-more-alienated-than-i-have-seen-at-any-time-in-my-50-years-in-politics-3179294 26/03/2021

159 Archer, B, 'QUB academic reveals year-long "campaign" of political pressure', *The Irish News*, irishnews.com/news/northernireland-news/2019/11/05/news/headline-1756474 05/11/2019

160 Carroll, R, 'Backlash after O'Neill says there was "no alternative" to conflict during Troubles', *The Guardian*, theguardian.com/uk-news/2022/aug/04/backlash-after-michelle-oneill-says-there-was-no-alternative-to-conflict-during-troubles-northern-ireland-ira 04/04/2022

161 Winters, R, 'Racist intimidation in the Village in south Belfast "going on for years"', *The Detail,* thedetail.tv/articles/racist-intimidation-in-the-village-in-south-belfast-been-going-on-for-years

162 Winters, R, 'Racist intimidation in the Village in south Belfast "going on for years"', *The Detail*, thedetail.tv/articles/racist-intimidation-in-the-village-in-south-belfast-been-going-on-for-years

163 Dalby, D, 'In Northern Ireland, A Wave of Immigrants Is Met With Fists', nytimes.com/2014/11/29/world/europe/in-northern-ireland-immigrants-are-increasingly-met-with-fists.html 28/11/2014

164 Winters, R 'Racist intimidation in the Village in south Belfast "going on for years"', *The Detail*, thedetail.tv/articles/racist-intimidation-in-the-village-in-south-belfast-been-going-on-for-years 26/05/2020

165 'Union flag protests cost Belfast businesses £15m', BBC News Northern Ireland, bbc.co.uk/news/uk-northern-ireland-20972438 10/01/2013

166 'Loyalist paramilitaries "behind some Northern Ireland trouble"', BBC News Northern Ireland bbc.com/news/uk-northern-ireland-20651159 08/12/2012

167 'Union flag dispute: Cost of policing protests exceeds £15m', BBC News Northern Ireland, bbc.com/news/uk-northern-ireland-21369953

168 Garsd, J, 'Gun Violence Can Be Diffused By Community Members Called "Violence Interrupters"', heard on All Things Considered, NPR, npr.org/2021/08/09/1026274452/gun-violence-can-be-diffused-with-community-members-called-violence-interrupters?t=1661769978925 09/08/2021

169 Caterall, P, McDougall, S, The Northern Ireland Question in British Politics, Palgrave Macmillan UK, pp.26

170 Newsroom, 'Orangemen in the past had no problem with the Irish language', *News Letter*, www.newsletter.co.uk/news/politics/orangemen-past-had-no-problem-irish-language-1131062 19/04/2017

171 'Census 1911: Belfast's Shankill had as many Irish speakers as Falls', Belfast Telegraph, belfasttelegraph.co.uk/news/northern-ireland/

census-1911-belfasts-shankill-had-as-many-irish-speakers-as-
falls-28733198.html 02/04/2012

172 Stewart, A T Q, *Edward Carson,* Gill and Macmillan Ltd,
pp 125, 1981

173 Mahon, B, 'United Ireland could need UK judges on constitutional
court', The Times, thetimes.co.uk/article/united-ireland-could-need-
uk-judges-on-constitutional-court-8sbzckvp8 30/11/2019

174 'Rules of procedure of the Presidency of Bosnia and Herzegovina',
Bosnia and Herzegovina, predsjednistvobih.ba/nadl/default.aspx?id=
53748&langTag=en-US

175 'Joint Declaration 1993 (Downing St Declaration)', Department
of Foreign Affairs Ireland, dfa.ie/media/dfa/alldfawebsiteme-
dia/ourrolesandpolicies/northernireland/peace-process--joint-
declaration-1993.pdf

176 Douglas, F, Blessings of Liberty and Education, 1884, taken from
frederick-douglass-heritage.org/quotes/

177 'Dyson says UK government does not need its COVID-19 ventilator', Reuters, reuters.com/article/us-health-coronavirus-britain-dy-
son-idUSKCN2262PU 24/04/20

178 'Human Development Insights', Human Development Reports, hdr.
undp.org/en/content/latest-human-development-index-ranking

179 Stephens, D, 'Food bank users "reject potatoes' because they can't
pay to boil them, says Iceland boss', LBC, lbc.co.uk/news/pressure-
mounts-rishi-sunak-spring-statement/ 22/03/2022

180 Syal, R, 'Rishi Sunak admits taking money from deprived areas', *The
Guardian,* theguardian.com/politics/2022/aug/05/video-emerges-
of-rishi-sunak-admitting-to-taking-money-from-deprived-areas
05/08/2022

181 Badshah, N, 'Elsie "disappointed" with Boris Johnson's response,
says Susanna Reid', *The Guardian,* theguardian.com/business/2022/
may/03/elsie-disappointed-with-boris-johnsons-response-says-
susanna-reid 03/05/2022

182 'Irish passport again ranked amongst the most powerful in the
world', IrishCentral, irishcentral.com/travel/irish-passport-third-most-
powerful-world 01/04//2022

183 Hutton, B, 'UK passport applications in North dip as more Irish
passports issued', *The Irish Times,* irishtimes.com/news/ireland/irish-
news/uk-passport-applications-in-north-dip-as-more-irish-passports-
issued-1.4442342 21/12/2020

184 Nelson, M, 'Sport has the power to change the world' speech, Lau-
reus World Sport Awards, Monaco, 2000, youtube.com/watch?v=y1-
7w-bJCtY

185 Winter, J, 'Ireland's Call – Lyrics and Background Explained', Rubgy
Dome, rugbydome.com/irelands-call/ 19/09/2021

186 Moore, C, 'The talks that could have produced an all-Ireland soccer team in the 1970s', *The 42*, 20/12/2015

187 Professional Ulster Rugby player who tragically died in an accident on a farm trying to save his family.

188 Dirs, B, 'Carl Frampton: The boxer following where McGuigan dared to tread', BBC Sport, bbc.com/sport/boxing/28973146 03/09/2014

189 McCurry, C, 'Rory McIlroy wades into united Ireland debate after Brexit vote', *Belfast Telegraph*, belfasttelegraph.co.uk/news/northern-ireland/rory-mcilroy-wades-into-united-ireland-debate-after-brexit-vote-34868384.html 09/07/2016

190 Leeson, D, 'Death in the Afternoon: The Croke Park Massacre, 21 November 1920', *Canadian Journal of History, Vol 38* No 1pp 43–68, 2003

191 Moran, S, 'Sporting Controversies: How Rule 42 and England were both shown the door', The Irish Times, rishtimes.com/sport/gaelic-games/sporting-controversies-how-rule-42-and-england-were-both-shown-the-door-1.4254698 18/05/2020

192 O'Donovan, D, '50 Years since GAA scrapped its ban on "foreign games"', *Echo Live*, echolive.ie/corklives/arid-40198971.html 02/01/2021

193 Willis, A, 'Oh dear… An MP was recorded "agreeing" to "get the ethics out"', Metro, metro.co.uk/2016/03/01/oh-dear-an-mp-was-recorded-agreeing-to-get-the-ethnics-out-5726531/ 01/03/2016

194 Newsroom, 'Belfast City Council seeking more powers over planning', *News Letter,* newsletter.co.uk/news/politics/belfast-city-council-seeking-more-powers-over-planning-3687215 10/05/2022

195 McBride, S, *Burned*, Merrion Press, 2019

196 Dollar, D, Victor, D G, 'Fixing the climate crisis will require local experimentation and solutions' www.brookings.edu 22/08/2022

197 'Systems, Not Structures – Changing Health and Social Care – Full Report', Northern Ireland Department of Health, health-ni.gov.uk/publications/systems-not-structures-changing-health-and-social-care-full-report 25/10/2016

198 'The Constitution of Ireland', 2020 [1937] states:
The number of members shall from time to time be fixed by law, but the total number of members of Dáil Éireann shall not be fixed at less than one member for each thirty thousand of the population, or at more than one member for each twenty thousand of the population. The all-Ireland Dáil 160 TDs in 26 counties and 63 TDs in 6 counties = 223 total.

199 'The Homelands', South African History Online, sahistory.org.za/article/homelands

200 'Franklin D Roosevelt's last message to the American People', Library of Congress loc.gov/resource/rbpe.24204300/?st=text 13/04/1945

201 Mandela, N, 1995, 'Address by President Nelson Mandela at the end of the snap debate on the Shell House incident in the National Assembly, Cape Town', mandela.gov.za/mandela_spee-ches/1995/950607_shellhouseend.htm

202 Luther King Jr, M, 'Martin Luther King Jr Acceptance Speech', The Nobel Prize, 1964 nobelprize.org/prizes/peace/1964/king/acceptance-speech/

203 'Mcguinness: These Killer Are Traitors To Ireland', *Daily Record*, dailyrecord.co.uk/news/uk-world-news/mcguinness-these-killers-are-traitors-to-ireland-1013400 11/03/2012

204 'About the Archives', National Centre for Truth and Reconciliation Archives, University of Manitoba, nctr.ca/records/view-your-records/archives/

205 Murphy, C, '"Vietnam and Ireland share a path"- President', Indepen-dent.ie, independent.ie/irish-news/vietnam-and-Ireland-share-a-path-president-35200582.html 09/11/2016

206 Byrne, D, McCullagh, D, 'Haughey backed Kohl over German Unity', RTÉ, rte.ie/news/ireland/2020/1226/1186480-state-papers-1990-unity/27/12/2020

207 'CFTA – Continental Free Trade Area', African Union, au.int/en/ti/cfta/about

208 'Continental Free Trade Area to Boost Intra-Africa Trade', Repu-blic of Kenya Ministry of Industrialization, Trade and Enterprise Development, industrialization.go.ke/index.php/media-center/blog/350-african-union-warms-up-for-cfta-negotiations

209 Koumoullis, G, 'If only we had accepted the Annan plan', Cyprus-Mail, cyprus-mail.com/2017/08/27/accepted-annan-plan 27/08/2017

210 'John Hume Nobel Lecture', The Nobel Prize, nobelprize.org/prizes/peace/1998/hume/lecture/ 10/12/1998

211 'John Hume Nobel Lecture', The Nobel Prize, nobelprize.org/prizes/peace/1998/hume/lecture/ 10/12/1998

212 Garbor, D, *Inventing the Future*, Pelican, 1964

213 Anderson, B, *Imagined Communities: Reflections on the Origin and Spread of Nationalism*, Verso Books, 2006 [1983]

214 McWilliams, D, 'Truth is the union with Britain has been an eco-nomic calamity for Northern Ireland', *The Irish Times*, irishtimes.com/opinion/2022/06/18/david-mcwilliams-truth-is-the-union-with-britain-has-been-an-economic-calamity-for-northern-ireland/18/06/2022

215 'Legislative acts and other instruments', Council of the European Union, data.consilium.europa.eu/doc/document/ST-6393-2018-INIT/en/pdf 01/03/2018

Luath Press Limited

committed to publishing well written books worth reading

LUATH PRESS takes its name from Robert Burns, whose little collie Luath (*Gael.*, swift or nimble) tripped up Jean Armour at a wedding and gave him the chance to speak to the woman who was to be his wife and the abiding love of his life. Burns called one of the 'Twa Dogs' Luath after Cuchullin's hunting dog in Ossian's *Fingal*. Luath Press was established in 1981 in the heart of Burns country, and is now based a few steps up the road from Burns' first lodgings on Edinburgh's Royal Mile. Luath offers you distinctive writing with a hint of unexpected pleasures.

Most bookshops in the UK, the US, Canada, Australia, New Zealand and parts of Europe, either carry our books in stock or can order them for you. To order direct from us, please send a £sterling cheque, postal order, international money order or your credit card details (number, address of cardholder and expiry date) to us at the address below. Please add post and packing as follows: UK – £1.00 per delivery address; overseas surface mail – £2.50 per delivery address; overseas airmail – £3.50 for the first book to each delivery address, plus £1.00 for each additional book by airmail to the same address. If your order is a gift, we will happily enclose your card or message at no extra charge.

Luath Press Limited
543/2 Castlehill
The Royal Mile
Edinburgh EH1 2ND
Scotland
Telephone: +44 (0)131 225 4326 (24 hours)
Email: sales@luath. co.uk
Website: www.luath.co.uk

www.ingramcontent.com/pod-product-compliance
Lightning Source LLC
Chambersburg PA
CBHW010143270326
41928CB00020B/3250